POVERTY, U. S. A.

THE HISTORICAL RECORD

ADVISORY EDITOR: David J. Rothman

Professor of History, Columbia University

THE PERSONAL SIDE

JESSIE A. BLOODWORTH
AND ELIZABETH J. GREENWOOD

Arno Press & The New York Times
NEW YORK   1971

Reprint Edition 1971 by Arno Press Inc.

Reprinted from a copy in
The State Historical Society of Wisconsin Library

LC# 71—137156
ISBN 0—405—03094—0

POVERTY, U.S.A.: THE HISTORICAL RECORD
ISBN for complete set: 0-405-03090-8

Manufactured in the United States of America

WORKS PROGRESS ADMINISTRATION

F. C. HARRINGTON, Administrator
CORRINGTON GILL, Assistant Administrator

DIVISION OF RESEARCH
(Formerly Division of Social Research)
HOWARD B. MYERS, Director

THE PERSONAL SIDE

By

Jessie A. Bloodworth
Elizabeth J. Greenwood

Under the supervision of
John N. Webb
Coordinator of Urban Research

1939

14355

CONTENTS

THE PERSONAL SIDE

BEHIND THE STATISTICS

When human beings are counted the identity of the individual is lost in the single measure of the size of the group.   To know that about 15,000,000 workers were unemployed and that nearly 28,000,000 persons were dependent on public assistance at the bottom of the depression is necessary and useful information.   But it is impersonal; it tells us nothing about who these persons were, what they did, or how deeply they were affected by their experiences.

Back of the impressive figures on unemployment and relief is the individual who lost his job and made the weary rounds from one "No Help Wanted" sign to another; the family which reluctantly cashed its insurance policies, sold or mortgaged its goods, and then— too often—found that no amount of economy or deprivation could stave off a trip to the local relief office.

The statistics of unemployment and relief measure the magnitude of distress with all the efficiency and accuracy of an adding machine tape, but they do not show what it means to the individual to be out of work or on relief—they leave untold the personal side.

Lacking a careful account of the human side of economic distress the reader of the voluminous statistical reports must draw upon his own knowledge of people in need. Moreoften than not it is the exceptional, rather than the typical, case that is recalled. Utter destitution has been widely publicized under such headings as "The Twenty-five Neediest Cases"; the indolent have been excoriated by a righteous press; and "chiselers" have been exposed at regular intervals during the past 5 years.

These and other extreme cases do exist, but they have received a disproportionate amount of attention. The real problem of unemployment and relief lies with the great majority who are just ordinary people in trouble, men and families whose difficulties have not been considered good "copy" and who have, therefore, remained numbers to be summed up in the reports.

These personal histories represent an attempt to supplement the statistics of unemployment and relief by recapturing the personal side; the means employed are intimate accounts of the individual's experiences during the depression and his reactions to those experiences. The 45 personal histories in this volume are not "sob stories"; there is no fiction, and there is no dramatization for effect. Indeed, there is no need for artificial touches. The experiences of these families, told soberly and painstakingly by the individuals as they recalled the events of the troubled years, are dramatic to a degree that needs no artifice.

Selecting the City

The 45 stories told here were selected from a total of 103 personal histories that were obtained in one city, Dubuque, Iowa, between December 1937 and April 1938. Dubuque was selected as the location of this study because it seemed to meet the specifications for this experiment more nearly than any of the other cities considered. The criteria of selection were: a city of diversified industry with a total population between 35,000 and 50,000 persons, a city that was neither satellite to a larger city nor was itself the economic center for dependent communities, a city with a high

proportion of native white citizens, and a city that had felt the full
impact of the depression.

The governing factors behind these specifications were the
need to avoid the exceptional situation and the importance of working
in a city whose social and economic fabric was not of too complex a
design.   The city of moderate size is still the rule rather than the
exception in urban America; it is large enough, when its economic activities are diversified, to display the variegated character of
urban-industrial life; and it has not yet reached the complex stage of
the metropolitan center where communities within communities make
unified description a lengthy task.

How well Dubuque, Iowa, measured up to the specifications
may be seen from a few simple figures. In 1930 the population number-
ed 41,675 persons. Over 90 percent of its inhabitants were native
white stock, and nearly half of its working population was dependent
upon the city's manufacturing industries.   Although Dubuque contains
two of the largest sash-and-door mills in the country, it is primarily
a city of diversified industries of moderate size.   Some 90 factories
(including one of the few inland shipbuilding yards in the United
States) produce more than 300 different articles.

The city is situated on the Mississippi River directly opposite the Wisconsin-Illinois boundary line, 80 miles west of
Rockford, Ill., 60 miles northwest of Cedar Rapids, and 70 miles
north of Davenport, Iowa.

Dubuque is the largest city in an extensive farming area
which it serves as the trade center. As a city of varied activities,

sufficiently removed from other cities to "stand on its own feet,"
Dubuque is the type of fairly self-contained urban center that could
be studied as a unit in a reasonably short period of time.

The depression affected Dubuque in much the same way that
it did hundreds of cities in the country. Local pride tends to
minimize Dubuque's economic difficulties. In the preface to the 1937
city directory the chairman of Dubuque's "25-year plan," sponsored
by the Chamber of Commerce, had this to say:

> "Dubuque is one of the most important manufacturing
> cities in Iowa. More than 146 factories and whole-
> sale houses furnish employment to many thousands of
> men and women. A striking thing about these indus-
> tries is that they keep right on producing quality
> products with seldom or never a shutdown."

This somewhat optimistic picture of economic stability in
Dubuque fails to find substantiation in the stories told by the workers or in the records of the local relief office. Nor does a report
of the Iowa State Planning Board leave any reason to doubt that the
depression came to Dubuque. According to the Planning Board's
Housing Survey of 1934, 30 firms employing 2,200 workers had closed
or left Dubuque between 1927 and 1934. The largest of these was
a phonograph and radio plant that figures repeatedly in the personal
histories. At the peak of production in the early 1920's this one
plant employed from 1,500 to 1,600 workers. By 1927 employment had
dropped to 900, and in 1931, the plant was closed permanently. At
about the same time one of the railroads moved its shops out of the
city. These railroad shops had employed 1,500 workers in the early
twenties, and at the time of removal there were 600 men involved.

The planning Board's study continues:

> The other large employers of labor, (the two
> sash-and-door mills) employing, the one 950,
> and the other 700 workers back in the middle
> 20's are now (1934) employing little over one-
> third their former number. The disappearance
> of many other small firms has added much to
> this situation. Decrease in the payrolls of
> these firms has been even greater than decrease
> in employment due both to decrease in wages
> and in time of employment of those still em-
> ployed.

Less than 8 months after the closing of the phonograph and
radio plant four local banks were closed. According to the local
press, these were the first bank failures since the late 1880's.
Clearly, then, the depression did not miss Dubuque.

There would be nothing gained from an attempt to show that
Dubuque is "representative" of moderate sized industrial cities.
Cities, like people, differ or correspond in degree only. It is
enough to show that Dubuque has a background in common with hundreds
of cities scattered across the country, and with them, shared a
common experience during the depression years. Unemployment meant
much the same thing to Dubuque workmen that it did to workmen in
Lima, Ohio; Columbus, Georgia; Bellingham, Wash., and many other
cities throughout the country. In a sense, then, the choice of a
city was the choice of a background in which the story of a common
experience was to be told.

Finding the Families

The desire to avoid extremes was likewise the guiding
principle in the selection of the families whose stories are told.
The specifications for selection were simple enough to be applied
rigorously. The families had to belong to the wage earning group as
distinguished from the professional, proprietary, and managerial groups.

The families had to have experienced at least one period of unemployment lasting 4 consecutive months during the depression years. And the families had to be chosen completely at random from among the total wage earning population of Dubuque. These specifications were broad enough to insure the inclusion of a wide variety of families whose livelihood depended upon the ability of the worker to find a job in the commercial or industrial life of the city. And the method of choosing the families insured that the "problem case" would be included in no more than its proper proportion.

A new city directory, issued in the fall of 1937, was used to select a cross section of the Dubuque family population. The names were chosen by systematic random selection before the interviewers went to Dubuque. In all, 433 families were chosen from the directory which listed, among other items, the names, addresses, and occupations of the family heads. The occupational entry was used to eliminate all families whose heads were in the professional, proprietary, or managerial class. The amended list was then sent to Dubuque where the exclusions were first checked for accuracy. The names remaining on the list were compared with relief records and the records of the public employment office to determine eligibility under the specification of at least one period of unemployment. Finally, the families themselves were visited and asked the few questions necessary to determine eligibility for inclusion.

Of the total list originally drawn, 103 families remained which had had at least 1 major period of unemployment and whose heads were wage earners. It is from the detailed personal histories of

these 103 families that the 45 histories in this report were chosen.
In making the selection for publication, care was taken to include
as wide a variety of family situations as the limitation of space
would permit.

Getting the Stories

The stories were obtained by personal interviews with each
family. In most instances, several visits were made: one to explain
the purpose of the study and to obtain willing cooperation; others to
get from the head of the family a full account of his experiences as
a worker; and still other visits with the whole family to get the
opinions and attitudes of the entire family group.

There was no printed questionnaire, no statistical card, no
check list of questions. Each visit was less an interview than a
friendly, even neighborly, talk about things in general and the depression in particular. The interviewers met the family and the
relatives; the neighbors frequently dropped in to add their own recollection of common experiences. There were long talks—sometimes
spirited arguments—around the stove during the winter evenings, talks
that dealt with many things besides the family's own troubles. Local,
national, and world politics and the personalities thereof were
overhauled. War and the prospects of war and whether they or their
sons would go were discussed at length, craftsmanship and the machine
age, relief and the Works Program, Bill Green and John Lewis, the
Chamber of Commerce and what it had done for or to Dubuque, marital
affairs, "getting a little place in the country"—all these and more
were the subject of friendly discussions.

From these talks came the histories, one at a time, slowly, as the family and its experiences developed in full detail. The task was not to get these people to say enough, but to sift the much that they said so as to fit the confines of the printed page. The experiences, emphases, and opinions came directly from the families themselves; there has been no editorial interpretation.

What the Stories Tell

On the subject of relief---their opinions contain some of the most cogent criticisms and evaluations of public assistance and the WPA that could be found. Although the families were close enough to reality to know that not everyone who really wanted work could find it, some thought that "relief just made bums of people." Another said, "Sure, some of them leaned on their shovels; if you've ever tried to buy milk for a family of kids and still have enough meat and good food to do a hard day's work outdoors you'll know why!" Others felt that WPA workers took as much pride in their work as any other class of workers. All preferred work relief to direct relief.

On politics and economics---they were not certain where the blame for the depression lay. They inclined to the theory that mechanization and concentration of wealth had much to do with it, but they were positive on one point: they felt that "people just weren't paid enough to buy what the manufacturers had to sell."

On Social Security and Old-Age Pensions---there was strong endorsement of old-age security which was regarded as a pension, not as a relief measure. Those who owned, or had owned, homes were indignant at the Iowa law that requires the grantee to sign over his

property. They had not yet had enough contact with the provisions
of unemployment insurance to be certain as to its effects on them.

On war—well, it was a racket; and a sorry day that they
went and it would be a hard job getting them to go again; but they or
their sons would probably be called whether they wanted to be or not.

On Dubuque—there was a deep and persistent conviction that
the forces in control of the city's economic life had too narrow a
point of view. Low wages might mean big profits and prosperity for
a few people; but in the long run Dubuque would suffer, for it was a
working—man's town and if the workers didn't prosper the city couldn't
prosper.

Generally—most of these families were deeply concerned over
the failure of the country to come out of the long slump. They felt
there must be something basically wrong somewhere. Above all,
they didn't want their children to work and save and plan as most
of them had done, and then see their lives go smash in some future
economic cataclysm they had no part in making.

There are no neat morals to be drawn from these personal
histories. Some of the families through a lifetime of thrift, hard
work, and ingenuity under adversity managed to keep off relief. Some
of them, with equal thrift and industry, bought homes, more farm land,
or put their savings into industrial securities and savings banks only
to have the efforts of many years canceled through foreclosure, bank
failure, or industrial collapse. Relief was more than a bitter
necessity to these families; it marked the destruction of the landmarks
by which they had ordered their lives. Still others spent as they
made and went on relief with little more than a wry smile. While most

were reluctant at first they drew some comfort from finding their friends
and neighbors in the waiting room. None of these families like relief,
though some of them know they are on the relief rolls to stay. Those who
are back at work hope the experience of unemployment need never be repeated,
but then it happened once and might again.

These are not dull-minded or broken-spirited people. They are
troubled people, a little bewildered perhaps, but still hopeful that under
wise leadership the country can regain its former prosperity and thereby re-
store to them the means of satisfying their modest desires.

It would be most unfitting to close this introduction without expressing deep appreciation of the sympathy and cooperation obtained in Dubuqu
during the conduct of this study. Officials, clerics, and laymen alike took
time off from their duties to assist and advise. There was no attempt to
mislead or to obstruct any line of inquiry. Differences of opinion were
frankly stated and stoutly defended. Dubuque is a friendly city. But the
greatest debt is due the families themselves who, through their willingness
to retrace the unpleasant past, make this study possible.

The names of the families and the establishments they worked for
have been changed for obvious reasons. Though many of the families said that
they didn't care who knew how they **felt**, the reader will readily recognize
the possible ill effects of complete identification of the speaker in such
matters as the attitude of the Chamber of Commerce and the leading industrial
ists toward the local wage scale.

For brevity and convenience 45 of the case histories are presented
here as representing all of the types included in the total of 103 histories
collected. The families fall into three main groups. Those who had been on

relief and have now returned to private employment are included in the
first section, "From Relief to Private Employment." Those who received no
relief while unemployed and are now working in private industry are included
in the section, "By Their Own Boot-straps." In the last section, "Still
Without Jobs," are the stories of families, relief and nonrelief, which
have failed to get back in private industry. Among them are construction
workers caught in the prolonged depression of the building trades, young
workers handicapped by lack of training and experience, and the physically
handicapped and the old who have been discarded by industry. The families
tell their own stories.

FROM RELIEF
TO PRIVATE EMPLOYMENT

THE YOUNG

PARK

Mr. Park	32
Mrs. Park	31
Claud, Jr.	11
Mary	9
Dorothy	4

Interviewing completed
January 2, 1938

When Claud Park was granted a pay raise a year ago at the Mississippi Milling Company, where he had been hired in August 1935 after 4 years of unemployment, the Parks thought the depression was ended for them. Now, however, with working hours reduced to 25 a week, the Park family fear that they are "getting right back" where they were 5 or 6 years ago.

At 32. Claud is weatherbeaten in appearance and shows the effects of worry and anxiety. Though frank and spontaneous, he is slow of speech and drawls out his words as he discusses the family's depression experiences. After the long siege of unemployment and dependency on either direct relief or work projects, Claud considers himself an "authority on the depression."

The Parks live in a rented five-room brick house in a neighborhood of small homes in the north end of town. Martha Park, the mother of three children, has found time to take an active part in the Parent Teachers Association and the Mothers Club of the church, despite her desperate struggle to make ends meet on a limited budget. She considers that her high school courses, especially home economics, have stood her in good stead in managing her household on a limited budget. Believing that the family's depressed circumstances should not be permitted to interfere with

the proper rearing of the children, she has always taken advantage of anything that would help her to become a more understanding mother and home-
maker. Claud Jr., 11 years old, is in the sixth grade and Mary, 9, is a
fourth-grader. Dorothy, 4, a "depression baby" is the pet of the family.

Claud and Martha Park "grew up" in a small town in southern
Minnesota, but have lived in Dubuque during most of the 13 years of their
marriage. Claud's education was cut short when he had to leave school
after completing the eighth grade to help his father support a large family.

The Parks moved to Dubuque immediately after their marriage in
1924, when Claud, through a relative, got a job as a spray painter at the
Iowa Foundry. His entrance rate was 45¢ an hour and he worked 54 hours a
week. After 2 years, Claud was advanced to the position of foreman of the
paint department; his rate of pay was increased to 50¢ an hour. The paint
did not agree with him, however, and after he had lost considerable weight
and suffered from ulcers of the throat, he decided to quit early in 1927 and
go to Chicago where he had heard of a chance to "get on" as a janitor in
a new building at $200 a month. Soon after the Parks arrived in Chicago,
they both came down with typhoid fever; by the time Claud had recovered,
all jobs in the new building had been filled. He found a janitorial job
in another building, but it paid only $100 a month. After having worked at
this job for about 2 years, he decided that with the higher cost of living
in Chicago, he would be better off working at the foundry in Dubuque.

On his return to Dubuque, he worked at the Iowa Foundry for a
year before he was laid off during the general reduction in force in February 1931. From February 1931 to the fall of 1932 he worked irregularly for
a barge line and at an insulating plant, averaging from $5 to $25 a week,

depending on the amount of work available. The family began running in debt and it was necessary for Claud to borrow $200 from his "folks." When this was exhausted, $80 was borrowed on a $1,000 insurance policy, which was later allowed to lapse. Claud regrets very much losing his only insurance policy. On their return from Chicago, the Parks lived in a five-room house for which the rent was $18 a month, but as circumstances became more strained, they moved to a small four-room house for which they paid only $10.

By December 1932 the situation had become desperate. The temperature was below zero, and there was little fuel or food left. As the Parks owed a coal bill of $40 and a grocery bill of $25, they expected credit to be discontinued at any time. To add to the seriousness of their plight, Mrs. Park was pregnant. After talking things over one night they could see no alternative except to apply for relief; yet they both felt that they would be "disgraced." Mrs. Park bitterly opposed going on relief, but during the night Claud got "scared about the kids," and thought "we can't let the kids starve just because we are proud." The next morning, without telling his wife his intentions, he went to the courthouse to make application for relief. When he arrived at the courthouse he couldn't go in. "I must have walked around the block over a dozen times--it was 10 below zero, but I didn't know it." Finally he got up sufficient courage to make his application.

The family was "investigated" and after about 2 weeks "a lady brought out a grocery and coal order." This was just in the "nick of time" as they were completely out of provisions. Mr. Park considered that they got along very nicely on the weekly grocery order. Part of the time they

were also allowed milk from the milk fund and "this helped a lot." The
Parks feel that they were well treated by the relief office and did not
find the routine investigations obnoxious. "It's part of the system and
when you ask for relief, of course you have to cooperate." "The questions
didn't bother us so much as the idea of being on charity."

Mrs. Park's confinement created less hardship than the Parks
expected, as Mr. Park did all of the housework and a visiting nurse came
in once a day to care for Mrs. Park.

Claud Park "never felt right about accepting the relief slip."
He says, "Later, when they let me do some work for it, I felt better."
The relief office allowed only $7.50 a month for rent and Claud did odd
jobs for the landlord to make up the difference. In the fall of 1933 he
was placed on a CWA road construction project at $80 a month. He was
delighted to be paid in cash and didn't feel that he was "getting something
for nothing." At the close of CWA in the spring of 1934, he was placed by
the public employment office on the lock and dam project, and his wages
were cut to $50 a month and later to $48. He was intermittently employed
on emergency work projects until August 31, 1936, when he got a job as a
benchman **finishing sashes** at the Mississippi Milling Company. Claud had
made application at all the factories in town, but he feels that he would
never have been taken on at the Mississippi Milling Company had not an old
employee there spoken for him.

The Parks kept a detailed monthly account of their income from
all sources, including work relief, direct relief, and odd jobs, from 1933
through 1935. The total income in 1933 was $450.96, and for 1935 it was
$698.64. Included in these amounts is work for back rent totaling $85.15

in 1933 and $107.25 in 1935. The Parks feel that 1932 and 1933 were their "hardest years." After Claud started to work on emergency projects, the family had "a little more to live on."

During the lean years of the depression the Parks barely "subsisted," and Claud feels that it would be impossible "even to subsist" on this low income over an extended period as clothing and furniture would have to be replaced. The Parks thought they were very economical in 1926, when their total expenditures were $1,095.15, including payments on furniture, medical bills, insurance, and a move to Chicago. At that time, there were only three in the family, but in 1933 there were five. The Parks are keeping the calendars on which they marked every item of income for the depression years as "relics" to look at when they are old, and, Claud hopes, "better off."

At the Mississippi Milling Company, Claud had worked 9 hours a day, $5\frac{1}{2}$ days a week, for about 7 months. The time was then reduced to 35 hours a week, and about 2 months ago, a 25-hour week went into effect. His entrance rate was 45¢ an hour, but when he requested a raise a few months after starting work, his rate was increased to 47¢ an hour. At present, the weekly pay check amounts to only $11.75, and the family is again getting behind with bills. Because of the uncertainty of the working hours at the mill, it is impossible for Claud to "fill in" with odd jobs. He feels that there is no use to look for more regular work in other factories, for in most of them work is just as irregular as at the Mississippi Milling Company. Then, too, if he quits to take another job, he might never be able to get on again at the Mississippi Milling Company.

After Claud's pay raise, "things began to look bright again," and the family moved to their present home where the rent is $17 a month. Mrs. Park felt that the overcrowding in the other house was bad for the children. After paying up back bills, she had even started some long-needed dental work, which she discontinued before completion when Claud went on short hours. She told the dentist he could keep the bridge he had finished in his safe, but he said that it was of no use to him and he was willing to trust the Parks.

In an attempt to make ends meet with the reduced income, the Parks now take 1 quart of milk for the children instead of 2, and buy meat only once a week. They have enough canned and dried vegetables from their garden on "the island" 1/ to last through the winter. The biggest problem is warm clothing for the children. Claud Jr. and Mary both need shoes, overshoes, and winter underwear, but so far it has been impossible for the Parks to do more than buy food and pay the rent, gas, and electric bills. In bad weather "the children will have to be kept home from school," and Mrs. Park "feels terrible" about that. She thinks "employers don't begin to realize how much hardship they cause by reducing the pay checks of the workers."

According to Claud, there is much gossip at the factory regarding the employer's policy in reducing hours. The reason given by the company was "reduction of orders," but the men believe that it is "an attempt to demoralize the workers and break up the union." The plant is only about 50 percent organized, but the employers are "strongly opposed to unionization and fear the influence of the CIO." The men think that "sufficient stock was accumulated while the mill was running at top speed to permit the recent drastic cuts in hours."

1/ The island, owned by the city, was turned over to needy families for gardens early in the depression. Garden projects were sponsored by local civic organizations.

Claud Park is not a member of a union, but he favors unions if they have proper leadership. He feels that the union in Dubuque is too weak to accomplish much and that the quality of the local leadership is responsible for this situation. He also thinks that too much of the dues goes to national headquarters. Then, too, many of the workers are afraid to take a stand during a crisis. "But no wonder: the big manufacturers have the town tied in a knot." Mr. Park feels that the discord in the ranks of the AFL and the CIO also "plays into the hand of the employer." He adds, "Both Lewis and Green have their good points and their weaknesses, but Lewis is much the stronger of the two."

Unemployment, Claud believes, is due largely to the introduction of labor saving machinery and the general speeding up in industry, combined with the low purchasing power of the workers. "When a guy can't afford even to buy what he produces, how can there be any prosperity? Look at me--it would take a week of my wages to buy one of those windows I work on by the thousand."

Consumers cooperatives would do much to relieve unemployment and help equalize wealth, in Mr. Park's opinion. While unemployed he read everything the city library had to offer on the subject of cooperatives. Claud firmly believes that a nation-wide system of cooperatives would do more to relieve unemployment and distress than any other reform. He thinks they would break up monopoly trusts and eventually equalize the wealth of the country. As to the Townsend Plan, "I wouldn't give a nickel for it."

Claud feels that the Social Security program "is a step in the right direction, but needs reform in order to benefit the poor man." The Old-Age Pension system benefits primarily the man with a "good, steady" income. "If my security in old age depends on my present 25-hour week employ-

ment, I will probably starve." While Claud believes that the State should
assume more responsibility for the unemployed, he thinks that States and
counties were not financially prepared to take adequate care of their destitute people during the recent depression, and in consequence, the Federal
Government had to institute emergency measures on a national basis.

The Iowa State sales tax the Parks consider "vicious," because it
works the greatest hardship on poor people who make small purchases. "The
guy who thought up that tax should be run out of the State." The Parks
estimate that about 6¢ out of each dollar they spend goes for sales tax.

If the Parks could "only be sure" of $35 a week, they could keep up
their usual level of living, take care of all their needs, and "lay aside"
enough for emergencies. It is the "terrible uncertainty of the weekly pay
check that keeps us worried. We've always kept up our morale for the sake
of the children even though the situation was often discouraging."

Gardening on the island has afforded a certain amount of sociabil-
ity for the Parks, as they meet most of the neighbors there during the gardening season. Claud had hoped to be well enough off by next spring to turn his
plot over to some needier family, but now "those hopes are dashed."

All Claud Park asks of the future is a chance to work and the security of a regular weekly pay check. He hates to think of ever going on relief
again, but with his present irregular work, he feels that"we are getting
right back where we were in 1932-1933."

Employment Chronology for Mr. Park

1924 - 1926   Spray painter, Iowa Foundry.

1926 - 1927   Foreman paint department, Iowa Foundry.

1927 - 1929   Janitor, office building.

January 1930 -
February 1931   Spray painter, Iowa Foundry.

February 1931 -
November 1932   Irregular work at common labor, barge line, and insulating company.

November 1932 -
August 1936   Unemployed except for emergency work.

August 1936 -
Present   Benchman, Mississippi Milling Company.

CUPP

Mr. Cupp	27
Mrs. Cupp	28
Betty	4
Junior	2
Sue	1

Interviewing completed
February 25, 1938

Jim Cupp is 27 years old, a tall lean fellow, with a shock of brown
curly hair and a gay smile. He likes to talk and to speculate about general
problems, building up his arguments and sorting out his ideas as he goes
along. The family's difficulties he discusses rather impersonally, but
frankly and unreservedly. Mrs. Cupp is placid and pretty, except for the
great gap left by the extraction of her front teeth. ("Your health runs down,
too, when you ain't got no money.") She is a competent housewife, whose
philosophy is neatly summed up in her own phrase: "You've got to get along
on what you've got". The three little Cupps—Betty, 4; Junior, almost 3;
and the 10-months-old baby Sue—are healthy, attractive youngsters. Betty
and Junior, rowdy and not too well-trained, play elaborate games of their
own invention and chatter unceasingly, in spite of the shouts of the older
Cupps and their vague threats of punishment.

The Cupps live in three sparsely and shabbily furnished rooms
of the first floor of a brick house in a downtown residential district.
From the fall of 1932 when the Cupps were married until September 1937,
Mr. Cupp had no regular full-time employment except on work projects. As
steel worker, rigger, and foreman on the Dubuque lock and dam project, he
had valuable experience which qualified him for the work he is now doing
for a private construction company in Dubuque. Mr. Cupp hopes now that he
will have employment whenever there is private construction work under way,

for he is young and healthy—an excellent "Insurance risk"—and experienced.
He hopes, too, that in the future he will be able to save enough during the
good months to tide the family over the lean winter months. Until now,
it has been necessary for the family to return to direct relief rolls each
time that Mr. Cupp has lost a job, for with accumulated bills to pay he
hasn't been able to save money.

     Until the spring of 1932, when Jim Cupp first went to Chicago, he
had lived on his father's farm about 8 miles from Dubuque. He had finished
eighth grade work in a country school, but had "never had time to go to
high school." Though the school district would have paid his tuition if
he had chosen to come to the Dubuque senior high school, it would have been
necessary for him either to board in town or to pay transportation, which
he could not afford. So he stayed on the farm. He wishes now that he
had a high school education, for it would be of considerable help to him
in his construction work.

     Between 1928 and 1930 Jim Cupp's folks had all the tough luck
they could have"; almost half of the livestock died, and Jim lost a
brother. By 1932 there was scarcely enough work to keep Jim busy on the
farm, and his parents urged him to try for work in the city. So Jim went
to Chicago, where he worked for some 6 weeks in the spring of 1932 on a
paint and carpentry job with a fellow who is now his brother-in-law, but
was then just a friend. "Before I was married I didn't care when I worked
and when I didn't." Even though he tried everywhere to find work, jobs
"didn't seem so important then." He had no other regular work in Chicago
until the fall of 1932, when for a few weeks he packed stationery; the job
had been contracted for by Mrs. Cupp's father, and all members of the

family and Jim helped with the packing in the basement of the home.

In November 1932 the Cupps were married. Mrs. Cupp had been employed, except for odd jobs of housework paying usually no more than $3 a week, for about a year previous to her marriage. Earlier, she had worked for 3 years in the office of a mail-order house, earning from $13 to $17 a week; and for about 1 year as timekeeper, at $20 a week, for a postal products company. Mrs. Cupp is proud of having done office work so long as jobs were available, even though she had only an eighth grade education.

Not long after their marriage the Cupps left Chicago because they were "financially embarrassed." Since Jim Cupp could not find work and Mrs. Cupp's parents were in no position to support him, he decided to take his wife to his father's farm, where they could at least always be certain of "having enough to eat." From "1932 on were the hardest times" the Cupps had. During the year or so that the Cupps spent on the farm, Jim tried to find regular employment but had only odd jobs. One winter, he spent a part of his time cutting wood at $1 a cord, and during most of the summer he earned $1 a day working for a farmer "from daylight to dark; a fellow doesn't squander any of his money then."

During the winter of 1933-34 Mr. Cupp couldn't find even odd jobs in the country, and in February 1934 he moved to town in the hope of having CWA employment, which had been half-promised him. But on inquiring now about the CWA job, he learned that just the day before a telegram from Washington had indicated that no more men could be assigned to projects. In the next 4 months Mr. Cupp had just 4 days of work. He had already, in 1932, borrowed as much as possible—$38—on his $1,000 20 year-payment life insurance policy, and he was now entirely without resources, but with a wife and a child to

support. It was necessary for him to apply for direct relief almost immediately after he came to town, even though he "put it off till the last
minute" and in the meantime looked for work. He applied for relief only with
misgivings and reluctance, for he "was ashamed to be in a place like that":
he doesn't "like to get something for nothing."

       The family considered the relief grants reasonably adequate. It's
all a matter of good management; families who complain about the meagerness
of relief grants, the Cupps think, simply don't know how to economize. The
Cupps "economized all right": before her marriage, Mrs. Cupp had never even
thought of baking bread, but now that baker's bread was out of the question,
she baked her own; she also canned great quantities of vegetables, and she
made her own clothes and the children's.

       Mr. Cupp had a garden lot on the island, where he spent many hours
that first spring uprooting stumps and clearing the ground. The many island
gardeners used to laugh together—though "it wasn't anything to laugh at
really"—when they saw good 10-acre fields near Dubuque lying idle and then
went down to the island and dug stumps and stones out of their meager plots
of ground; meanwhile the farmers were garnering benefit checks for not raising
crops. "There was something wrong somewhere." The second spring when Mr.
Cupp put in his garden, he "worked just as hard," except that there were no
longer any stumps to be dug. Soon after he had finished his planting, the
floods came, and the island was buried under 6 feet of water. From that day
to this, the Cupps haven't bothered with gardening.

       The Cupps were on direct relief, that first time, from February to
July 1934, when Mr. Cupp was assigned as a cement worker to the Dubuque lock
and dam project. Mr. Cupp believes that relief has been well handled. Of

course, "there is some drag," but it is better to feed "a few people who
don't really need help" than to let others who have no resources "starve."
What the Cupps minded most while they received direct relief grants was
their inability to pay rent. The relief office paid rent for the family
only every other month, and Mr. Cupp was "put in an embarrassing position"
when he had to ask the landlord to wait for the remainder of the rent.
But then, Mr. Cupp found himself in lots of embarrassing positions while he
was out of work and unable to meet bills for rent and for groceries and for
dental and medical care; after a while he "got used to embarrassing positions."

Mr. Cupp is inclined to think that the depression hit hardest
the young men who, like him, began to look for jobs only when jobs were
hardest to find. Older men may become "discouraged" too, but at least they
can look back on "the good years" with the comfortable feeling that they've
"had part of their lives." For a young man to grow discouraged is a more
serious thing. Mr. Cupp believes that depression unemployment has made for
an increase in crime, especially among younger men, though the CCC camps
have helped to minimize this trend toward crime. The camps have "made men"
of some of Mr. Cupp's acquaintances who might otherwise have become "bums
or crooks."

The Works Program and employment offices have also offered excellent opportunities to young men; Mr. Cupp himself had never really had a
chance to work until he was referred by the local employment office to
the locks project. At the employment office he had never been classified
"above a truck driver or laborer," and it was as a laborer that he was

first assigned to the work project. Later, he was transferred to work
requiring more skill, at a higher rate of pay.

From July to December 1934, when the locks were completed, Mr.
Cupp did cement work at 50¢ an hour---$15 a week. He much preferred work-
ing to depending on relief grants and found that the men took the project
work seriously. When the cement work was finished, Mr. Cupp again applied
for direct relief. Until the following September, when he was again assigned
to a work project, Mr. Cupp's only employment was an occasional odd job.

From September 1935 until May 1937 Mr. Cupp was regularly employed on the construction of the Dubuque dam. He began work as a rigger,
earning 80¢ an hour. After a few months the PWA contractor said that having
"made a rigger" out of Mr. Cupp, he would now "make a steel-worker" out of
him; so he became a steel-worker, earning $1 an hour. Near the end of
April, when the contractor decided that Mr. Cupp was ready to learn to be
a foreman, he "promoted" Mr. Cupp to a job paying $35 a week, less than he
had earned in many a week while working at the hourly rate of $1. As foreman,
he continued to work overtime, sometimes putting in 12 or 13 hours a day,
but with this difference: he was no longer paid for overtime. Still, when
a man is offered a job as foreman, he "doesn't turn it down," for the experience is valuable. Mr. Cupp jokes about his satisfaction with the job
as foreman; he thinks that his reactions were similar to those of a hero
of a recent movie who, when asked how much his new job would pay, answered,
"What do I care what I make? I'm gonna be the boss!"

Soon after the completion of the Dubuque dam in May 1937, Mr.
Cupp was transferred to a PWA construction project in New Boston, Ill., where

he worked for about 8 weeks as a rigger, under the direction of the same
construction company but under a different foreman. He was "alone" in
Illinois for 3 weeks before he rented furnished rooms for his family. Only
a few weeks after Mrs. Cupp and the children had gone to New Boston, Mr. Cupp
was laid off because of "hard feelings between the boss" and him. Immediately
after he returned to Dubuque, Mr. Cupp was employed by a private contractor,
then doing some repair work at an insulating plant. Though his hourly rate
was now only half as much as before---40¢---he was well enough satisfied with
the change. There was no great disparity in his weekly earnings, for he now
worked longer hours---regularly 48 hours a week, and some weeks considerably
more than 48 hours.

When this job was finished in November 1937, the Cupps again
applied for direct relief. They managed nicely on the relief grant of a
little more than $9 for groceries and 1/2 ton of coal for a 2-week period.
The Cupps never requested clothing, as Mr. Cupp always managed when he was
working to buy enough clothing to "tide him over" periods of unemployment,
but he can understand why the men who have been on WPA over a long period
of time want to "stock up on clothes" when they return to direct relief
rolls; from a $12 weekly pay check, not much can be spent for clothing.

Then, too, Mr. Cupp had 5 days of work on odd jobs during the
5 weeks he was on direct relief---an unusually good record, he thinks. Besides, when the Cupps applied for relief for the third time, they had some
food on hand, as flour and other staples had been purchased in large quantities. Thus, the Cupps were not entirely dependent on the $9 food order.
Though they could manage for several weeks or even several months on direct

relief without going deeply in debt, they fear that they couldn't "manage for
a year" without supplementary income or credit, for replacements of clothes
and household equipment must be made. On January 3d Mr. Cupp was assigned to
a WPA clearing project, on which he worked until the middle of February, when
he was called by the same private contractor for whom he had previously worked.

Mr. Cupp found the WPA "a great thing in time of need." He doesn't
"know what Dubuque would have done this winter" if it hadn't been for the WPA,
but he wonders sometimes "if the Government will have to go on forever"
creating jobs for men who have no employment in private industry or only seasonal employment. For the past 7 years even when employment in Dubuque has
been relatively high during the summer months, "hundreds of men have been laid
off" during the winter.

Mr. Cupp believes that there may always be seasonal peaks in certain
industries—such peaks may even be justifiable—but in Dubuque in recent years
the problems of seasonal employment have been intensified by the efforts of
the largest manufacturing concerns to "break" the newly organized millworkers'
union. In the summer the factories can hire high school boys who, working
only during the vacation season, "won't want to join the union." Warehouses
can be stocked with enough materials to fill such orders as are received during the winter months, and many men can be laid off. All this is considered
"none of the men's business until they make it their business." Mr. Cupp believes that although collective bargaining and legislation may help to raise
wage scales, the industrial situation in Dubuque will probably not be improved
so long as the town depends largely on the woodworking mills; for woodwork is
already "doomed."

"Unless something unforeseen happens or some drastic changes are
made," Mr. Cupp thinks, unemployment will continue to be a serious problem.
He attributes unemployment largely to the introduction of new machinery.
Since "every employer is only thinking of his own profits," he doesn't realize
that if he cuts total wages by installing machinery he may also cut purchasing
power to such an extent that he will have no markets for his product. "The
profit in the machine should go to labor." Employment can be spread by shortening hours of work, and purchasing power can be preserved by "guaranteeing
living wages" to the employed men, even though they may work short hours or
during only a part of the year. What a man earns by the hour or by the day
or by the week is not very important; "the annual wage" is what really counts,
for a man "has to go on living all the year" whether he works or not. Mr.
Cupp thinks that unions may help to raise wage rates, but that minimum wages
should be set by law. He regrets the lack of a structural steel workers'
local which might raise the steel workers' wages above the present 40¢ hourly
rate.

Mr. Cupp favors the Social Security Act; if only he had continued
to earn $35 a week, he would have "a good start on a tidy little pension."
The NRA, too, was "a fine piece of legislation," but there was "enough capital
to have it outlawed." So far as war is concerned, Mr. Cupp, like "all other
Americans," can only "wonder" and "hope" that America can stay out of war.
As the father of "three kids," he "wouldn't fancy a war," though he would be
glad to fight if America were actually invaded, or if a war fought on foreign
soil could forestall a threatened invasion.

Mr. Cupp has evidently given much thought to the Works Program. He
can understand the point of view of the WPA workers who see as "big things"

the minor disadvantages which WPA administrators consider "little things."
For instance, there is the question of transportation, which the men think
should be paid by the WPA. The administrators, thinking that "$12 a week is
an adequate wage," don't realize that 20¢ a day for transportation cuts a
big slice out of the weekly wage. Then, too, there is the matter of illness;
if a man misses 1 day of work because of illness, he is expected to present
a doctor's statement that he was unable to report for work. "No fellow
earning $12 a week," says Mr. Cupp, "can afford to pay $3 for a doctor's call
unless it is absolutely necessary."

The WPA clearance project, on which Mr. Cupp worked for about 6
weeks, seems to him worthwhile enough to justify a little extra expenditure
for transportation of workers to and from the project, which, being 6 miles
out from town, can scarcely be considered within walking distance. Most of
the WPA workers, Mr. Cupp feels, are anxious to have private employment whenever possible; he himself, on leaving WPA for private employment, thought that
he wouldn't mind if he "worked 7 days a week" instead of 3, and if his earnings fell a little below the $12 weekly wage, so long as he could manage at
all. In private employment he feels so much more "independent" and more as
though his earnings depend entirely on his own efforts.

When the contractor for whom Mr. Cupp had worked for 2 months in
1937 first contracted for the construction of a new building in February 1938,
Mrs. Cupp urged her husband to ask for a job, but Mr. Cupp told her, "He'll
pick out his men." Sure enough, that very day the contractor called Mr. Cupp
to work; he was one of the first men to be hired on the new job.

Mr. Cupp likes Dubuque as a place to live, but not as a place to
work. Chicago, he thinks, would offer more opportunities for employment, but
he has no contacts there, while in Dubuque he has an excellent record with

two different construction companies. The Cupps are most anxious to remain
off direct relief and WPA rolls in the future, and just now Mr. Cupp finds
his prospects for continued employment unusually good. So long as there are
construction jobs to be had in Dubuque, he expects to continue working.

                    Employment Chronology for Mr. Cupp

          Until 1932   -   On father's farm.

          Spring 1932   6 weeks--painter.

          Fall 1932   6 weeks--packer of stationery.

          November 1932 -
          September 1937   Unemployed except for emer-
                            gency work.

          September -
          November 1937   Steel worker, private contractor.

          November 1937 -
          February 1938   Unemployed except for emergency
                            work.

          February 1938 -
          Present   Steel worker, private contractor.

<u>WHITNEY</u>

Mr. Whitney	28
Mrs. Whitney	30
Betty	6
Billy	1

Interviewing completed
January 24, 1938

The Whitneys live in a tall, narrow, four-room house set high
above the street level in a neighborhood of scattered small homes. The
house is rickety and in need of repair. Too poorly constructed to be
entirely weatherproof, and heated only by the one great stove in the
living room, the house is cold in winter months. The wind whistles under
the front door and pushes the thin rug up into great bulges. At bed time
Betty, the little girl, undresses behind the stove and then races upstairs
to jump under the bed covers.

Garf Whitney, 28 years old, was unemployed for almost 4 years
between 1931 and 1935. During most of this period the family was dependent either on direct relief or on Mr. Whitney's earnings from emergency
work projects. For more than 2 years now, he has been regularly employed
at the Iowa Foundry.

The Whitneys are a happy family group. Mr. and Mrs. Whitney are
friendly with strangers, to whom they talk freely and without reserve. Mr.
Whitney, though not tall, is solid and husky-looking. His dark hair grows
ragged on the back of his neck which is gouged with the deep scars of old
carbuncles. His nose, too, is pitted with little scars. His eyes are
small and squinty behind puffy eyelids, but they twinkly while he talks
and laughs a little at his own misfortunes.

Almost every evening friends come to the Whitneys' home to play cards or to listen to the radio. Mr. and Mrs. Whitney go out only on Saturday nights when they usually see a movie while Mr. Whitney's sister stays with the two children. Mrs. Whitney would prefer not going out at all to leaving Billy in the care of a "young girl."

Garf Whitney's mother died when he was 4 years old and he was brought up by an older sister. Since his father had a large family to support, Garf found it necessary to leave school and go to work when he had finished the eighth grade. He began work as a cutter at Hall's clothing factory. Except that the pay was low, he liked this "good clean work" which he did not find too monotonous. Some of the men, high school graduates, who began work at Hall's when Garf did, were rapidly promoted from machine operation to the shipping room to the sales force, but Garf Whitney continued for almost 7 years as a cutter. His pay was increased, over the 7-year period, from $15 to $19 a week. He feels that he might have stayed at Hall's forever without going beyond the $19-a-week job. Even so, he might have continued at Hall's indefinitely had he not wanted to marry. Surely, he thought, he couldn't support a family on $19 a week; and surely he thought again, there was some place where he could earn more money.

So Garf, who had lived all his short life in Dubuque and Violet, who had grown up in Wisconsin but came to Dubuque to work after her graduation from high school, went to Rockford, Ill., then generally recognized as a "booming" town. There they were married one Saturday afternoon in the spring of 1929. On the Monday morning the two of them went their separate ways to look for jobs. The job-seeking they called their honeymoon. Before the day was over, both had found work: Mr. Whitney was in a machine shop and Mrs. Whitney in a dime store. Jobs were still plentiful

in 1929---so plentiful, Mrs. Whitney recalls with some awe, that she
actually left one store "just because she didn't like the girls" and
promptly went to work in another.

Mr. Whitney worked for a little less than 2 years as a helper and as an electric welder in the machine shop, earning 44¢ an hour for
the regular 9-hour day, and extra pay for overtime, which almost always
included two evenings a week and Saturday afternoons. He left this job
only when there was a general layoff late in 1930. By then, jobs were
no longer to be had for the mere asking in Rockford; so the Whitneys decided to come to Dubuque, where Mr. Whitney had a lot of friends.

For a time, however, it seemed to him that he no longer had
friends in Dubuque since he couldn't find a job anywhere. Finally, at
the end of about 2 months, Mr. Whitney was taken on as a saw operator
in an insulating plant. He was paid 35¢ an hour for 12 hours a day 7.
days a week. The plant was then working 24 hours a day on two shifts.
The men were paid for the full 12 hours "straight through the lunch
hour"---but then they had "no full hour for lunch" either; they were expected to gulp down their food in about 10 minutes. Mr. Whitney didn't
really mind the long hours; he was so glad to be working. But it was a
little disconcerting to be earning only $28 a week for "all them hours."
In the spring of 1931 the insulating plant shut down altogether. Quickly,
Mr. Whitney got a job at the Midwestern Foundry as buffer---a highly routine job, but one which didn't last long enough for Mr. Whitney to grow
bored with it. At the end of about a month he was laid off again, and
now, though he tried everywhere, he couldn't find another job---not even
a 35¢-an-hour, 12-hour-a-day job.

The Whitneys had no savings. In Rockford they had bought furniture, some of which they sold rather than move it to Dubuque. In Dubuque
they had bought more furniture--little enough, but still enough to preclude
the possibility of saving any money. Soon after the marriage Mr. Whitney
had taken out insurance policies for himself and Mrs. Whitney, but these
had no cash surrender value and were allowed to lapse. The Whitneys lived
on credit until they owed money to "everybody in town"--the grocer, the
landlord, the coal dealers, and to whom not? Mr. Whitney had got to "hanging around outside the courthouse," where the county poor relief investi-
gator--this was before the days of the ERA--had her office. But even after
he had gone down to the courthouse for several days in a row, he "couldn't
get up enough courage" to go in and make an application for assistance.
"It took a lot of guts--pardon my language, but I don't know any other way
to say it--to go in and apply for relief."

Then one day one of the county supervisors, a friend of Mr.
Whitney, offered to take Mr. Whitney to the office. He didn't mind so
much going with this supervisor, and once he had made his first application
"it wasn't so bad." He explains, "of course, it wasn't any disgrace, as
far as that is concerned." Every day the first floor of the courthouse
was jammed with people waiting to see the supervisor, and every time Mr.
Whitney went in to make some request he met a lot of his friends. Mr.
Whitney didn't want to "complain," for he realized that funds were
limited and the staff inadequate; but he didn't like having to go to the
office repeatedly to make minor requests. "If he had waited for a worker
to come to the house," Mr. Whitney thinks, "we would have got nothing."
Sometimes he "couldn't help feeling" that the fewer the needs that the
workers met--and the more money they saved for the county-- "the bigger
the feather they got in their caps."

Mr. Whitney has forgotten—he has "wanted to forget"—many of the
details of relief experiences. Mrs. Whitney "gets the creeps" at the mere
mention of the word relief, for she can't help but wonder if she may sometime have to relive those depression days. For grown people, relief
wouldn't be so bad—"they can live on bread and potatoes"—but the children
must have a variety of food. Living on relief was "just existing from hand
to mouth; you couldn't call it really living." The grocery order of $2.50
a week was increased to $3 with the coming of the emergency relief setup,
but it still wasn't "any too much." When Mr. Whitney was on work relief,
grocery orders were a little higher, he thinks about $5 a week. He worked
for some time on the county airport project on a relief basis, the number
of weekly hours being determined by size of the family and amount of the
food allowance.

Food orders were supplemented by surplus commodities. The
Whitneys ate so much canned beef that the very sight of it made them ill,
and once Mrs. Whitney was really ill from eating the beef. The salt pork
she rendered into lard. The Whitneys also supplemented grocery orders
with their own garden produce. Mr. Whitney said that they had to have a
garden to maintain their eligibility for relief, but that they would have
had one anyhow he had gardened before receiving relief, and since returning to work has continued to put in a garden every spring. Now, the
Whitneys have a large garden plot at the side of the house. While they
lived in an apartment, Mr. Whitney gardened "2 acres—well, no, "that's a
little exaggeration," but at least he gardened a huge lot which he was
permitted to use rent-free. And Mrs. Whitney did a great deal of canning.

Over one period of time, a $7 rent allowance was made every
other month. Since the actual rent was $9 a month for the two rooms which

the family then occupied, whatever was not paid by the relief office was
added to the rent bill. Mr. Whitney kept looking for all kinds of jobs
while he was on relief and on work projects, and he was usually able to
put in at least 1 day a week at some sort of work. Rates of pay were
very low: Mr Whitney unloaded carloads of coal more frequently than he
did anything else, and for the unloading he was paid from 10 to 15¢ a ton.
"They knew they could get fellows to do it for that." Whatever Mr.
Whitney earned was applied on the rent. Even so, he ended by owing the
landlord more than $70; this he considered an enormous bill in view of the
fact that the rent was only $9 a month.

Since that time the Whitneys have moved twice; they lived for a
time in another apartment but found the arrangement unsatisfactory,
especially as the woman living downstairs worked at night and slept during
the day just when Betty wanted to romp and play. So they moved again, this
time to the house which they now occupy and which rents for $12 a month.
Here, there is plenty of space for Betty's play and for Mr. Whitney's gardening. But, because the rent is so little, the Whitneys cannot expect the
landlord to make any repairs, or even to take care of the painting and
papering. The paper, which the Whitneys themselves hung more than 2 years
ago, is now dingy and blackened with coal smoke.

While they were on relief the Whitneys managed for the most part
without new clothes, but once, when neither Mr. nor Mrs. Whitney had a
shred of night clothing, they got through the Red Cross some very dark
blue flannel from which Mrs. Whitney made, without patterns, two pairs of
pajamas; they happened to be much too large. When Mrs. Whitney's brother-
in-law, who had refused to contribute to the Red Cross, saw these huge
"almost black" pajamas, he said that if Violet could actually wear those
things, he could send his dollar to the Red Cross, and he did. Since

then, Mrs. Whitney has learned to sew better; she has a decrepit but still
usable sewing machine, and she makes all of Betty's attractive little print
dresses for school.

In the fall of 1933 Mr. Whitney was assigned to CWA work on the
county roads. He was paid $15 a week, which seemed like "big money." Soon
after the CWA program ended, Mr. Whitney was assigned to emergency work,
first on the Dubuque lock and dam project, then on a paving job. Between
jobs, the family again received direct relief for about 6 months. Mr.
Whitney preferred project work to direct relief, chiefly on the basis of
the increased income, and the income in cash instead of grocery orders
and commodities.

So far as the Whitneys are concerned, the relief days are over.
In the fall of 1935 Mr. Whitney, on one of his usual rounds of job-hunt-
ing—he worked only 3 or 4 days a week on WPA and spent all of his spare
time looking for regular full-time, or a little supplementary, work—
stopped at the Iowa Foundry and asked for a job. He was told that the only
work to be done at the moment was the unloading of a 36-ton carload of
coal. Promptly he said that he would unload the coal, and he said to himself that maybe—just maybe—if he unloaded that coal in record time he
would be offered a regular job. So he set to work, and he unloaded the 36
tons of coal in 8 hours. When he paused briefly at noontime, he took time
to telephone to his wife and tell her of his "hunch" that he might get a
job. She said, "If you do, I think I'll faint." Then she remembered that
Garf was wearing, to unload a carload of coal, his only white shirt and
his only decent shoes.

"Well," she thought, "if he gets a job out of it, I guess we can
get him a new shirt." Sure enough, at the end of the day, the boss looked
at the 36 tons of coal and said, "Suppose you report for work in the

morning." And so it was that Mr. Whitney got a new shirt—not to mention
a full-time job that he has held up to the present time. Oh! some weeks,
of course, he has had short hours, "but there has always been a pay
check coming in."

Mr. Whitney was first put to work as a molder's helper and was
paid 37½¢ an hour. The work did not differ a great deal from the job in
the machine shop in Rockford, and on the whole he found it quite satisfactory. His wage-rate was soon raised to 40¢ an hour. At the end of
about a year he was given a regular molder's job at a piecework rate.
He now earns, on an average, 60¢ an hour for a 45-hour week. Occasionally, when there are rush orders, the molders work longer than 45 hours;
and sometimes there is work enough to last only 3 or 4 days a week. A
group bonus plan is in effect at the foundry, but the molders rarely make
the bonus, as the task has been set high, and any materials ruined in the
molding process are counted against the record of work accomplished by
the department. The highest bonus payment Mr. Whitney ever received was
40¢ for a week's work. Still, the bonus plan "gives the fellows something to work toward."

In the foundry Mr. Whitney's weekly pay is about the same as at
the insulating plant, but his weekly hours are little more than half as
long. He prefers the Iowa Foundry as a place of employment to every other
plant in Dubuque, for wages are higher and the work more regular than in
most local factories. But there are some disadvantages, of course;
though the plant has never shut down entirely since Mr. Whitney began to
work there more than 2 years ago, the hours are somewhat irregular. In
summer months the extra heat of the great furnaces is almost unbearable.
Not a single molder in the foundry is a member of a union. On principle

Mr. Whitney believes in the unionization of all workers. The AFL, to his
way of thinking, has protected only carpenters and other skilled workers;
it has never been really concerned about "the laboring man." The needs of
the "laboring men" the CIO has sought to meet. If the CIO and the AFL can
work together--and Mr. Whitney has some faith in the "peace" negotiations--
they may really accomplish something in the way of extensive and powerful
labor organization.

      Mr. Whitney would "like to be a booster" for his town, but the
wish to boost cannot blind him to the fact that "wages in Dubuque are
wretchedly low." A daily paper recently ran an article pointing out that
wages in Dubuque are among the lowest in the United States and do not
compare very favorably with the low wages in the Southern States. Thus,
in Dubuque more than in many other cities, there is need for "strong
labor organization."

      Mr. Whitney, who favors most of the recent social legislation,
is very much interested in the wage and hour bill. "Wage and hour legislation will have to come." He believes that a limitation of hours of work
will serve both to spread employment and to smooth out seasonal peaks of
production. For example, instead of working 50 hours 1 week and perhaps
only 30 the next, Mr. Whitney, if wage and hour legislation were a
reality, might work regularly 40 hours a week. Any man is inclined to
"spend all he earns," and in slack seasons may find it hard to make ends
meet. For himself, Mr. Whitney would prefer working a definite number of
hours and counting on a regular wage week after week, even if his total
earnings were a little lower than at present. The NRA Mr. Whitney considers "one of the best laws ever passed"; except for opposition of "the
big shots" the act would have been workable. The Social Security Act also
offers excellent protection to the working man.

Though Mr. Whitney doesn't "know enough" to understand the
causes of depression unemployment or the various proposed solutions, he
has some few ideas of his own. Unemployment can be minimized through
the spreading of employment as a result of limiting hours of work and
pensioning older employees. Mr. Whitney sees in the "recession" only a
"manipulation" by business men. He does not anticipate that it will be
long-lived or that it will threaten his own job-security.

Employment Chronology for Mr. Whitney

1922 - April 1929   Cutter, Hall's clothing
                     factory.

April 1929 - December
1930   Helper, machine shop.

February 1931 - spring
1931   Saw operator, insulating
                     plant.

Summer 1931-- 1
month   Buffer, Midwestern Foundry
                     Company.

Summer 1931 - fall
1935   Unemployed except for
                     emergency work.

Fall 1935 - present Molder's helper and
                     molder, Iowa Foundry.

THOMPSON

Mr. Thompson 32
Mrs. Thompson 30

Interviewing completed
January 3, 1938

Gerry Thompson, 32 years old, has made his own way ever since
he was 17. Within the past 15 years, during 2 of which he had no regular
employment, he has worked for 11 different companies. He laughs about
the number and variety of jobs he has held, but prides himself on having
"stuck" with even the most unpleasant jobs either until they ended or
until he had better jobs in sight. He "kind of enjoyed" outlining his
work history in terms of hours, wages, and dates of employment, even
down to the precise hour of the day when he began work on one new job;
he thinks that a summary of his varied jobs would make a "good magazine
story."

Mr. Thompson is tall and lean. His black hair, growing a little
thin, has receded from his already high forehead. The skin of his neck
is slightly mottled as the result of a chronic skin infection. His
manner is cordial, and he talks freely.

As the oldest of six children, Gerry Thompson found it advisable
to leave school when he was 17 and go to work. He had completed high
school work and begun a business school course. Though his father did
not insist on his leaving school, Gerry knew that he could not well afford
to support all of the children in the home. The father, a tavern keeper,
had found it necessary to move on to another county each time the one in
which he had been running a tavern "went dry." When Dubuque County

went dry Mr. Thompson, senior, had only to move his business across the
Mississippi River to East Dubuque, Ill. When the whole country went dry,
the father got factory work with the Mississippi Milling Company in
Dubuque.

At 17, Gerry Thompson began work for the Yough Marble Company in
Dubuque. During 6 years of continuous work for this company he was
transferred frequently from one department to another and ended by knowing
marble-cutting thoroughly. His earnings were $24 a week. At the end of
4½ years Mr. Thompson was transferred to a plant of the same company in
another Iowa town, where he remained, working at the same rate of pay, for
about 18 months. He left to go to Chicago with a fellow-employee. Mr.
Thompson had anticipated the bankruptcy of the company by a few weeks.
He lost only 2 days' pay, which was tied up in a receivership.

Through his work in the shipping room of the Yough Company, Mr.
Thompson had learned of the Chicago plant which had recently undertaken
the same general type of work. As Mr. Thompson was familiar with a
special cutting process, he and his friend were immediately hired by the
Chicago firm. In the department in which the two of them worked, they had
pretty much their own way; special tools were ordered on their request.
But no sooner was the work well started than both were fired, presumably
because the company had learned from them all that was necessary. Mr.
Thompson had worked here for about 2 months; his earnings were $30 a week.

Almost immediately after he was fired, Mr. Thompson and a friend
secured jobs with a Chicago firm of contractors, building cement culverts.
The friend had formerly worked for this same company on a construction
job in Florida. Mr. Thompson's particular job was running the cement
mixer. Though this work was heavier than any to which he had been

accustomed, he "stuck" until the job was finished at the end of 3 months.
He had been paid 90¢ an hour; hours of work varied, but he made about $48
a week. He had hoped that he would be transferred to similar jobs in
other parts of the country on the completion of the Chicago job, but he
now learned that the company usually picked up laborers at the scene of
each job. He was again out of work, then, at the beginning of July 1928.

Early in July of the same year Mr. Thompson was married to a
Dubuque girl, 2 years younger than he. Mrs. Thompson, now several months
pregnant, is very pretty with her brown wavy hair, soft brown eyes, and
flushed cheeks. She is quieter than her husband but occasionally enters
into the conversation with a remark which shows a nice sense of humor.
Before her marriage, Mrs. Thompson had operated a power machine in Hall's
clothing factory; since her marriage she has never been employed outside
the home. The Thompsons are happily anticipating their first child.

At the time of their marriage 9 years ago, Mr. Thompson was not
working, but saw no point in postponing the wedding, the date for which
had been set far in advance. The Thompsons began married life in Chicago,
where in mid-July Mr. Thompson found a job as an extra dock worker for a
railroad. He was paid 50¢ an hour, $24 a week, and a bonus figured on the
amount of freight handled. The work of handling and hauling the freight
was still heavier than the construction work, but "a man can get toughened
into any work," and Mr. Thompson did get toughened. At the end of 6 weeks
he was referred to a job with a carloading company following a request
that the railroad send a good workman. This job was approximately the
same as the other, except that it promised to last longer. For the
carloading company, Mr. Thompson worked 48 hours a week; the 8-hour day
began at 7:30 A.M. Mr. Thompson gave up the job at the end of 2 weeks,

"the truth of the matter" being that "she got homesick." Mrs. Thompson
defends herself against this charge; the Thompsons were then renting a
furnished apartment for $65 a month, which was about as low a rental as
could be found but more than Mr. Thompson could pay except by drawing on
his meager savings. Furthermore, because of the early starting time, it
seemed practical for the family to live near the warehouses; the neighborhood was not a particularly good one and neither Mr. nor Mrs. Thompson was
well satisfied with the living arrangements.

Whatever the truth of the matter may be, the Thompsons returned
to Dubuque in August 1928 and moved in with Mrs. Thompson's parents and
her younger brother and sister. The arrangement was a reasonably
satisfactory one, for all members of the family got along well together.
The Thompsons did not do their own cooking but lived as a part of a single
household. They explained, "We were just like two kids there." They paid
$10 a week for board and room. Almost immediately, Mr. Thompson got a job
at the Stevenson Phonograph and Radio plant, where Mrs. Thompson's father
and brother were working. As a so-called "cabinetmaker" Mr. Thompson
couldn't be said to have had "a trade" since he merely fitted together the
parts of the phonograph cabinets that came to him ready-cut by machine.
He worked on an average of 9 hours a day, occasionally as many as 10
hours, and earned 64¢ an hour. Many of the men worked very long hours
during the busiest seasons, but the amount of work varied from department
to department.

In December 1931 the Stevenson plant closed, and Mr. Thompson,
and Mr. Shearer and Ralph Shearer, Mrs. Thompson's father and brother, all
were laid off at about the same time. The Dubuque railroad shops had
closed only a few months earlier. Since at least one member of almost

every family in the north end of town where the Shearers owned their home
had been employed either in the shops or at Stevenson's, the entire
neighborhood was "hard hit." For a time the Stevenson workers assumed
that the shutdown was only a temporary one. But gradually, when no men
were recalled to work, they began to realize that the shutdown might be
more serious than they had thought. Fears were confirmed and suspense
was ended when they heard that machinery was being moved out of the
Stevenson buildings.

After the closing of the Stevenson plant Mr. Thompson had no
work for almost 2 years. He resented most having no satisfactory way of
spending his time; Mr. Thompson, Mr. Shearer, and Ralph all "just sat"
except when they could find odd jobs or could garden in a vacant lot owned
by Mr. Shearer. Mr. Thompson, following a habit of long standing, read
every magazine he could lay his hands on—not "trash," of course, but
"good" magazines. Because he read so many articles and had such decided
opinions, the family—"just to tease him"—labeled him "a Bolshevik." He
was "kind of radical" and might have grown more so if he had been unemployed a little longer. But he is now less "radical," for "a fellow
doesn't think so much about those things when he has work to do, and after
all, I've been working for 4 years now." He does not elaborate on his
"radicalism" or on the differences between his attitude when he was unemployed and his present attitudes, but he explains that he is still
vigorously in favor of unionization and "can put up a good argument" in
defense of strikes for higher wages. Mr. Thompson considers it "an old
story that this town clamps down on the working man." But he understands
that wage scales have been greatly increased by union activities and by
the strikes in the Dubuque factories during the summer of 1936.

Mr. Thompson has had many a rousing argument with his present
employer, a wholesale grocer, who, never having worked for anyone but his
father, has no understanding of what it means to be entirely dependent on
a job. Mr. Thompson recalled one occasion when somebody had asked what
the striking factory workers wanted anyhow--money to put in the bank? Mr.
Thompson's answer was a suggestion that this man should "try taking care
of a family on $10 or $15 a week and see how much money he would have to
put in the bank." For that matter, Mr. Thompson feels that any man's
earnings should be high enough to enable him to save a little for an
emergency. Mr. Thompson has no car and no "envy" of men who do have cars;
he "can get along without one." He doesn't drink beer and he doesn't
often go to the movies, and "That's all right, too"; he "can get along
without beer and movies." But he does "want to know if there is any
reason" why he shouldn't have a radio or a new suit of clothes when he
needs one.

While Mr. Thompson had been working at Stevenson's, he and Mrs.
Thompson had continued to live with the Shearers. As Mrs. Shearer is
never very well and has had several serious illnesses, it was virtually
necessary for Mrs. Thompson to remain at home to care for her; the younger
daughter was working outside the home. When Mr. Thompson lost his job, he
found himself unable to make regular payments to the Shearer family. He
secured what cash he could by borrowing $200 on his and Mrs. Thompson's
insurance policies and by selling his old car for $100. These amounts
were for the most part applied on the board bill. Mr. Thompson also helped
the Shearers in other ways. He worked for a coal company to pay off the
Shearers' coal bills and worked out the family's water bill. Amounts of
these bills were deducted from the total amount owed by the Thompsons to

the Shearers. Mr. Thompson found that when people living together get
along well with each other, they have no difficulty in making financial
adjustments. Mr. Thompson helped with the gardening and Mrs. Thompson
with the canning and the sewing. The Thompsons bought no new clothing,
and they cut expenses to a minimum. They did run a grocery bill and a
doctor's bill as well, for Mr. Thompson had treatments for his "annual
bronchitis" and for the chronic skin infection.

        In the spring of 1933 both the Thompsons and the Shearers made
application for relief. This "didn't bother" Mr. Thompson any. Other
families "no worse off" than the Thompsons were making applications.
Besides, he felt that he had worked when jobs were to be had and was now
"willing to work at anything"available; "if I couldn't find a job there
wasn't any reason why I shouldn't get work relief"; he had not requested
direct relief. Because the Thompsons had no children and the larger
families were "naturally enough" given first consideration, Mr. Thompson
had only 1 or 2 weeks of work cutting wood for the county. He was paid
$19 a week in cash. "There has to be relief"; Mr. Thompson knows that,
but he believes that "men should be made to work for what they get." As
a matter of fact, most men prefer work to direct relief, at least in the
beginning, but it is easy for them to come to depend on relief grants and,
after a time, lose the ambition to work.

        Evelyn Shearer's employment at Hall's, where she earned $2.50 a
week, made the Shearer family ineligible for more than occasional work relief.
Evelyn is still employed at Hall's, but she estimates that she has work
for only about 7 months of the year, when time lost because of layoffs
and short hours is counted out.

While he was unemployed, Mr. Thompson sought work wherever he could, but local factories, having laid off men in great numbers, would not take new applications; there were "plenty of old workers" waiting to be recalled when any hiring was done. Whenever Mr. Thompson heard that a company was taking on new men, he went to the plant in the hope of being among those hired. But he had no luck until August 1933 when he got a job with a firm of wholesale grocers, for whom he worked 10 hours a day as driver, packer, salesman, and so on.

Mr. Thompson got this job through another employee, a friend of his; almost no one was being hired anywhere unless he had "pull." When Mr. Thompson was told that he could begin work, he wasted no time asking about the rate of pay, for he knew of no other job available at the moment and was willing to work for any wage. However, he had thought that he would get "at least $15 a week," and when, on the first pay day, he found only $12 in his pay envelope he was "sick." He was "put in such a position" that he couldn't very well ask for a raise, but his pay was increased to $13 a week with the coming of NRA, and hours were reduced to 8 a day.

It was Mr. Thompson's understanding that the NRA code agreement stipulated wage payments of $19 a week for truck drivers, but he was told by his boss that he could be paid no more than $13. "If anyone happened to ask me what I was doing, I was to say that I wasn't a truck driver. It was true that I spent only part time on the truck." The invalidation of NRA made for an increase in his hours to 8½ a day but no decrease in the rate of pay. A year later he was granted another increase of $1 a week. He was now earning $14 a week, and "mind you, we were trying to pay up back bills."

On July 14, 1936, Mr. Thompson left the grocery firm, where he had worked for almost 3 years, and on the following day began work as a gas station attendant, earning $15 a week. However, he did not complete a week's work, for at the end of 3 days someone at the Electric Power Company who had learned from a relative that Mr. Thompson was anxious to have a better job suggested that he apply for work on a construction gang. Accordingly, Mr. Thompson went to the Electric Power Company, was hired immediately, returned to the gas station to give up his 3-day-old job, and that same day began work as timekeeper on a construction job. Here he was paid 45¢ an hour; hours varied with changes in the weather, but earnings averaged about $30 a week. Mr. Thompson worked on a job in Dubuque for 10 days. At the end of this time he was sent with a gang to a Wisconsin town, where he worked for about 1 month.

Though expenses were higher away from home, with his own board bill amounting to $8.50 a week, Mr. Thompson sent home, from his pay of $65 or $70 for a 2-week period, more than he would have earned at the gas station. In September 1936 he was transferred to a job in Nebraska. Still later, he worked with the gangs in Minnesota and again in Wisconsin. Mrs. Thompson was with her husband for about 1 month of the 4 months he worked for the Electric Power Company, but she returned to Dubuque when the Thompsons found it difficult to meet the extra expenses of her room, board, and travel.

At Thanksgiving, Mr. Thompson returned home and looked around in Dubuque for another job, for he knew that the construction work would peter out during the winter months. In short order, he got a job as driver of a coal truck. He returned to Wisconsin to collect his pay and pack his clothing and was back in Dubuque in time to start work on the following Monday morning.

As truck driver for the coal company Mr. Thompson earned 45¢ an hour for an irregular number of hours, earnings averaged $25 or $26 a week. After 3 months' work he broke an arm when he fell from the truck as it skidded on an ice-glazed street. For 2 months he received compensation of $14.01 a week. Doctor bills were paid by the company. He returned to the job the middle of March, but he had worked for only about a month when he was told that there would be no work on the following day. He interpreted this to mean that there would be no work, or at best only a few odd jobs, before the next fall.

Mr. Thompson at once filed application with the State employment office and also went to the Dubuque Woodworking Company, where he stated that he was "a cabinetmaker." He was told that he might start work immediately. It was then 10 A.M. Mr. Thompson had neither work clothes nor dinner pail and didn't want to "waste money" by buying lunch downtown, so he said that he would begin work at 1 P.M. On this job, he earned 35¢ an hour for 50 hours a week. He was also granted a bonus but never learned how it was calculated: "It was extra, and you just took it." His highest bonus payment was $9 for 2 weeks.

Mr. Thompson had hoped to remain at the woodworking mill at least for the summer. But by June the work was already slack, and he was half expecting to be laid off at any moment; so he was glad enough to return to the wholesale grocery company when he was called back. "After all that moving around," he has ended by returning to the company where he had had his first job after the Stevenson closing. He is, however, now earning more than he previously did—$18 a week. And he is well satisfied with the job, for he knows that the work is steady; it is also more varied than the factory work. He has not been docked for time lost, even though he was

once out for 2 weeks during an illness; he has been promised a raise,,and
he is now gaining valuable experience which may lead to a better job with
this or another similar company. Mrs. Thompson fears that, at 32, he is "
"too old" to secure other work easily, as the first question asked by a
prospective employer usually relates to age, and the preference is for
younger men. Mr. Thompson, on the other hand, feels that experience has
more weight than youth when it comes to getting jobs in the wholesale
grocery business.

During the past 3 months the Thompsons have been living in a
four-room, first-floor apartment not far from the Shearer home. The
Thompsons had once before left the Shearer home and rented an unfurnished
apartment in the downtown section. But after a few months, they returned,
for Mrs. Shearer was again ill, and it had been necessary for Mrs.
Thompson to spend more time at her mother's than in her own home. They
are better satisfied with the present arrangement: Mrs. Thompson can visit
her mother frequently, and the Thompsons will have their own home when the
baby is born. The Shearers have been managing fairly well, as Mr. Shearer
and Ralph have been employed for some time in one of the woodworking mills,
and Evelyn has continued to work, though irregularly, at Hall's. However,
because of shutdowns during inventory-taking at the end of the year, all
three have recently been at home for several days. Once again, all the
wage-earners of the family have been laid off at the same time.

Mr. Thompson has been much interested in recent social legislation, especially the old-age benefits provisions of the Social Security
Act; he finds the tax payment scarcely noticeable, though Mrs. Thompson
fears that when the rate rises to 3 percent and the tax on wages for an
entire month is deducted from the pay for a single week, the family may
have more difficulty in managing. Mr. Thompson fears that wage and hour

legislation, if the law as passed stipulates a minimum of 40¢ an hour,
will result in the lowering of wages of men now earning more than 40¢ an
hour. In Dubuque, under the NRA, the minimum wage tended to become likewise the maximum, and "what has happened once can happen again." Mr.
Thompson has more faith in unionization as a means toward the raising of
wage rates.

Mr. Thompson has heard many men attribute the depression of the
early thirties to "machines," but he inclines to the belief that the
manufacture of machinery may create more jobs than the use of the machinery
eliminates. Mrs. Thompson thinks that perhaps the depression resulted from
the fact that "all the money was in one place." The present "business
recession" does not worry Mr. Thompson very much, as he feels that he is
secure in his own job, though he agrees with Mrs. Thompson's statement
that he would be worried if he were a factory worker. For the Dubuque
factories, recently shut down for inventory-taking, have not all reopened,
and even those workers who have been recalled to work have no assurance
that their jobs will last. But the grocery business is a little different,
for "people will always have to eat."

Employment Chronology for Mr. Thompson

1922 – 1928	Cutter, Yough Marble Company.
February – March 1928	Cutter, marble company.
April – July 1928	Cement mixer operator, construction company.
July – August 1928	Loader, railroad and carloading company.
August 1928 – December 1931	Cabinetmaker, Stevenson Phonograph and Radio Company.
December 1931 – August 1933	Unemployed.
August 1933 – July 1936	Packer, salesman, and truck driver, wholesale grocery company.
July – November 1936	Construction worker, Electric Power Company.
November 1936 – April 1937	Truck driver, coal company.
April – June 1937	Cabinetmaker, Dubuque Woodworking Company.
June 1937 – present	Salesman, wholesale grocery.

<u>COLLER</u>

<u>Mr. Coller</u>	31
Mrs. Coller	28
Jane	6
Roy	4

Interviewing completed
March 28, 1938

Don Coller, 31 years old, a truck driver for 12 years, was unemployed and on direct relief or work relief for 2 years during the depression. Employed for the past 2 years as a night-loader for a trucking
company, Mr. Coller now receives the highest wage he has ever made and
his outlook for the future is optimistic. Mr. Coller, his wife, and
their two children, Jane, a first-grader, and Roy, 4, occupy a small,
two-story frame house in a good residential neighborhood on the hill.
The house is in excellent repair; the interior is neat and clean, and
the furnishings are of fair quality. The Collers pay a rental of $17
a month.

Mr. Coller is somewhat striking in appearance. Of medium build,
he has large black eyes, heavy black brows, and black hair brushed back
from his face. Friendly and well-poised, he discusses his depression
experiences with franckness and spontaneity. Mrs. Coller, also a brunette,
is attractive and gracious. The children are healthy-looking and well
mannered. Roy, undecided as to whether he wants to become a fireman or
a cowboy when he grows up rides around proudly in his red fire truck.
Both Mr. and Mrs. Coller are happy that they are now able to provide
adequately for the children's pleasure as well as their actual needs.

Mr. Coller was born in Dubuque. Being 1 of 10 children, he
had to quit school at the age of 15 to contribute to the family budget.

His first job was that of general "handy man" for a neighborhood grocery.
After a year, however, he was employed at the Jefferson Dairy where he
worked for the next 7 years. As driver of an ice cream truck he was
paid from $20 to $23 a week and worked a 7-day week. He did not like
the Sunday work; so he quit to take a job as truck driver for the Elite
Laundry, where the pay was $25 for a 6-day week. During a slack season
2 years later Mr. Coller got a job driving a truck for the Western Milk
Company. Here he was paid $25 a week and worked only 6 days a week for
a period of 2 years. Early in 1934 Mr. Coller lost his job when the
company discontinued bottling milk altogether and began the production
of casein.

There was a delay of about 1 month before relief was granted,
At the time Mr. Coller became unemployed he had no savings,
but an insurance policy on which he had paid a weekly premium of 23¢
for 8 years was cashed in for $28. Two other policies allowed to lapse
have since been renewed. Six weeks after losing his job, Mr. Coller applied for relief. Feeling that relief was a "disgrace," he put off applying as long as possible. When he realized there was no other way to
feed his family he made application.

There was a delay of about 1 month before relief was granted,
and the family was completely out of provisions. Had not Mr. Coller's
father, also unemployed, helped the family with food, Mr. Coller doesn't
know what would have become of them. Mr. Coller feels that the family
never "fared" very well on direct relief as it was always a struggle to
get anything in addition to the grocery order. They were threatened
with eviction for nonpayment of rent, and Mr. Coller worked out his coal
bill. After being on direct relief for 3 months Mr. Coller was assigned
to work relief at the quarry. He much preferred work relief to direct
relief, but after 1½ years on project work he was glad to get back in

private industry. During most of the time that Mr. Coller worked on
projects he was paid at the rate for unskilled labor, but for about 3
months on the lock and dam project he drove piling and was paid 80¢
an hour. While working on this job he fell into "80 feet" of water
one winter day and his clothing was frozen stiff before he could get
across the bridge. He believes that most men put in their daily stint
on project work just as conscientiously as in private employment.

Mr. Coller had kept his employment office application active
and frequently applied directly to various dairies. On "Father's Day
2 years ago" he met an acquaintance who had just bought a transfer and
trucking company. When Mr. Coller asked this man for a job he was told
to report for work the next night. On this job he works from 12 to 13
hours a night loading trucks and is paid $32 a week. He has from 7 Sun-
day to 7 Monday off. Mr. Coller considers this the best job he has ever
had and does not object to the night work though it did take him some
time to get used to sleeping during the day. He especially likes having
2 full days free to spend with his family. A year ago he bought a secondhand car for $165 and last summer he took his family on trips to Milwaukee,
Chicago, and other points of interest. In the course of the summer he
drove 12,000 miles on pleasure trips.

During Mr. Coller's unemployment the family had gone in debt
about $75, but this has been paid in full and the last payment was made
on the car 2 months ago. He said he plans to start his first savings
account after they have bought some much-needed clothing and a few pieces
of furniture. He feels that conditions have greatly improved during the
past 2 years and minimizes the seriousness of the recent recession.

Mr. Coller considers the Social Security Act "a wonderful
piece of legislation" and gladly pays his 32¢ a week. Unemployment and

old-age insurance are, in his opinion, "much superior to relief," but he
"supposes relief too will have to be continued for some time." It "was
only right" that the Federal Government should assist the States in caring
for their unemployed, but Iowa perhaps should have assumed more financial
responsibility; "they could and they should." Dubuque is "all right except
for the domination of the Chamber of Commerce." There is no doubt in Mr.
Coller's mind that "the Chamber of Commerce has kept out" such industries
as the Ford plant and the Quaker Oats Company. Mr. Coller has never worked
in a mill and "hopes he never will." Dubuque mill owners have "always opposed unions"; the millworkers' organization is the weakest in Dubuque as
too many of the men are "afraid of losing their jobs if they join." Mr.
Coller, a member of the truck drivers' union, believes that organized labor
is stronger in Dubuque now than ever before. If the labor candidates for
the City Council are elected, and Mr. Coller thinks they will be elected,
"industrial conditions in Dubuque will be improved and new factories will
be brought in." Formerly, the business men "sided with the big-shot manufacturers," but now, Mr. Coller believes, business men are more sympathetic
with labor.

Mr. Coller is well satisfied with his present job and feels secure in it. He is sorry for people who have to go on relief and hopes
that he "will never have to do it again." His family now has plenty to
eat and just about everything it needs; all Mr. Coller asks of the future
is that this happy situation will continue.

Employment Chronology for Mr. Coller

1921 – 1922	Handy man, grocery store.
1922 – 1930	Milk truck driver.
1930 – 1932	Laundry truck driver.
1932 – 1934	Milk truck driver.
June 1934 – June 1936	Unemployed except for emergency work.
June 1936 – present	Night loader, motor express company.

HETZEL

Mr. Hetzel	30
Mrs. Hetzel	29
Billy	6
Dickie	5
Betty	3
Jack	1

Interviewing completed
January 12, 1938

The Hetzels live in a little box of a house near the ragged end
of one of the best residential streets in the town. Emerich Hetzel, 30
years old, a husky, bulky chap, was married in the fall of 1929. In August
1930 he lost the job as checker and loader which he had held for more than
2 years. From August 1930 until January 1937, when he was taken on at the
Mississippi Milling Company plant, he was unemployed except for work on his
father's small pig-feeding farm and on work projects.

Mr. Hetzel calls his wife "Mother." They have four children,
ranging in age from 6 years to 14 months, all attractive, well-trained
youngsters, "nice to have, so long as they are well." Billy is a self-
important first-grader, and Dickie goes to kindergarten in the afternoons.
Betty prides herself on "helping Mommie" with cookie cutting.

Both Mr. and Mrs. Hetzel are intelligent and responsive, though
she is rather more quiet than he. Emerich Hetzel left school when he was
16 years old and before he had completed his high school course. As the
oldest of a large family of children, he felt some pressure to begin earning
his own living, and he did not then consider education very important.

Just after he left school in 1924, Emerich began work as an apprentice automobile mechanic, earning from $10 to $12 a week. Though he liked

the work--he has always been interested in any sort of mechanical work--he
left the job before the apprenticeship was ended in the hope that he could
become a railroad engineer. His father was then working in a Dubuque roundhouse, where Emerich was taken on as a wiper in 1925. Because the boss "sort
of liked" him, he was soon given many other duties in addition to those of
wiper, and he became a "general flunky," filling in wherever he was needed
and working a part of the time as machinist's helper. Earnings varied with
the hours of work which were sometimes very long; over a 3-year period his
pays averaged perhaps $25 a week.

         Since the waiting list was very long and his name near the bottom,
Emerich lost hope of becoming an engineer. He left the roundhouse at the
end of 3 years to take a job in Rockford, Ill., with a firm manufacturing
farm machinery. This was in February 1928. He was hired as a loader and
later became also a checker, accounting for all of the equipment loaded or
unloaded from the freight cars in the company yards. He had at first been
paid 40¢ an hour; the rate was later raised to 45¢. For the loading he
was paid by the ton instead of by the hour. The work was very heavy and
the hours long, for the ordinary 12-hour working days were stretched in busy
seasons to 16 hours.

         Nevertheless, Emerich liked the work. "It didn't seem hard to me
because I worked under a nice boss and with a fine, jolly bunch of fellows,"
to many of whom he still writes occasionally. And he was well satisfied
with his earnings of approximately $55 a week.

         In the fall of 1929, while he continued to work in Rockford, he
was married to a Dubuque girl. They bought furniture enough to fill the
four-room house that they rented for $30 a month. Prices were high, and
food purchases for two cost about the same as the present purchases for the

family of six. When Emerich, along with some 2,000 others, was laid off in
August 1930, the Hetzels had almost no resources except their furniture and
a "lizzie," which Emerich still drives to work and to church on Sunday mornings; '"at least it still runs."

After returning to Dubuque, where both Mr. and Mrs. Hetzels' families. lived, the Hetzels managed to get along, "catch as catch can," until
April 1931, when they moved to Emerich's father's farm. Relatives had not
been able to help very much, for the parents had to care for large families.
Mrs. Hetzel's father had been a factory worker until he was laid off when
he was nearing 65. Now he has little hope of being reemployed on any regular full-time job. In the summer of 1937 he was "lucky enough" to find work
as a caretaker; he hopes to have the same job again next summer, but at best
he earns only a meager living.

By 1931 Emerich's father had gone into the business of feeding
pigs on a 30-acre farm some 6 miles from Dubuque. In order to help him
and in the hope of making money, Mr. and Mrs. Hetzel moved to the farm in
April of 1931. The Hetzels, father and son, invested in a samll truck,
bought on credit, and about 140 pigs. For the "thin pigs" they paid 8¢ a
pound; they expected to sell the hogs at 10¢, then the going rate. But the
price of hogs went lower and lower, until finally the Hetzels were forced
to sell at 3⅓¢. Meanwhile, they had had to live up to their agreement with
the Dubuque restaurants to collect their garbage daily for swill. Gasoline
required for the daily trip to town was an added investment on which there
was no return. The Hetzels figured that they lost about $1,000 on the deal,
including the cost of the truck. They were deep in debt; they owed money
for the truck and for mash, and even the family's day-to-day expenses
couldn't be met. Mrs. Hetzel "couldn't tell you how little we lived on."

Nor do they know just how much they owed; they do know that they "never
could pay a doctor's bill."

Finally, while they were still living on the farm, the family applied for relief. Of course, they didn't "like it," but there was nothing
else to do. They were well satisfied with the food allowance of $3.50 a
week for the family of four (there were then two children), as they had
never been accustomed to "anything fancy." They did not request fuel, for
Mr. Hetzel cut his own wood and they managed with what clothing they had.
He thinks that "investigators do the best they can," under the limitations
set by rules and regulations.

In November 1933, when the Hetzel family had moved back to town,
Mr. Hetzel was assigned to CWA work in the county stone quarry. He earned
$15 a week and much preferred working for what he got. When the CWA work
ended in the following March, he again went to his father's farm, where
the family remained for more than a year. In November 1935 he was assigned
through the State employment office to the Dubuque lock and dam project as
"a skilled worker"--rigger and cement finisher. He was paid 80¢ an hour
for a 30-hour week. The family again moved to town to be nearer Mr. Hetzel'
work. His employment was interrupted for 6 months after the locks were finished and before work on the dam was begun. During this 6-month interval
the Hetzels were again dependent on direct relief.

In March 1936, just after Mr. Hetzel's grandmother died, his
grandfather and his uncle persuaded the Hetzels to move to the grandfather's
farm. The arrangement was more satisfactory for the grandfather than for
the Hetzels---Mr. and Mrs. Hetzel helped with the farm and house work and
bought the groceries for the entire household group instead of paying rent.
There was no saving in expenditures, and Emerich's trips to his work were

long. At the end of about 7 months the Hetzels again moved to Dubuque,
this time to an apartment in the downtown section. They were not satisfied
with an apartment; the children had to be kept indoors, for there was no
other place for them to play except on the streets. So a little less than
a year ago they moved to the house where they now live. Here there is
plenty of space for the children's play and for Mr. Hetzel's gardening.
They have always counted on canning several hundred quarts of vegetables
each summer; "that means canning a little every day."

Early in 1937, when the dam was almost completed, Mr. Hetzel
found work with the Mississippi Milling Company. He had been looking for
private employment all along, but frequently without much hope. In the
earlier depression years, the local factories would take no new applications
and did almost no hiring. Mr. Hetzel kept in touch with the situations
in various fields of work through his many friends, and whenever there
was the slightest rumor that a plant was hiring new men, he went in search
of a job. But he was frequently very much discouraged. "When a man's
willing to work and willing to sacrifice, and then can't even sacrifice,
it's pretty bad."

Mr. Hetzel was asked to go to New Boston, Ill., to work on another
dam and lock project on completion of the local project, but he felt that,
with the family of six, it would not be advisable to begin the endless
moving about from one construction job to another. Consequently, he "snapp-
ed up" the chance for work with the milling company.

Mr. Hetzel is enthusiastic about the relief and work programs,
which he believes have done much for "the poor man." The various work
programs have also been valuable to the country as a whole. If the unemployed men had been left "to sit on direct relief," the Nation would

probably have gone just as deeply into debt, and "the roads wouldn't have been graveled, and the locks and dams wouldn't have been built." He had found real satisfaction in the construction work on the lock and dam project.

Mr. Hetzel is not so happy about his present job. In fact, he likes it less than any job he has ever held. It has been difficult for him to grow used to the "inside work." And there are many other disadvantages, though conditions under which he works and his rate of pay are now somewhat more satisfactory than when he began to work a year ago. He first took the place of a checker who had been confused by the noise and the dust and had made many mistakes in the sorting of the window frames. Mr. Hetzel was paid $37\frac{1}{2}\cent$ an hour for a $9\frac{1}{2}$-hour day on this same job. He didn't like the noise and the dust, either, but did the job well enough to be made an inspector several months ago.

Two raises have brought his hourly rate up to $42\frac{1}{2}\cent$, but his total earnings are no higher now than before, since with each raise in pay there has been a corresponding reduction in hours. When he was granted his first $2\frac{1}{2}\cent$ raise, his weekly hours were cut from $51\frac{1}{3}$ to 40. When a second raise was granted, hours were cut from 8 a day to 7, or even, sometimes, 5. He understands that a raise can be granted no oftener than once every 6 months; "even then, you have to fight for it." And no one raise amounts to more than $2\frac{1}{2}\cent$ an hour. Thus, there is little "chance for advancement." Skilled men who have worked for the Mississippi Milling Company for many years earn "little more" than he. If he were to remain with this company "for the next 50 years," he would probably never earn more than $50\cent$ an hour. He further resents being "classified as an unskilled worker"; almost any job, he believes, requires a certain amount of skill.

Of course, the greatest difficulty is the low earnings, averaging only about $16 a week—"not enough for a family of six to live on." For instance, the Hetzels now pay a rental of $17, though Mr. Hetzel believes that a family should not pay rent amounting to more than 1 week's pay, if other items in the budget are to be adequately met. Since the house now occupied by the family has been sold, the Hetzels must move again as soon as they can find another place. "But we can't find anything within our range." The very lowest rental for enough rooms for the family seems to be $20 a month, and that is for an apartment, where they would not want to take the children. Even aside from the difficulty of finding another place, Mrs. Hetzel dreads the task of moving; they have "moved so much" already.

Mr. Hetzel estimates that in order to support his family even reasonably well, he should have an income of $25 or $30 a week. At the barest minimum, he must have about $5 a week more than he earns at the milling company. This he has been able to make by tending furnaces, cleaning walks, and doing other odd jobs which require all told some 3 hours each day for a well-to-do family in his own neighborhood. He thinks that he possibly manages better than many workers in larger cities, for he can learn from time to time of such odd jobs. "Oh, people can live this way, but it takes all the joy out of it." Though the Hetzels would like to have "a little recreation," they haven't been able to go to a dance for more than 3 years. And it was more than 3 years ago that Mr. Hetzel last saw a movie. "It's not that I don't want to go to movies, but if I spend 30¢ for a show, I think I'm just beating the kids out of a pair of stockings or something."

Mr. Hetzel spends considerable time studying. For the past 8 months he has been working on a correspondence course in mechanical engineering. On a table in the living room, there is a great stack of books to which he points with some pride while explaining that he puts in as much time as possible reading and studying. But he knows that he is "handicapped" by lack of education, for he always has to keep a dictionary beside him while he reads. Even so, he has some difficulty in understanding everything that he reads, and sometimes becomes so discouraged and "disgusted with myself" that he flings his book aside. He realizes, too, that a regular course in mechanical engineering usually covers 4 years of full-time work. How then, he wonders, can he hope to accomplish anything with his part-time study? And yet he keeps on trying.

Since Mr. Hetzel believes now that a college education is a prerequisite to almost any kind of really satisfying, well-paying job, he hopes to send his children to college. Recently he has heard that managers of gas stations operated by one particular company must be college graduates. In his opinion, college-bred people do get along better than others, for they can "understand things" more readily, and have had more experience in dealing with other people. Without college educations his children may be "handicapped all their lives." But unless there is a vast change in his own work, and in his financial situation, the children will be "lucky if they can finish high school."

Mr. Hetzel sees little hope of any such change so long as he remains with the milling company. The proposed wage and hour legislation would not affect his status. He becomes a little confused as he tries to express his ideas as to what changes should be made in the present industrial setup, but eventually makes it clear that he does not see low rates of pay as the basic difficulty. What is needed is not higher wages, which may only make for higher prices, but such an adjustment between wages and prices that "the lowest-paid worker can live on his earnings." Mr. Hetzel himself would never expect to have so much, or be able to give his children so much, as a really "wealthy person" may do. But it does seem to him that business men and industrialists should be able to work out, in cooperation with the government, a wage scale adjusted to current prices. He has little faith in unionization as a means of making such an adjustment and does not believe in strikes. Employers and employees should reach agreements through "discussion" of problems.

Mrs. Hetzel remarks matter-of-factly that "they say another depression is beginning, when we haven't got over the last one yet." Mr. Hetzel, too, is concerned about the "business recession" though he does not expect it to affect his work in the near future. But depression or no depression, it is probable that his work will be slack during the next few months as a result of the usual seasonal slump. He has only recently been called back to work, following a layoff of 1 month during the taking of inventory. He assumes that he will be kept on at the Mississippi Milling Company as long as he wants to stay, but believes that he would have more "chance for advancement" in construction or railroad work, or at the Rockford factory where he once worked. Since he considers that he has had some good experience in each of these fields, "it may be possible" to get another job. Of course, making a change is not so easy. He is still in debt; moving would be expensive; and he cannot afford to give up one job until after he has found another. And yet he is far from hopeless; he fully believes that some day he will have his "chance for advancement."

Employment Chronology for Mr. Hetzel

1924 - 1925   - Apprentice automobile mechanic.

1925 - February
1928   Wiper, railroad roundhouse.

February 1928 -
August 1930   Checker and loader, farm machinery
                       factory.

August 1930 -
January 1937   Unemployed except for work on
                       father's farm and on emergency
                       work projects.

January 1937 -
present   Checker and inspector of window
                       frames, Mississippi Milling Company.

WATSON

Mr. Watson   28
Mrs. Watson   30
Johnnie   3

Interviewing completed
February 16, 1938

Guy Watson has been on either direct relief or work relief most
of the time since his marriage 4 years ago, though he is at present employed in a local battery factory. His employment prior to the depression
had been with construction contractors, and of a highly seasonal nature,
averaging only 7 or 8 months out of the year.

Mr. Watson, 28 years old, is large and healthy-looking. He has
a ruddy complexion, blond hair, and blue eyes. Boyish in his appearance
and reactions, he blurts out his ideas impulsively without a great deal
of thought. He is forthright in manner and seems to have considerable
insight into his situation, though he finds it a bit difficult to express
some of his ideas. Somewhat rough in his speech, he storms out at the
badly spoiled, 3-year-old son, Johnnie, whose reactions to his father
show that the father's vicious-sounding threats are never carried out.
He is proud of the child's precociousness and would like to send him to
kindergarten now, though the schools will not admit children under 5 years
of age.

Mrs. Watson, 2 years older than her husband, is more mature in
her thinking, and expresses her views with more clarity and humor than
does Mr. Watson. She, too, storms at Johnnie, who obviously does not
know the meaning of obedience. Johnnie, after showing all of his
Christmas presents, climbs to the top shelf of the cupboard to sample a

cake baked for his father's lunch box; then he rolls in the middle of the
floor, singing at the top of his voice.

Mrs. Watson is rather attractive in appearance, though she is
thin and somewhat stringy. Her hair and eyes are very black, and her
skin is clear. She was born in Dubuque and has never been out of the
State. She was a power-machine operator at Hall's Manufacturing Company
for 10 years prior to her marriage. "Never very smart in school" and
"never able to learn arithmetic," Mrs. Watson started to work at 15. She
was required to attend part-time school, but she thinks it didn't do her
any good. At Hall's she earned from $5 to $10 a week on piecework until
the NRA boosted the rate to $13. Whenever the girls failed to make $13
they were called on the carpet and severely scolded. As she was not a
very fast worker, she found herself "on the carpet every week."

The Watsons live in a four-room upstairs flat, a block from the
Mississippi Milling Company. Sawdust from the mill often covers the floors
and furniture when windows are left open. The property, owned by the mill,
is occupied for the most part by mill employees. They rented the flat
while Mr. Watson was employed at the mill for a few months in 1935. The
rent of $8 a month is somewhat lower than the rentals for similar flats
in the down-town district. The rooms, orderly and clean, are sparsely
furnished, as the Watsons have never been able to buy more than the
barest necessities. The rooms are heated by a coal circulating heater in
the large living room, which is bare except for a small old-fashioned day-
bed, three chairs, a couple of small end tables, and a cabinet radio.
The floor is covered with cheap linoleum. Each year since her marriage,
Mrs. Watson has hoped to be able to buy a rug, but now she is beginning
to wonder if they will ever get enough ahead to buy anything for the home.

Mr. Watson, born in the western part of Iowa, came to Dubuque 9 years ago. Having left school at 16 after completing the ninth grade, he worked for paving contractors until 1928, when he was employed at the Stevenson Company where he worked for 2 years, repairing phonographs. The paving work usually lasted from April to November; during the winter he picked up occasional odd jobs. For the paving work he was paid $30 a week. At Stevenson's the pay was 45¢ an hour. During a layoff in 1929 Mr. Watson was employed for a few months by another paving contractor. From 1929 to the beginning of CWA in November 1933 he worked irregularly on road construction, filling in with occasional odd jobs during the winter months.

The Watsons were married in September 1933 and made their first application for relief in November. Mr. Watson was certified for common labor on CWA almost immediately. After his layoff from CWA in March 1934, he worked on a road construction job for a private contractor for 2 months. In June he reapplied for relief and was assigned to the lock and dam project where he continued until the late spring of 1935. In July 1935 he was hired in the packing room of the Mississippi Milling Company, but he had worked only a short time when the men went out on strike. Mr. Watson had joined the union and supported the strike. He resumed work at the mill in the fall of 1935, only to be laid off again in December.

Shortly after he started work for the Mississippi Milling Company, a collection agency had tried to garnishee Mr. Watson's wages for a clothing bill he had been unable to pay. The foreman told him he would have to pay the bill or be fired. Mr. Watson arranged to pay it at the rate of $2 a month. Since that experience he has refused to go in debt for anything.

The Watsons reapplied for relief about 3 months after Mr.
Watson's layoff from the Mississippi Milling Company; he was immediately
certified for WPA and was placed on the dam in July 1936 at $48 a month.
After working about 7 or 8 months on the dam he was transferred to the
rock quarry. During the time that Mr. Watson had worked on projects, he
had constantly sought work in private industry. His efforts were finally
rewarded when the State employment office referred him to a battery
company in September 1937.

Though Mr. Watson had been grateful for the project work, he was
glad to quit the quarry job for a "real job." Work at the battery company
was steady up to December 22, when the men were laid off for 5 weeks,
though they had expected to return to work January 1. On the strength
of this assumption, the Watsons had a "nice Christmas"; had they known
that the layoff would last 5 weeks they would not have spent any money
for Christmas. Mr. Watson is paid $40\frac{1}{2}$¢ an hour, and works from 9 to 11
hours a day; before Christmas he earned from $48 to $50 a week.

Mr. Watson is enthusiastic about this job and considers it by
far the best he has ever had. The boss has promised an increase in wages,
and the future looks quite hopeful "unless the unions start trouble." The
factory is unorganized, and Mr. Watson hopes that no attempt will be made
to unionize it, as the company moved from "down east or somewheres to get
away from labor trouble." Though he joined the union at the Mississippi
Milling Company, he has little confidence in the union's ability to
better working conditions in Dubuque, because the town is controlled by
a "few big shots who have all the money and control the Chamber of
Commerce." Had the Quaker Oats Company, when looking for a desirable
location some years ago, located in Dubuque instead of Cedar Rapids, Mr.
Watson believes that Dubuque would have fared better during the depression,

as he hears that this plant has given steady work to its employees
throughout the depression.

Mr. Watson also feels that "pull" is the only thing that gets a
workman anywhere in any of the big mills. Unless a workman has the
backing of a foreman or some of the old employees, he has little chance
for a permanent job.

Though Mr. Watson "made good money" on the paving work, he had
never been able to save anything because he had helped his parents whenever he had money; then every year there were 3 or 4 months of unemployment which ate up his reserves. Mr. Watson had a $1,000 insurance policy,
but it had not been carried long enough to have any loan value. Neither
had Mrs. Watson been able to save anything from her small earnings at
Hall's; after she bought her clothes and paid board to her mother there
was nothing left.

Mr. Watson is unusually frank about his feelings in respect to
relief. Though he disliked the idea of having to seek aid, he felt no
embarrassment whatever about going to the relief office to make his first
application. "We needed help; the money had been appropriated for needy,
unemployed people; so I went after it." Mr. Watson was anxious to get off
relief, as "I know the money will have to be repaid some day and my son
will have to help pay for it." He had learned his lesson, however, about
going in debt; he much preferred going to the relief office, when he got
up against it, to asking for credit.

While Mr. Watson stood his ground with the relief office
investigators and usually got what he requested, he is critical of the
administrative setup. He feels that there are "too many young girls
trying to tell families how to get along on nothin', and what the hell do

they know about taking care of a family?" He also feels that the
investigators are paid too much for what they do. He sees "no sense" in
their getting "$100 a month for walking around town with big envelopes
under their arms" while the men at the rock quarry are paid only $48 for
"back-breaking labor." The Watsons were never able to manage on their
direct relief allowance of $7.48 every 2 weeks, because, Mrs. Watson ex-
plains, Mr. Watson is such a "big eater." They used 1 peck of potatoes
every week and quantities of beans, but even so, the food never stretched
out for the period it was supposed to cover. When he would start "lunch-
ing between meals" Mrs. Watson would ask him, "How do you expect that
grocery order to last if you eat between meals?" Whereupon Mr. Watson
replied, "When I work I gotta eat."

Mr. Watson much preferred work relief to direct relief and never
objected to any assignment, no matter how hard the work. Some men turned
down the lock and dam project assignment because some of the projects in
town required lighter work, and it was not necessary to pay $2.50 a month
on transportation. He believes that his willingness to do any type of
work may have been responsible for his getting his present job through the
employment office. Mr. Watson always "stuck on" any job to which he
was assigned. He does not blame the men for taking the relief work a
"little easy"; "why should they do $40 worth of work for $12 pay?"

Mr. Watson is enthusiastic about all recovery legislation with
the exception of relief to farmers. The administration, he believes, has
favored farmers to the detriment of working men in industrial communities.
In his opinion, Iowa farmers have always been prosperous and have had
reasonably good crops; "for the last year or two they have been excellent.
After all," he says, "the farmers depend on the working man and as long as
the working men are employed, the farmers get along all right."

Mr. Watson does not know how to explain widespread unemployment except that the "few capitalists who control the wealth of the Nation refuse to let go of their money." He discredits the idea that machinery has thrown men out of work, though Mrs. Watson quotes an article she read about the number of miners displaced in West Virginia when loading machines were introduced. Mrs. Watson points out that her husband has had little experience in millwork and probably doesn't know about new machines. Mr. Watson thinks the Social Security legislation is a fine thing, and approves of the wage and hour bill, though he is "against all the farm legislation." He thinks that legalizing beer has stimulated business to some extent, but Mrs. Watson feels that most people can't afford to buy even a glass of beer. She can scarcely remember the last glass of beer she had, it has been so long ago. Mrs. Watson shows much curiosity about conditions in other parts of the country and can't believe that conditions elsewhere can be as bad as they are in Dubuque.

Mr. Watson believes that war is inevitable, though he is much opposed to this country's "mixing up in foreign wars." His outlook for America and for the world in general is somewhat gloomy. "There is a lack of confidence everywhere"; Nations distrust each other, and business is run on a "cut-throat basis." The Watsons' social life does not extend beyond occasional card games with friends, visits to Mrs. Watson's mother in the north end, and, on very rare occasions, a movie. They enjoy listening to the radio and always attend church on Sundays.

Mrs. Watson has thought that she might try to get a job at Hall's again, as Hall's does not object to hiring married women. Her earnings would make it possible to buy furniture and "get us out of the hole." Mr. Watson, however, objects to his wife's working. He feels that many

married women are taking the jobs that should be given to men--for that
matter, single women are taking men's jobs, too. Married men, in his
opinion, should be given preference in all jobs. Mrs. Watson thinks,
though, that it would be better for her to work than for them to go on
relief every time Mr. Watson is laid off from a job, as has been the
case ever since their marriage. Mr. Watson feels now that he has a year-
round job with a future, and sees no reason why they should not get on
their feet within a few months with his present earnings; then, too, he
is looking forward to the promised raise.

Employment Chronology for Mr. Watson

1925 - 1928   Laborer, construction company.

1928 - 1929   Repairman, Stevenson Phonograph
               and Radio Company.

1929 - July
1935   Unemployed except for odd jobs and
               emergency work.

July 1935 -
December 1935 Mill worker, Mississippi Milling
               Company.

December 1935 -
September 1937 Unemployed except for emergency work.

September 1937 -
Present   Battery factory worker.

<u>STETSON</u>

Mr. Stetson   33
Mrs. Stetson   28
Jimmie   6
Jean   1½

Interviewing completed
March 3, 1938

The four Stetsons live in a little house of yellowish-green up-
and-down boards with a red roof. The lean-to kitchen is built on a lower
level than the two front rooms which serve as bed- and living-rooms. The
chief disadvantage of the house is the lack of running water. Though the
Stetsons hope to move in the spring, just now they don't quite know how
they could manage to pay a higher rent elsewhere. Emil Stetson, who had
been unemployed for almost 3 years, returned to the Julien Foundry in
April 1934. He says that periodic layoffs and illnesses of all members of
the family have made it difficult for them to get on their feet.

Mr. Stetson is an excellent talker, although he "ain't very well
educated" and depends solely on the daily papers for keeping in touch with
world affairs. He has evidently given much thought to causes of unemployment and proposed solutions, which he discusses spontaneously and emphatically. Mrs. Stetson, as well informed as her husband, makes an
occasional pertinent comment; and she supplies dates of Mr. Stetson's employment and unemployment and details of the family's depression experiences with a nicer attention to accuracy. Jimmie, 6, and Jean, 1½, are
well-trained and well-behaved youngsters. Already Jimmie dreams of becoming a farmer. Last summer, he tended his patch of corn in the backyard
quite as well as his father took care of the rest of the garden.

Emil Stetson began doing "a man's work for a man's wages" when he was only 14 years old. His father, a foundry employee, had "tough sledding" after the older sons were drafted for service in the World War, and in 1917 it seemed inevitable that Emil, who had never been much interested in school, should go to work. Emil thinks now that if he'd had any "sense" he would have stayed in school, for he has suffered from having been "put in harness too young." At 33, though still very strong physically, he is exceedingly "nervous." He thinks that this condition is the result of having worked as a riveter in extreme heat and nerve-shattering noise for many years.

His first job was with a contractor who was razing a brewery building. Emil worked for about a year at all sorts of heavy hauling, for which he was paid 20¢ an hour for the 10-hour day. When the building was demolished, he got a job as rivet-passer, at 30¢ an hour, with the boat works. At the end of 2 or 3 weeks, he was given a job as rivet-holder at 50¢ an hour; and only a little later he was told that he was working as hard as any man on the riveting gang and his wage was increased to the maximum rate of 55¢ an hour. Mr. Stetson finds it disconcerting to be earning now less by the hour, and considerably less by the day, than he earned when he was "a boy." After he had worked for more than a year on the fleet of oil barges built by the boat works, Mr. Stetson left the job in 1919. There was then only one scow under construction; many men had already been laid off, and more layoffs were anticipated.

Mr. Stetson then "walked in" to the Julien Foundry at 2 o'clock one afternoon, asked for a job and began work as a rivet-driver that same day. He worked as rivet-driver for $3\frac{1}{2}$ years before he was given a job as helper of the hydraulic press operator. His wage-rate on both jobs was the same—50¢ an hour. Total earnings were fairly high, for he frequently

worked until 9 or 10 or even 11 o'clock in the evening, always at

"straight pay." Some 3 months after he began work at the foundry, Mr.

Stetson decided to take a week off; he thought that after having worked

"day and night" for several months he needed "a little holiday." But as

he passed the foundry on his way downtown one afternoon, the foreman hail-

ed him and insisted that he should resume work that very minute. In those

days there were signs saying "Men Wanted" "every hundred feet" along

Central Avenue, but "them days are gone." Now, all the signs read "No

Men wanted."

From 1919 to 1924 Mr. Stetson continued at the Julien Foundry.

At the end of this period, being "all in," he went to Chicago in the hope

of finding less strenuous work. He had only the clothes on his back and

$25 or $30 in his pocket; the rest of his belongings he had left at home.

"In Chicago," Mr. Stetson says, "I had the finest picnic I ever had in my

life." When he was just walking down the street, a fellow called to him,

"Are you looking for a job?" and he answered, "You've got the fellow right

here." For the next 2 years, he worked in a small Illinois town, first as

lead-monkey, later as pipe-corker, for a contractor laying a water line.

He had taken the job without asking what the rate of pay would be, and

when he got his first check for 90¢ an hour, he "nearly fell over." A

few months after he began work for the contractor, he was given a job as

pipe-corker paying $1 an hour.

As soon as the pipelaying job ended, Mr. Stetson went to a

Wisconsin town, where he worked from October 1926 until the spring of 1931

as a riveter for a boiler and tractor company; he earned 75¢ an hour. In

1929 the Stetsons were married. Except during the first year of their marriage when Mr. and Mrs. Stetson were both regularly employed, they have had "tough sliding all the way." After her marriage Mrs. Stetson continued to work for the telephone company for $16 a week, which she considered excellent pay. Though they spent money more freely then than now— bought furniture, had some recreation, and "thought nothing of paying 80¢ a dozen for eggs"—the Stetsons regularly saved money.

But soon work at the boiler and tractor company began to be slack. Early in 1931 Mr. Stetson was working only 3 days a week, and when, in the spring of the year, his work was limited to 2 days a week, he wrote to his father asking about the opportunities for full-time employment in Dubuque. Learning that Dubuque had not yet been very seriously affected by the depression, Mr. Stetson determined to return. As the cost of moving furniture to Dubuque would have been about $200, the Stetsons sold all of their furniture except the radio, which Mr. Stetson transported in his car. With his savings of $800 and a car, he felt that he was well prepared to meet the depression.

In Dubuque the Stetsons bought minimum household equipment with the money cleared on the sale of their furniture in Wisconsin and rented a house at $15 a month. Almost immediately Mr. Stetson got a job running a riveting-hammer at the American Foundry, where he earned 40¢ an hour for about 2 months before he was laid off in July 1931 when there was a general reduction in force. Jimmie was born just after the layoff.

Then Mr. Stetson began the long search for another job. He drew on his savings to pay his rent regularly, and the family "kept on eating." In 1932 he bought no license for the car, which he could not afford to run. When savings were almost exhausted, he decided to borrow money on his 20-payment life insurance policy, on which he had paid the annual premium of $32.50 only a month earlier. He took the policy, which

should have had a loan-value of $244, to a private loan company and asked
for a loan of just $100. Now he was told that he had been "a fool" to
continue paying premiums to an insurance company which had been in
bankruptcy for 2 years; this company was later taken over by another insurance firm, which likewise went into receivership. The policy has
never netted Mr. Stetson one cent, though he had "paid in to that son of
a gun for 11 or 12 years."

It was almost impossible for Mr. Stetson to find even an odd
job in the years from 1931 to 1934. Once he earned 50¢ a day for 2 days
when he helped with a moving, and again, he worked for some time cutting
wood for a farmer who said he didn't really need the wood, but would pay
Mr. Stetson $1 a cord if he needed work badly enough to cut the wood at
that price. Another time Mr. Stetson and a friend decided that they would
go from farm to farm offering to do any sort of work "from digging
potatoes to handling a team of horses," not for cash but for whatever
produce the farmers could give them. But even this scheme wasn't effective, as almost every farmer said that he had farm hands working only for
board and room. Once Mr. Stetson did get a 1-day job on a threshing
machine. When the threshing on one farm was finished, he offered to help
another farmer, who said that he had no money but would be willing to pay
Mr. Stetson in produce. On the two threshing jobs, he worked from very
early in the morning until it was "pitch dark." One farmer paid him 50¢
and the other gave him a leghorn rooster, with which he was well satisfied.

Finally, early in 1934, when savings were exhausted and the
family owed a $75 grocery bill and several alarmingly large doctor bills,
the Stetsons applied for relief. Earlier, in an effort to reduce expenses,
they had moved to a house renting for $8 a month. Now, there was nothing

to do but apply for relief, though there "ain't anything" that makes Mr.
Stetson "more sick than to ask for something and stand in line" when he's
"healthy and able to work," but simply can't find a job. Much as he
hated applying for relief, he's "not too proud" to ask for help if he
can't get work; "it would be foolish" to let his family suffer for the
sake of his pride. The relief investigator told Mr. Stetson, "You ought
to be ashamed of asking for relief, with the size family you've got," to
which his reply was, "You get me a job if it's only 50¢ a day, and I won't
ask for anything." Since the investigator never referred him to any job,
he "guesses" she heard of none.

The Stetsons were on relief for only 3 months before Mr.
Stetson was recalled to work at the Julien Foundry in the spring of 1934.
They found the food orders adequate enough, though Mrs. Stetson thinks
that "a person feels more like eating if he earns his own money." Mr.
Stetson is puzzled about relief, which he believes has been handled as
well as possible, but yet has made for such deterioration of some "good
honest workers" that they will "never be any good any more." Yet "they
gotta do something with the unemployed; they can't leave 'em starve—
that's a cinch." He considers work projects superior to direct relief;
still, he thinks that some of the WPA workers have not been anxious to
shift to private employment, since they "can manage on $12 a week better"
than many Dubuque factory workers can manage on their low and irregular
earnings.

Shortly before he was called to work at the Julien Foundry, Mr.
Stetson, having determined to "try anything before we'll go in debt any
more," moved his family to a shack in the country. He paid a rental of
$50 a year for the one-room hut to which a second room was added, the
landlord furnishing the materials, and Mr. Stetson, his brother, and his

father doing the building. He had almost lost hope of ever having
regular work again; "this way," he could "at least put in a big garden."
But when the relief worker first called at the Stetsons' new home, he
had already returned to his job as helper at the foundry. The Stetsons
were especially appreciative of the garden seeds that the relief worker
left, even though it was not necessary to have another food order
delivered.

When he first went back to his old job, Mr. Stetson made only
40¢ an hour for an 8-hour day, though he had previously been paid 50¢ an
hour at the same job. But the family's expenses were now not very high;
Mr. Stetson had his garden; he began to save money and to anticipate
really "getting ahead." That spring he bought chickens and a cow, and
soon after he bought a pony to draw the cultivator. Then just as things
were going along well he was laid off in July 1934. During a 6-month
period of unemployment, he worked for a neighboring farmer, earning $1 a
day making hay, picking corn, and doing various odd jobs.

Mr. Stetson was recalled to the Julien Foundry in January 1935,
and he worked until fall when he was again laid off; he was unemployed
until January 1936. When he returned to work at the foundry, Mr. Stetson
began once more to save money, but resources were again exhausted while
he was out on a prolonged strike beginning in the summer of 1936. Jean
was just 2 weeks old when the strike was called. Hospital bills had been
paid in advance, but doctor bills are still to be met. Mr. Stetson feels
that the strike was worthwhile. A series of wage-increases based on a
sliding scale established as "a direct result of the strike" has brought
his hourly rate up to 50¢. During the strike, orders enough to last
through the winter had piled up at the foundry, and there were no layoffs
later in the year, as there might otherwise have been.

In January 1937 the Stetsons moved to town, as the two-room
house was difficult to heat and too cold for the baby. They sold the cow
and the chickens for enough to enable them to get along during Mr.
Stetson's 3-month illness in 1937. During this same period Mrs. Stetson
and the two children were also ill, and they had to depend on Mr.
Stetson's father to carry the water and take care of the garden, and on
neighbor children to make trips to the store. "Every time" that Mr.
Stetson has felt that he was at last getting ahead, illness or a layoff
has pushed the family back into debt.

Since the first of the year he has been working no more than 5
days a week, and recently his time was cut to 4 days. The union agreed to
a reduction of hours for all workers in place of further layoffs. Though
some of the men, sure of their own jobs, wanted to continue working 5 full
days a week, Mr. Stetson thinks it better to work only 4 days than to
allow some men no work at all. He is willing "to share a day's work any
time."

The chief disadvantages of his present job are "the low wages,"
the uncertainty as to how long the work will last, the grease with which
his clothes are always covered, and the extreme heat of the furnaces.
Winter and summer, he works where the temperature is 120° or higher;
sometimes when he comes out of the plant "everything swims" before his
eyes. He wears out a pair of work gloves in about 3 hours, but since
he can't afford to invest $1.50 in gloves each week, he makes one pair
last until there's "nothing left but the backs." He buys new overalls
every 2 weeks; no matter how much Mrs Stetson scrubs his work-clothes
they never come clean. His skin, too, is caked with grease at the end

of every working-day, and though he's "always scrubbing" himself, even
the bed clothing is sometimes stained with grease.

Mr. Stetson thinks that the depression, which "isn't licked
yet," was caused by "mass production" and increases in the productive
capacity of workmen without corresponding increases in wages or decreases
in prices. A purely temporary "boom" was created only by Government
spending. "If employers had tried as hard as the Government to give
men work," all of the unemployed men might have been reabsorbed by
private industry, but he says that industrialists have "fought Roosevelt
all the way," and will continue to "fight him for the next 2 years."
Wage increases and shortened hours would help to improve business
generally and spread employment, but few men realize that by working
long hours "they are automatically laying the other fellow off."

If a man could be sure that "barring ill health" he would work
the year around, or even if he could be sure of working 10 months out of
the year, he would feel "free to spend his money and business would be
improved." The Stetsons, for instance, would like to buy new furinturo,
but can't risk buying anything not absolutely essential. Mr. Stetson
revises his statement that the family has no luxuries by explaining that
he does spend "a quarter a week" for tobacco, and "sometimes on payday
nights" he buys three cans of beer which he and Mrs. Stetson share. But
they never go out in the evening except to visit with Mr. Stetson's
family. They haven't seen a movie for more than 4 years.

Mr. Stetson has heard industrialists say that "no one can
dictate to industry. We have to make profit regardless--regardless,"
he thinks, "of whether the men have work or not. Americans are warned
'Beware of dictatorship,'" but he thinks that if a dictatorship is ever

established in this country, it will be "a dictatorship by the million-
aires," who should be "corralled." The employers who object to unionism
are "the very ones" who have forced men to organize by "paying low wages
and working the men long hours." Mr. Stetson has been a member of an
A. F. of L. union only since he returned to work at the foundry in 1934.
He doesn't know a great deal about the CIO, but suspects that John L.
Lewis may be "less radical" than some people try to lead him to suppose,
and the idea of "one big union" may be sound. "Certainly," he says,
"Green himself forced Lewis to go his own way," and that if the A. F. of
L. had been more "alert" the steel workers and the automobile workers
might have been organized long ago. Industry has "encouraged" conflict
between the A. F. of L. and the CIO, for, as Mrs. Stetson puts it, "when
laborers fight each other, they don't fight the employers."

Mr. Stetson has heard many men say that a war might bring new
prosperity, but he believes that "no war ever did anyone any good" and
that America should not enter into a war under any circumstances. "Let
the industrialists protect their own property without leaving the blood
of young men laying over there." In the World War "thousands" were killed
and "thousands" more were injured, and "today nobody could tell you what
it was all about."

Mr. Stetson has not much hope for any change in his own
economic status or in the industrial situation in Dubuque, where "wages
have been low even when there were booms" elsewhere because local factories have not had enough "competition" in a labor market. Nor does he
see any prospect of immediate improvement in the industrial situation
of the United States as a whole. There is the question of what is to be

done with men between the ages of "45 and 65," for as soon as a man has
"one gray hair" or has reached the age of 45 he is considered "too old"
for factory work. Mr. Stetson states that he is "nearly 40" now, and
though he is as husky as ever he may be discarded by industry in the
near future. If he could do what he wants most, he would buy a 3- or
4-acre plot of ground in the country, continue with his factory work in
Dubuque, but spend his leisure time gardening and taking care of his cows
and chickens.

Employment Chronology for Mr. Stetson

1917 - 1918	- Helper, private contractor.
1918 - 1919	- Riveter, boat works.
1919 - 1924	- Riveter and helper of hydraulic press operator, Julien Foundry.
1924 - October 1926	- Lead-monkey and pipecorker, contractor.
October 1926 - Spring 1931	Riveter, boiler and tractor company.
May - July 1931	Riveter, American Foundry.
July 1931 - April 1934	Unemployed.
April 1934 - present	Helper of hydraulic press operator, Julien Foundry; employment irregular.

BEUSCHER

At home

Mr. Beuscher	62
Mrs. Beuscher	60
Paul	13
Katherine	17
Jeannette	19
Bob	21

Married and away from home

Charles	23
Celia	25
Butch	26
Eileen	28
Helen	30
Caroline	32

Interviewing completed
December 13, 1937

Mr. Beuscher, 62 years old, had been working for 29 years for the Dubuque railroad shops when they closed in 1931. He was recalled to work at the shops after he had been unemployed for 4 years. Tall, gangling, weather-beaten, he stoops forward when he talks so that he may follow the conversation with greater ease, for he is more than a little deaf. He expresses opinions decisively and vigorously, his black eyes gleaming from under bushy black brows.

Mrs. Beuscher is 2 years younger than her husband. She is the mother of 11 children, but has found time to make dresses and coats and suits, not only for her own family, but also for customers outside the home. A genial, mild-mannered woman, she is earnest in her speech, but always ready to laugh at her own and other people's foibles. Her eyes, merry but tired, are protected with spectacles that slide down on the bridge of her nose when she bends over reading or sewing and that are pushed up on her forehead when she raises her head to talk or to listen to an especially amusing radio program.

Four children remain at home: Bob, 21, a high school graduate, has had only short-time employment and is now out of work; Jeannette, who completed a high school commercial course last spring, is now clerking in a 5-and-10-cent store on Saturdays; Katherine, a high school junior who goes out occasionally with her "boy friend," cleans the house on Saturday mornings; Paul, attending junior high school, is privileged as one of the "Knothole Gang" to see the local ball games at 10¢ a game and contributes his proceeds from the sale of magazines, sometimes as much as "a whole 15¢," to his mother's purse.

One daughter died several years ago. The other children are married and now have their own households. But during the early years of the depression Charles, then unmarried, was at home; and Celia and Butch, who had had their own homes, came with their families to the Beuscher home when they could no longer pay rent.

Mr. Beuscher was educated haphazardly in country schools in Wisconsin during the seasons when work was not too pressing on his father's farm and his "old man" didn't "make him saw wood" in preference to sending him to school. He worked as a "hand" on his father's and neighboring farms until he came to Dubuque, with his wife and two children, in 1902. He was employed at the boat works for a few weeks before being taken on as a boilermaker's helper in the railroad shops. Promoted to a job as boilermaker in 1910, he continued at the same job, except for brief interruptions because of illness, a disagreement with his foreman, and, again, a general railroad strike, until the closing of the shops in 1931.

When Mr. Beuscher began work in the shops as a boilermaker's helper in 1902, he was paid 10½¢ an hour for a 60-hour week, though he actually worked but 55 hours, for Saturday afternoons were free. In those days jobs in the railroad shops were more plentiful than job-seekers, for there was much work to be done and the pay was so low that the shops could not successfully compete for workers with neighboring factories.

Such a thing as a standard wage was unknown, for this was before the time of shop unions, and the highest paid of all the boilermakers in the shop earned only 29¢ an hour. There had been "floaters" before 1905, but it was not until that year that workers in the Dubuque shops were organized. In the beginning all of the helpers were organized in a separate union; only later were the boilermakers' helpers taken into the boilermakers' union, blacksmiths' helpers into the blacksmiths' union, and so on. When the helpers were first banded together, Mr. Beuscher, representing the boilermakers' helpers, along with two representatives of the other helpers, went to Chicago to negotiate for wage increases. They were successful in a measure, for irregular increases were granted; a standard wage came only much later.

The effect of organization on Mr. Beuscher's own wage rate was to increase it to 18¢ an hour. Mr. Beuscher attributes the general wage increases for shop workers in 1908 partly to the rising cost of living which had its effect on wages in various industries and partly to increasing union strength. He is a staunch believer in craft unionism and in the A. F. L.; he would not belong to the boilermakers' union if it were affiliated with the CIO, which to him symbolizes "one big union" and the interference of men skilled in one craft with the actual methods of work of those skilled in other crafts. There is disagreement, good-tempered

but vigorous, between Mr. Beuscher and his 21-year-old son on this score;
Bob believes that the CIO may help to equalize wages by reducing differen-
tials in rates.

Mr. Beuscher's highest earnings as boilermaker's helper amounted
to 28½¢ an hour. In 1910 he became a boilermaker, earning 40½¢ an hour
for a 10-hour day. It was in 1913 that hours were shortened to 9 a day.
During the World War Mr. Beuscher's wage rate was increased several times,
finally reaching a peak of 72¢ an hour. The ground gained during the war
was held but only with a struggle; rates were reduced 5¢ an hour for a
short period after the war, but pay-cuts were soon restored. In 1922 an
announced pay reduction led to a general railroad strike, the only one af-
fecting the Dubuque shops since the "Debs strike of '94." The strike was
short-lived and successful, so far as the workers' effort to avoid a general wage reduction was concerned; Mr. Beuscher continued to earn 72¢ an hour
until the shops closed in 1931 and earnings ceased altogether.

During the 29 years that Mr. Beuscher was regularly employed in
the shops, the family managed to live comfortably and happily, though they
never had "luxuries"--they "never had a car"--and never got very far ahead,
for with 11 growing children, frequent unanticipated bills, such as doctors'
bills and dentists' bills, had to be met. But Mrs. Beuscher enjoyed planning in advance for small purchases from the "next pay"--curtains for the
living room windows or special items of clothing--even though the plans
could not always be carried through. Almost every weekend the Beuschers
had guests or visited their friends; "the children didn't stop us from
going."

In 1915 the Beuschers bought an attractive though unpretentious
seven-room frame cottage on a payment-purchase plan. Until Mr. Beuscher

lost his job, he paid $20 monthly to the real estate agency carrying the mortgage; this amount covered payments on the principal and interest of 7 percent. The home is in a north end neighborhood of well-kept single-family houses occupied for the most part by industrial wage-earners with families. Piece by piece the Beuschers' home has been comfortably furnished, and it gives evidence of the care and planning that have gone into its making.

The Beuschers never had a savings account--they thought it more practical to pay as much as possible on the house, especially as the rate of interest on the mortgage exceeded that on savings accounts--but they did invest in insurance policies for all members of the family. As the 10-payment life insurance policies carried for the older children had matured, they had been cashed in, but premiums on policies carried for Mr. and Mrs. Beuscher and the four youngest children were kept paid up to date until the spring of 1931, when the Beuschers found themselves with a mortgaged home, five children still largely dependent on the parents, and no regular income.

As they "look back on it," Mr. and Mrs. Beuscher scarcely know how they did manage to get along during the time that he had no regular work. The irregular income from Mrs. Beuscher's sewing continued, though she was forced to lower prices until earnings averaged no more than $3 or $4 a week. Instead of buying any new clothing, Mrs. Beuscher made over the old dresses and coats which, though discarded, had been packed away in the attic trunks. Insurance policies were cashed in one by one. Mrs. Beuscher's 20-payment life insurance policy, with face value of $500, netted her $137; cash surrender values of the four policies carried on the younger children averaged about $35. Though they were able to keep Mr. Beuscher's policy, $200 was borrowed against the face value of $1,000. Premiums have now been paid to date, but interest on the loan has been deducted from the value, now no more than $600.

For a year after Mr. Beuscher lost his job, the family's only cash income was the four hundred seventy-odd dollars obtained from the insurance policies and Mrs. Beuscher's irregular earnings, as contrasted with the pre-depression regular income of about $130 a month, Mr. Beuscher's full-time earnings. In spite of all the Beuschers could do to reduce expenses and to raise cash, not all of the bills could be met: payments due on the principal of the mortgage and the property taxes had to be disregarded, and Mr. and Mrs. Beuscher were harassed with worry over the $68 grocery bill, for they had never before asked for credit, except from week to week. Expenditures for replacements of household equipment were eliminated from the budget. By the time Mr. Beuscher returned to work, the family had almost no bedding; this was the first special item purchased when the family again had a regular income from private employment.

Although they had heard about other families, some of them in their own neighborhood, who had applied for relief grants, the Beuschers had never thought of requesting relief for themselves until one day, in the fall of 1933, Mr. Beuscher came home from a neighbor's to say to his wife, "Do you know what Jim said? He said we ought to try to get relief." Mrs. Beuscher was so "shocked" that she gasps, even 4 years later, when she recalls her emotion. But after talking things over, Mr. and Mrs. Beuscher agreed that application for relief was a virtual necessity. Mr. Beuscher remembers going down to the courthouse for the first time as the hardest thing he ever had to do in his life; his hand was "on the door-knob five times" before he turned it. The investigation, which the Beuschers recognized as necessary and inevitable, was so prolonged that Mrs. Beuscher "really didn't think" that the family would ever get relief. But finally, after about 2 months, a grocery order of $4.50 was granted. Mrs. Beuscher had long before learned to "manage" excellently on little, and though the order was meager, the family "got along" and "always had enough to eat." Mrs. Beuscher believes that investigators "did the best they could"; she resents only their insistence on the disconnection of the telephone, on which she depended for keeping in touch with her customers.

Soon Mr. Beuscher was assigned as a laborer to county relief work, for which he was paid, always in grocery orders, $7.20 a week; this increased amount gave the family a little more leeway. Yet they were still without much cash. Payments even of interest on the mortgage had had to cease. Because they anticipated foreclosure of the mortgage, the Beuschers applied for a Home Owners loan, which was refused, since there seemed to be little chance of Mr. Beuscher's getting back to work. "Things looked pretty bad then," and Mr. Beuscher was considered a "bad risk" because of his age. Though Mr. and Mrs. Beuscher were "terribly disappointed at the time," they are glad now that they are not burdened with such a debt.

Mrs. Beuscher cannot guess how the family could have managed during the depression without the home, but Mr. Beuscher found home ownership more of a handicap than a help, for relief grants made no allowance for taxes or interest payments, while "bums" who had never tried to save or look to the future had their rent paid "regularly."

While the relief grants continued, a married daughter whose husband, as a collection agent, found his commissions going lower and lower, and a married son, who "hadn't a sign of a job," moved in with the parents. There were then 13 living in the 7 room house. Of course, the children had come home only after a general discussion in which it was agreed that this was the

best plan, and everyone had though of the arrangement as quite "temporary";
actually Celia and Butch and their families remained in the household for
about a year. For a time, Eliot, the son-in-law, was able to contribute
$5 a week, which probably covered any additional expenditures for himself
and his wife and their two children, although there was no attempt to keep
separate household accounts. But soon he could make no collections at all,
and payments to the Beuschers ceased.

Eliot and Butch found that they could not obtain relief grants for
their families while they remained with the Beuschers, nor could the grant
for the entire household be increased. They did all they could to help the
family: worked with Mr. Bouscher for the gas company to pay the gas bills,
and for the coal company to pay the coal bills; they worked in the garden
and helped to saw wood for the family's use.

For a time Charles was able to contribute a little to the family
income by playing ball on professional teams in various towns; almost every
week end during the baseball season he accumulated $7 or $8 in this way. But
since he could find no regular work in Dubuque, he soon went to Detroit, where
he stayed with a married sister. Though it was not absolutely necessary for
him to leave home, in his absence there was "one less mouth to feed," and he
was in a better position to seek work. He has since paid his back board bills
to his sister, and is now married and working in a neighboring Iowa town.

The family's garden, for which the city furnished some of the seeds
and the plot of ground on the city island, added fresh vegetables to the list
of staples which alone could be purchased on the grocery orders; there were
even some vegetables to be sold from house to house, and Mrs. Beuscher canned
a little almost every day, just as the vegetables were ready for use. One
summer she put up 500 quarts of vegetables. The family had never had a garden

before 1932, both because there was little space and because they had "never

though of it," but Mr. Beuscher has continued to garden even now that he is

back at work. Since the island garden plot could be reached only by boat,

transportation was something of a problem, solved when Mr. Beuscher and three

of his neighbors chipped in $2 apiece for the materials from which they built

a jointly-owned boat. Only infrequently did two or more families set out to

work in their gardens at the same time; so they were forever having to halloo

across the water to ask that the boat be brought back to the town side to pick

up more gardeners.

Grocery orders were supplemented with surplus commodities. The

only other outside assistance which the family received was a sack of seed

potatoes for Mr. Beuscher's garden planting in the spring of 1932 and several

tons of coal during the winter of 1933-34 from a private charitable organiza-

tion to which the Beuschers had in previous years contributed with the thought

that they were "giving something away"; now they consider these contributions

the "best investment they ever made"; they have been "repaid a hundred-fold."

Although the Beuschers never felt comfortable about receiving re-

lief, it came to be more or less an accepted thing. "You know, you went

down to City Hall, and had to wait in line, and you saw all your friends;

it was funny in a way, though it was pitiful, too....People went down to

the relief office, and talked about going, just the way they might have

gone anywhere else."

The family received food orders for only a few months, as Mr.

Beuscher was soon assigned to the CWA Eagle Point Park project as a laborer,

earning 40¢ an hour. Later he worked on the lock and dam project at 50¢ an

hour. Mr. Beuscher cannot understand why there was so great a difference between the wage rates of laborers on work projects and those of skilled carpenters. Although he was glad to be assigned to projects, there was little essential difference in his feelings about direct relief and about "work relief"; he worked hard for his pay, but still felt that he was being "given something." He has heard many times that persons on relief do not want work and will not accept jobs in private industry, but he knows from project employees whose reactions were similar to his that such is not the case, except perhaps in a very few instances. Nothing makes him "more mad" than this criticism of project workers.

Mrs. Beuscher believes that relief, as such, has not fostered dependency. "Of course, there have always been some people who have wanted something for nothing," but "the right kind of people--the people we know, except maybe a very few--" have invariably tried to remain independent, applied for relief only as a last resort, and made every effort to go back to private employment. It may be true that some persons have become so discouraged and disheartened that they have ceased to look for jobs, but any such discouragement Mrs. Beuscher considers "purely temporary." Men will go back to private employment as soon as there are jobs to be had "without standing in line day after day waiting" on the chance that someone may be hired from among the men at the factory gates.

On principle, Mr. Beuscher decidedly favors work projects as against direct relief. "Men should be made to work for what they get," and the "majority of them--at least 70 percent--" prefer to work. In any event, however, Mr. Beuscher believes that some direct relief will always be necessary as there are a "few people who aren't eligible for pensions and can't work."

Some time before the time that Mr. Beuscher was called back to work at the railroad shops, Eliot and Butch had reestablished a household for their two families. They received relief for a time, but finally both found work in local factories, and Butch moved to a home of his own. Now, they are independent, as are the Beuschers, senior.

Bob tried at various times to be assigned to a CCC camp. The family does not fully understand the many delays, though they believe that boys from smaller family groups were sent in preference to Bob because other families were more demanding and insistent than the Beuschers. But Bob's turn finally came in the fall of 1935. He liked the woods work, except when the temperature was well below zero. During a prolonged cold spell he asked for and was granted a transfer to kitchen duty. He was chagrined when the temperature dropped still lower, and the woods workers were permitted to loaf indoors while he labored in the kitchen where the thermometer stood at 5 above zero. Again he requested a transfer, which was arranged just as the weather warmed up enough for the woods workers to be sent out every day. On the whole, he considers it quite a joke that he managed always to choose "the wrong thing." He was enjoying the work most "just when he came home," after a 10-month stay, to take a job as a saw-operator, paying 30¢ an hour, with the Mississippi Milling Company. Several increases had brought his hourly rate up to 37¢ when he was laid off because of a general reduction in the force in August 1936. During the winter months the plant "took on every kid they could find"; then when the warehouse was overstocked the younger workers were laid off in great numbers.

Although Mr. and Mrs. Beuscher "don't say the depression is over yet," times have been better for them since the late fall of 1935, when Mr. Beuscher was called back to his old work at the shops at the old rate of pay. Mr. Beuscher considers this "regular work," and, as such, far superior to relief work, especially as he now "feels more independent." Still, it is not as it was in the old days when 1,500 men were employed rebuilding damaged and out-worn cars. Of the 130 men taken back at the shop, only 25 remain at work, which now consists of wrecking instead of reclamation, and no one of the 25 men knows how long his work will last. Mr. Beuscher was one of those to be recalled and to remain at work because of his "seniority right."

While he was out of work, Mr. Beuscher had regularly made the rounds of the local factories looking for jobs and had kept active his registration with the State employment office. Though he frequently grew discouraged with looking for work, Mrs. Beuscher thinks that he "enjoyed it in a way." He and his neighbors used to get together in the evenings, air their many disappointments, and decide not to bother going out again to look for jobs. But invariably the following morning found them "off again." When Mr. Beuscher learned that a few men were to be rehired, he went to the shops to explain that he was available. Soon, he was called back. Since his return to work, the Beuschers have paid up all back bills, including interest on the mortgage, property taxes, and street assessments which totaled about $500. Within the past month, the Beuschers have been able to claim the deed to their home, as the principal of the mortgage has been reduced to $1,500. The interest rate from now on will be only $5\frac{1}{2}$ instead of 7 percent.

Mrs. Beuscher thinks that perhaps young people have had the most discouraging experiences in the search for work. After Bob was laid off at the mill, he made every effort to find other employment. He reported regularly at the State employment office, which referred him to only one job, a job as chronometer reader for a battery factory. Bob thought that he could do the work, as he had had some practice in chronometer reading in his high school machine shop work, but when he reported at the factory he was told that only a man of 35 years and 200 pounds could be employed. "The local factories will not file applications" and usually offer jobs only to those men who are waiting at the plants when openings occur. Thus, when the word goes around that some factory is "hiring"—which may mean only that one man, perhaps "a relative" of another employee, has been taken on the day before—the men all go to the factory to wait for jobs. Bob has spent many hours and days "waiting" at the gates of factories in Dubuque and in Illinois towns to which he has either hitchhiked or traveled on the **family's railroad pass.**

Bob has though of going to Detroit, where he would live with one of his sisters while hunting work, but Mrs. Beuscher tells him, "If you don't have a job, your place is at home, not with your brothers-in-law, who have a hard enough time taking care of their own families." One of the brothers-in-law has recently had his hours at the factory cut in half.

Finally, Bob heard that an insulating company was expanding and taking on more men. Next morning he went to the plant at 7 o'clock; he stayed all day. Of the 30 men waiting, only 1 was hired. On the second day Bob was given a job weighing and carting raw materials. He had worked 1 full 8-hour day and about 2 hours of the second working day when some of the machinery broke down and the plant was closed for repairs.

Jeannette, like Bob, has kept a registration active at the State employment office. She is now clerking on Saturdays in a 5-and-10 cent store and hopes to have several days' work just before Christmas. Although she would prefer stenographic work, she says that she has been willing to

take what she can get. She talks to the other kids and knows that none
of her friends has a regular full-time clerical job.

Mrs. Beuscher believes that "the depression has changed people's
outlook." In a way she is more "comfortable" now than when both she and
Mr. Beuscher worried about bills and tried to plan for the future. Now,
they "just live from day to day," with the feeling that since they "lived
through the depression" they can face anything to come. Of course, it was
fun to plan and look ahead, "and that's one way we've lost." This resignation and acceptance of what the future may bring, Mrs. Beuscher accounts
a "sign of age" as well as a result of the depression. Another "sign of
age" is Mr. and Mrs. Beuscher's being content to spend leisure time at
home; lack of money "was the start of it," and when they were once again
reasonably secure, they had "lost the ambition to go."

Mr. and Mrs. Beuscher would prefer to live through another and
longer depression rather than a war, which they fear may be inevitable.
All wars he considers only "legalized stealing," the result of "capital"
and "greed." "If the U.S. were actually invaded," Mr. Beuscher says, I
"would take up a gun myself." He sees no reason, however, for anyone's
fighting "across the sea."

Mr. Beuscher is intensely interested in discussions of the
causes of extensive unemployment. As a reader of 5¢ weeklies he cannot
agree with "editorial writers" that there is no serious "technological
unemployment." From his own experience, Mr. Beuscher knows the work of
many men has been taken over by machinery. When he first worked as a
helper, it was a good 10-hour job for 3 men to hammer by hand 300 rivets;
after the introduction of pneumatic drills, 1,200 rivets could be placed
in the same length of time with about the same effort. Once a freight

train crew of 5 men handled about 20 cars; now a crew may be responsible
for 5 times as many cars, "and not the old 40-ton cars, either, but 60-,
80-, or 100-ton cars." And so it goes, in railroad shops, on the trains,
and in other industries as well. Though it has been claimed that displaced
workers are absorbed by new industries, Mr. Beuscher believes that the
proper balance has not been maintained, as the new machinery wears longer
than the old and need not be produced in such great quantity.

Mr. Bouscher has only one suggested solution for the problem of
unemployment: persons of "wealth" should be persuaded to invest their
money in industries that might increase or create new employment. He believes also that there should be a better "distribution" of the money paid
for commodities. But Mr. Beuscher does not hold "radical" ideas. At one
time there was quite a group of Socialists in Dubuque; now the movement has
"died out." Mr. Bouscher expresses his feeling about the group by telling
gleefully an old story. A friend of Mr. Bouscher's approached one of these
Socialists, who had a remarkably fine garden, and asked, "John, you believe
in distribution, don't you?" "Yes." "Then I want you to give me your
carrots and cabbages."

Mr. and Mrs. Beuscher are agreed that they would not in any event
be willing to give up property which they might have struggled to accumulate.
However, they would not want great wealth, as they would scarcely know how to
spend or handle it. Mr. Bouscher is nearing his 63d birthday; at 65 he will
be eligible for a Railroad Retirement pension of $62 or $63 a month, the precise amount depending on the extent of his earnings during the intervening
period. His greatest present hope is that he can work steadily until he
reaches the age of 65; his greatest fear, that the work will peter out between one day and the next. When he leaves the shop, Mr. Bouscher would

like to be able to buy a small plot of ground, but this is only a wish,
not an expectation. He would not want to go back to farming as a renter
or laborer, but he would like to farm if he could own his land, just enough
to work comfortably with his efforts alone.

Though the Beuschers are reasonably well satisfied with remaining
in Dubuque, they consider it "the cheapest town there is," so far as wages
go. The local factories have "never paid what they should, but then rents
are low here, too." Mr. Beuscher thinks that he would not be "telling anything" by explaining the reason for the low wage scale, for "everybody knows
that a few factories control the town." Mrs. Beuscher says with some dis-
may that she has read recently that "even office workers in Dubuque get less
than in any other city in the United States." Then she rises to the defense
of the town, which has "good schools" and a comparatively new radio station;
it numbers among its famous people a movie star, the wife of a movie star,
and a great football player. On the whole, "it's not a bad place to live";
and anyhow, the **family** "can't leave now because you even have to pay to
get across the toll bridges" into the adjacent States of Wisconsin and
Illinois.

                    Employment Chronology for Mr. **Beuscher**

          Until 1902 - On father's farm.

          1902-1931 - Helper and boilermaker,
                        railroad shops.

          Spring 1931- Unemployed except for
          fall 1935   emergency work.

          Fall 1935 -   **Boilermaker,**
          present   railroad shops.

KROLL

Mr. Kroll   62
Michael   21
    Away from home
Victor   23

Interviewing completed
December 30, 1937

Mr. Kroll recalls dates and length of jobs with great difficulty. He explains that his memory "ain't what it used to be" since the
onset of the depression and its accompanying worry and grief. Deeply sad-
dened by his wife's death "of a broken heart" over the loss of the home
through foreclosure, Mr. Kroll says philosophically, "That is life, though;
you have to take the bitter along with the sweet."

At 62 he is wiry and active, though somewhat stooped and hard of
hearing. His jet-black wavy hair presents a striking contrast to his
deeply furrowed brow and almost toothless mouth. Since the age of 14 he
had been a sheet metal worker, except for 5 years on the railroad, and had
never experienced any major unemployment until the present depression
when he was unemployed for 4 years. Now he is working for the factory
where he was employed as a lad of 14 and where he had not worked for more
than 20 years until his reemployment 2 years ago.

Mr. Kroll is proud of his two sons, both of whom are working.
Victor, 23 years old, is married and lives in Omaha. Having studied
mechanical drafting in high school and in night school after he was graduated, he now has a job as a draftsman.

Michael, a fine looking boy of 21, is at home with his father.
He talks intelligently of his plans to save up enough money to be married

next summer. Since his graduation from high school 2 years ago he has worked as an elevator operator in a Dubuque office building. His regular salary is $70 a month. Michael's girl friend is employed as a stenographer.

Mr. Kroll, Michael, and a very old bulldog, treated as a member of the family, occupy a five-room flat in a good residential neighborhood on the hill. The flat is exceptionally well furnished but not very neat or orderly. A china closet is filled with fine old Haviland china and cut glass; the shelves and sideboard are covered with soiled filet doilies made by Mr. Kroll's mother some 70 years ago. Mr. Kroll would not think of parting with any of these articles as they were greatly prized by Mrs. Kroll. Michael and Mr. Kroll do their own cooking, cleaning, and laundry. The dishes are washed only when there are no more clean "every day" ones in the cupboard, and the laundry is done only once or twice a month or when they "run out of clean clothing."

Though the flat is equipped with a furnace, Mr. Kroll considers it more economical to use a coal heater and the kitchen range. In extremely cold weather he and Michael sleep on the davenport in the living room, as the upstairs bedrooms are unheated. Michael is thoughtful of his father; the two of them are companionable, and apparently they enjoy "batching." Michael, who likes a "nice Christmas," with the help of his girl friend had tastily decorated a tree in the living room; Victor and his wife came from Omaha, all trying to make a happy Christmas for their father. Mr. Kroll still grieves over the loss of his wife and seems to derive satisfaction from reminiscing about their happy life together in their own home "before the depression hit them."

When he had completed the eighth grade, Mr. Kroll began work at the American Foundry, owned by a friend. After 8 years in this factory, Mr. Kroll "got itchy feet to see the country"; so he went to Wisconsin, where relatives lived. Here he had been employed 2 years at sheet metal work when he decided to "push on" to Great Falls, S. D, where he remained about 5 years, working 2

years at the sheet metal trade and 3 years as a fireman on the railroad.
The railroad transferred him to St. Paul, Minn., where he continued to work
as a fireman for 1½ years. By this time he began to get homesick for
Dubuque; so he returned and shortly afterwards met his future wife.

Mrs. Kroll wanted to remain in Dubuque, and therefore Mr. Kroll
returned to the American Foundry, where he worked for the next 10 years.
From 1917 to 1921 he was employed at the Stevenson Company but quit after
a strike for higher wages was lost through the company's threat to bring
in outside labor. The men who were receiving 30¢ an hour struck for an increase of 5¢ an hour. The representative sent from the national office of
the sheet metal workers' union advised the men to return to work as the
local union was not strong enough to stand its ground.

Mr. Kroll was employed by the Marquette Sheet Metal Works for the
next 8 years, except for 18 months in Chicago during the building of a
factory. He heard of the Chicago job through a business manager of the sheet
metal workers' union. On this job he received 80¢ an hour which was 20¢ more
than most of the Dubuque sheet metal workers received at that time. At the
Marquette Sheet Metal Works, however, his rate had been increased from time
to time prior to 1928. When he left in 1928 to work for the Moon Company he
was receiving 80¢ an hour; the Moon rate was 90¢. Mr. Kroll was laid off in
October 1931; the slump in building had hit Dubuque and there was little or
no sheet metal work to be had. He was unemployed until January 1936, when,
through the influence of a friend, he was hired in the sheet metal department
at the American Foundry, where he had last worked in 1917. While he now
receives only 45¢ an hour, he feels that the inside factory work has many
advantages for a man of his age. He is protected from the weather and is
not required to climb around as would be the case on most outside jobs.
Then, too, he feels that his age is not a handicap at the American Foundry

where many older men are employed. Although he could now return to either
of the other sheet metal works where the hourly rate of pay is more than at
the American Foundry, he is reluctant to give up the security of his present
job.

In 1921 the Krolls had built a home through a realty company. The
purchase price was $6,500; a down payment of $1,000 was made and the realty
company was to receive $40 a month; the Krolls were responsible for the taxes
of $120 a year. Mr. Kroll landscaped the yard, planted fruit trees, install-
ed a new furnace, and made various repairs from time to time. All of Mr.
Kroll's savings had gone into the home and in consequence there were no cash
reserves to fall back on when he became unemployed in 1931. The family had
three $1,000 insurance policies on which $500 was borrowed early in 1932.
When Mr. Kroll was no longer able to keep up the monthly payments on the
home he made application for a HOLC loan, which he did not receive as he
could not meet the requirements.

Fifty-eight hundred dollars had been paid on the home at the time
the realty company foreclosed on it early in 1934. Mrs. Kroll, grief-
stricken over the loss of the home, suffered a complete nervous collapse,
developed an acute cardiac condition, and died 3 months later. Though the
family could have lived in the home for some time after receiving the notice
of foreclosure, Mrs. Kroll insisted on moving out immediately.

The family first received relief in April 1933, about 18 months
after Mr. Kroll had lost his job. Mr. Kroll attributes their ability to
manage for so long to the fact that Mrs. Kroll had canned over 400 quarts of
garden produce. While Mr. Kroll was unemployed he had been out looking for
work every day, but had picked up only a few odd jobs such as mending roofs,
putting up storm windows, etc. He had never thought of going on relief until
one day he met a friend who was working for his relief grant. Mr. Kroll says

"I got to thinking about it and I decided it wouldn't be so bad if they would
let me work for what I got."

The first application was "the worst of it," but he soon got used
to the idea. An investigation was made and the family received a grocery
order in less than a week. Mr. Kroll asked that he be permitted to work for
his relief and was soon placed on a road repair job. He continued to work
for relief in kind until the fall of 1933, when he was assigned to common
labor on a CWA project and later to other work projects and was paid in cash.
He thinks the Works Program is "a fine thing," and strongly favors cash payments over payment in kind.

Victor had been graduated from high school in June 1934, and his
inability to find work had been an additional source of worry to Mrs. Kroll.
One of Mr. Kroll's well-to-do friends in the neighborhood heard about the
Krolls' plight and arranged to have Victor given employment at the office
building, owned by the friend. Until now, this friend, who was later
instrumental in having Mr. Kroll reemployed, had not known that the Krolls
were on relief. The news of Victor's job cheered Mrs. Kroll greatly, and
the family had hoped she would take a new lease on life and recover. Her
condition, however, was critical; she died just 2 weeks later. The $1,000
insurance policy carried by Mrs. Kroll had been depleted by loans to such an
extent that only $200 remained after medical and funeral expenses had been
paid. This $200 was used to clear up the loan and premiums for the other two
policies on which Mr. Kroll could now borrow as much as $500 if necessary.

As soon as Victor began work the relief office was notified and
Mr. Kroll was dropped from work relief. Though Mr. Kroll feels that he was
well-treated by the relief office he was glad to get off relief. While he
worked on projects the family received surplus commodities from time to time.

The abundance of salt pork distributed as a surplus commodity caused Mr. Kroll to wonder "what became of the hams and bacon from all those pigs."

Mr. Kroll sees no reason why the State should not take more responsibility for needy people now that the Federal Government is doing so much through the Social Security program. Mr. Kroll considers this social legislation a fine thing and is thankful to know that others will benefit by it even though he may never benefit personally. He thinks too many people are finding fault with the program just because they personally are ineligible for benefits.

Victor was not satisfied with his job, as he had his heart set on drafting. He was married and moved to Omaha where his wife had relatives who helped him find a job as a draftsman. Michael, who had just been graduated from high school, took Victor's elevator job. Now Michael has his own car and drives his father to and from work. As Michael "likes things nice," he decided to trade in some "odds and ends" for a vacuum cleaner "so we can keep the house looking tidier." Mr. Kroll supposes "I will have to live with Michael and his wife after they are married." One day while they were talking about their plans for the marriage, Mr. Kroll remarked, "I guess I'll blow," whereupon the girl indignantly declared that she would "call the whole thing off" unless Mr. Kroll promised to live with them. Mr. Kroll thinks that both of the boys have shown good taste in the selection of their girl friends.

The present war talk is disturbing to Mr. Kroll as he knows his boys would be eligible for conscription in case of war. He feels that wars are a great waste of money and human lives. The bonus paid to the veterans of the World War was in his opinion no more than they deserved; "while we were making money they were over there getting cracked up physically and mentally and they were entitled to every cent they got."

Mr. Kroll feels that employment conditions are much better in Dubuque now than they were 2 years ago, but he believes that most of the workers who are employed lead a hand-to-mouth existence. He can see no hope for improvement in the wage situation, however, so long as "a few big manufacturers control the town and keep other manufacturers out." He believes that the managements of these mills are utterly selfish, giving no thought to the welfare of the town. He especially resents their policy of employing young boys just out of school in preference to men with families. "When they began to get busy" a year or so ago they had boys hired even before school closed, though many former employees walked the streets in search of work. "These young fellows of course are willing to work for lower wages."

The unions are not strong enough to accomplish anything, in Mr. Kroll's opinion. He had been a member of the sheet metal workers union for years, but lost interest in it some time ago when he discovered that it was not strong enough to improve conditions in respect to local wages.

Mr. Kroll doesn't spend much time reading, or for that matter "even thinking" about national problems. When evening comes he is content just to sit in his rocker and doze. He gets up at 5:30 in order to cook breakfast, pack his lunch pail, give the dog a run, and report at the factory by 7 o'clock. He stops work at 4:30, goes to market, prepares dinner, and perhaps does the laundry or "washes up a kitchen full of dishes." Then, too, the old dog requires a lo of attention at night as "he gets so lonesome" at home alone during the day. "That danged dog wants me to be doing something every minute. If the baby next door cries he even pushes me around trying to make me go over to see about it." The dog lies at Mr. Kroll's feet watching his every change of expression as he talks.

Mr. Kroll feels that he and his two sons are very fortunate to be working. He sees no reason why he cannot continue to work for years as he is in the best of physical condition. The fact that the company is controlled by a friend probably adds to Mr. Kroll's feeling of security in the present job, although he sees little of the friend socially. He thinks it is probably fortunate that they moved to their present address after the loss of the home, as the friend in the same block became interested in helping them. The pity of it was that the help came too late to save Mrs. Kroll.

For 12 years Mrs. Kroll had devoted herself to the home and "just couldn't stand to give it up." She was "a good sport about going on relief and amazed the relief worker with her skill at gardening and canning, but when that notice of foreclosure came, she just went completely haywire." Mr. Kroll hated to lose the home, too, but the loss of the home was nothing compared with the loss of his wife, and now he sometimes wonders if there wasn't something he could have done to prevent the foreclosure. Mr. Kroll is not particularly worried about the future. The boys, he believes, will prosper if they have half a chance and he will have a home with them when he is no longer able to work.

Employment Chronology for Mr. Kroll

1891 - 1899	Sheet metal worker, American Foundry.
1899 - 1903	Sheet metal worker.
1903 - 1906	Railroad fireman.
1907 - 1917	Sheet metal worker, American Foundry.
1917 - 1921	Sheet metal worker, Stevenson Company.
1921 - 1923	Sheet metal worker, Marquette Sheet Metal Works.
1923 - 1924	Sheet metal worker, building construction.
1924 - 1928	Sheet metal worker, Marquette Sheet Metal Works.
1928 - 1931	Sheet metal worker, Moon Company.
1931 - 1936	Unemployed except for emergency work.
January 1, 1936 - present	Sheet metal worker, American Foundry.

MALLOY

Mr. Malloy	59
Mrs. Malloy	54
Ruth	24
James	22
George	20
Donald)	9
Dorothy)	

Interviewing completed
January 22, 1938

The Malloys live in a well-kept two-story stucco house which Mr. Malloy himself built some years ago. He has worked as a carpenter ever since 1912, except during 4 years of depression unemployment.

Mr. Malloy is a stubby little man, cocky and self-confident. His wiry, sandy hair and eyebrows have given him the inevitable nickname—"Red." While he talks, aggressively and assertively, he puffs away on a huge black cigar. He has lived almost all of his life in Dubuque County, where his parents farmed. He worked on the family farm until he was 21 except for a few weeks when he stayed in Dubuque with a friend and without his parents' knowledge got a job as "student brakeman" on the railroad. He had made his first run with a regular brakeman who was to teach him the job, and had started on the second run, when his mother came in to town and hunted up his roommate, who was obliged to tell her that "Red" had got himself a job. "Red's" mother soon "put the skids under him" by telling his boss that he was not yet 21. the minimum age for brakemen. So he went back to the farm for a few more months.

On the whole, he does not regret having been forced to leave the railroad job, for, he says "1 always had carpentry in my mind ever since I watched carpenters working on a new farm building. But he had no actual experience as a carpenter until after he came to Dubuque in 1912. Beginning as a helper, he learned carpentry while he worked at it. Until

about 1926 his work for various contractors in Dubuque was fairly steady,
even during the winter months. Though he usually lost, all told, some 6
or 8 weeks each year because of bad weather, he was never entirely without
a job. In fact, he frequently worked at night and over week ends on small
jobs which he had promised to do for friends and neighbors and for which
he found no other time.

In 1916 Mr. Malloy did "inside work" instead of carpentry for 8
or 9 months, but only because following a long illness he had been advised
by his doctor to give up for a time the strenuous outdoor work through all
kinds of weather. Being a carpenter, he had no difficulty in obtaining a
job with the Mississippi Milling Company; he worked in the frame department,
earning 19¢ an hour for a 10-hour day. These wages of course did not
compare at all favorably with his usual wages at carpentry; so with the
coming of the warm spring weather, Mr. Malloy left the factory to go back to
his carpentry work.

Since 1917 Mr. Malloy has been a member of the carpenters' union,
affiliated with the A.F. of L. When he joined the union, the regular union
wage rate was only 45¢ an hour, but by slow and painful stages, this rate
has been raised to $1 an hour, the highest wage rate Mr. Malloy has ever received
on any private carpentry job in Dubuque. He feels that this wage scale is
too low, especially as "every other city in Iowa has a higher union scale."
Dubuque has "the cheapest wages in the United States." Sometimes when they
consider the low wages prevalent here, the Malloys wonder why anyone stays
in Dubuque; yet it is a byword in the town that those who do leave inevitably
return. Mr. Malloy knows why he has never left Dubuque permanently, and why,
after he had worked for a year or so in Chicago, he returned to Dubuque; he

had built his home here and thus tied himself down.

In the early twenties, while Mr. Malloy was working for a contractor on a school building, he bought a lot just across the street from the family's rented home with the idea of building his own home as soon as he had some free time. When he told the landlord of his plans, the landlord said that he might sell the house. Mr. Malloy advised him to "go ahead and sell it," but was a little taken aback when the rented house was sold before he had begun work on his own home. A large garage at the back of the lot was, however, completed in short order, and all that summer the family "camped out" in the garage. When the school building neared completion, and the time had come for the pouring of the cement floors, a number of carpenters were to be temporarily laid off. Mr. Malloy, though told by the foreman that he was not among those slated to go, asked to be laid off for 2 months; he had to get that house of his up before winter. He worked feverishly, and at the end of the 2 months, the family moved into the new house, though outside doors were not yet hung, and much of the inside finishing work was yet to be done. Mr. Malloy dovetailed the finishing of the house with his regular carpentry work.

In 1926, because carpentry work was beginning to be slack in Dubuque, Mr. Malloy went to Chicago, where he quickly found work which kept him busy very nearly night and day. For the regular 44-hour week he was paid $87; for overtime he was paid at double the regular rate. While in Chicago he earned more than ever before; for several weeks in succession, his pay amounted to $115. But then expenses were higher too; he had to pay his own room and board, while Mrs. Malloy and the three children remained in Dubuque. During the school vacation the rest of

the family spent 1 month in Chicago, but Mr. Malloy scarcely saw his
wife or his children--he was so very busy. When, after having worked
in Chicago for a little more than 1 year, Mr. Malloy returned to Dubuque,
the town seemed dead to him; nevertheless, there was construction work
going on. He found work almost immediately and continued to have fairly
steady employment until 1930.

From 1930 until 1933 he had virtually no work. Though he was
not entirely jobless for more than 3 or 4 months at one stretch, he
estimated that, over a 3-year period, he had no more than 1 full year of
employment. In the winter of 1933, Mr. Malloy applied directly for CWA
employment and was assigned to a tree-trimming park project. He makes
it clear that the CWA employment was not in any sense of the term "work
relief," and that he had not applied for, or received, any form of assistance before his assignment to CWA. For this work he was paid $15 a week.
Shortly after the CWA program ended in March 1934, Mr. Malloy was sent,
through the State employment office, to work on the lock and dam project
at Bellevue. Here, he was paid $1.20 an hour; his earnings of $36 a week
"looked like big pay", after 3 years of almost total unemployment and
about 4 months on CWA work.

In September 1934, when work on the Bellevue locks was almost
at an end, Mr. Malloy got a job at 46 cents an hour with the Dubuque
Woodworking Company. But work was slack in the mill, as elsewhere, and
in November 1934, when the second big layoff in 2 months took place, he
was among those to go.

After the layoff Mr. Malloy had several brief jobs, but he
found no regular work, either with contractors or in the factories.
Finally, in the early spring of 1935 he applied for relief, but only as

a means of getting work. He had been told by friends and neighbors and
by his grocer, who was perhaps beginning to worry over whether the Malloys
could ever pay their huge bills, that an application for relief was a good
means of being assigned to a work project, but that he mustn't be "too
proud to take a couple of slips" before being assigned to a project;
almost no one was put to work immediately. So Mr. Malloy went down to
the relief office and answered "one million five hundred thousand questions," which he resented considerably. Next, an "investigator" came to
the home and asked Mrs. Malloy "a thousand and one questions."

Mr. Malloy, when asked if he had a home, said, "Sure" he had
a home, but that it wasn't all his, and in any case he "couldn't eat it."
Finally, the investigator returned to the home, bringing with her "a
slip." With a sweeping gesture, Mr. Malloy indicates that he paid so
little attention to this "slip" that he doesn't even remember the amount
of the grocery order. Whatever the amount, it "wasn't enough" for the
seven Malloys to live on. Luckily, by the time the worker called at the
home with a second slip Mr. Malloy was able to tell her that no more
help would be needed; he had been assigned to carpentry work on the
Dubuque lock and dam project and was again earning $1.20 an hour.

Ever since his work on the lock and dam project ended late in
1936, Mr. Malloy has had fairly regular employment with various private
contractors in Dubuque. In December 1936 he began work for Smith and
Sons, contractors. His earnings now were not so high as his predepression
earnings as carpenter, and his hours not so long. Instead of 44 hours,
he was now working 30 hours a week; instead of the straight hourly rate
of $1, there was a "floating scale"--various rates of pay for various

types of work. Mr. Malloy has worked for a great many different local contractors. As it happened, he had never previously worked for the Smiths, but "one man's dollar is as good as another's." Mr. Malloy has worked fairly regularly for the past year or so, except that he "didn't earn a dime" during the 5 weeks just before Christmas of 1937.

With an elaborate sarcasm Mr. Malloy states that of course he had a "swell time" during the depression years. From 1930 until the fall of 1933, when he was unemployed almost all of the time, the family lived on amounts obtained by cashing in, or borrowing on, insurance policies, and on credit. Of course, they cut down expenses in every way possible. And as for new clothes--well, they "just didn't see any clothes" for 3 or 4 years. For each of the three oldest children, Mr. Malloy carried a 20-payment life insurance policy with face value of $125. When cashed in, these policies netted the family only about one-third of their total face values. On his own policy, Mr. Malloy borrowed $150.

Mr. Malloy was able to work out his coal and gas bills. He rather resents never having been paid anything in cash for his work for coal and gas companies; when he worked a few hours beyond the time necessary to pay off the outstanding bills, his pay was credited on the next bill. The Malloys ran in debt on groceries, taxes, doctor bills, and so on. Mr. Malloy figures that his debts, accumulated over a period of about 4 years, amounted to approximately $3,000. He includes, in this total, amounts borrowed on insurance and lost by cashing in policies before they had matured. Thus, the $3,000 just about covered the family's total expenditures for almost 4 years.

Mr. Malloy has been paying off his debts as rapidly as possible, but he is still "in the hole." He thinks that credit is an asset in times of

stress and that he should preserve it by paying bills as soon as pay checks
are again coming in.

The Malloys have three children of employable age and the 9-year-
old twins, Donald and Dorothy. Ruth, James, and George are all high school
graduates. After Ruth was graduated from high school, she was given a
scholarship covering tuition only at a Dubuque college. Textbooks and inci-
dentals were an added expense which Mr. Malloy found he could not meet in
1930; so Ruth left college at the end of her first year. Since leaving
school, Ruth has had very little work. For some time she clerked on Saturdays
and during preholiday rush seasons in a Dubuque department store. Last summer
she had full-time work in a restaurant for a few months, but she was laid off
in the fall, and since then has found nothing to do.

The two oldest boys have likewise had considerable difficulty in
finding regular full-time work. For several years both James and George had
newspaper routes which netted them enough cash to pay for their own clothing.
One summer when Mr. Malloy had no work and James was spending a month in the
country with relatives, Mr. Malloy delivered his papers; he was glad enough
to earn $2.60 a week carrying papers. A little more than a year ago, James,
who had previously had only odd jobs, found work as a truck driver for a
neighborhood grocery. His hours as a deliveryman are long and somewhat irregular; he goes to work at 8 a.m. and returns home at any time from 6:30 to
8 p.m. He comes in tired and hungry, flops down into a comfortable chair,
and waits for Mrs. Malloy to prepare his dinner, which he must eat alone.
In a month or so, he expects to begin work as a grocery clerk; his hours will
then be more regular and the work a little less strenuous. George has not
yet found full-time work.

Mr. Malloy believes that it is especially difficult for young
people to find work because older persons hold their jobs instead of retiring
On the railroads, for instance, many men eligible for pensions continue on
jobs which should be open to younger men. Mr. Malloy believes that railroaders should be forced to retire when they have reached the age of 65,
though he supposes that if he were 65 and able to work and to earn more at
his regular job than the amount of his pension, he would not want to give up
his job either. The employment of married women whose husbands are able to
support them has kept many young girls from getting jobs. Furthermore, Mr.
Malloy believes that in Dubuque there has been a definite trend toward factory employment of out-of-town men in preference to Dubuquers. He considers
the depression "just a business slump" and is inclined to believe that the
seriousness of the problem of unemployment has been somewhat overstated, but
he is concerned about the low wage scales in Dubuque.

Mr. Malloy, as a union carpenter, considers unionism the best means
of raising wages and improving working conditions. On principle, he approves
the A. F. of L. craft unionism, but thinks that the A.F. of L. "went to sleep"
a few years ago. Mr. Malloy feels that though the CIO may just "die out"—
indeed, he rather hopes that it will disintegrate—it has "at least waked up
the A.F. of L."

So far as he himself is concerned, Mr. Malloy has a great deal of
confidence in the future—a confidence that he considers justified by his
past record. He anticipates working fairly regularly at high enough wages
to enable him to pay off his debts. There are plans afoot in Dubuque for new
buildings on which Mr. Malloy hopes to work. And if the housing legislation
goes through, perhaps some of the houses in the flats where "people have to

live, even when they don't have floors" can be replaced with adequate homes.
Mr. Malloy thinks that such building, in addition to improving living conditions for the flats-dwellers, would provide jobs for carpenters and stimulate
business for Dubuque woodworking mills.

Employment Chronology for Mr. Malloy

Until 1912	— On father's farm
1912 - 1916	— Carpenter, construction company
8 or 9 months 1916	Fitter, Mississippi Milling Company
1916 - 1930	Carpenter
1930 - September 1934	Unemployed except for emergency work
September - November 1934	Cabinetmaker, Dubuque Woodworking Company
November 1934 - December 1936	Unemployed except for odd jobs of carpentry and emergency work
December 1936 - present	Carpenter, private contractor

<u>GARESCH</u>

<u>At home</u>

Mr. Garesch	58
Mrs. Garesch	52
Mae	26
Howard, Jr.	24
Dorothy	18
Leonard	16
Jean	13
Eileen	11
Waite	9

<u>Married and away from home</u>.

3 sons

Interviewing completed
March 25, 1938

"The depression has left me an old man, and now I never will own
my own home," says Howard Garesch, 58 years old. He is tall and lean. His
gold-rimmed spectacles and high forehead make him scholarly-looking. He
talks easily, and uses an excellent if somewhat overpompous vocabulary.
During the 15 pre-depression years that Mr. Garesch had his own business of
interior decorating, with his own shop and from 10 to 15 employees, he had
been saving money with which to buy a home. Now his savings are gone; he
does not own his home; he has no shop; his car and most of his tools have
been sold. He now has only enough tools for his own work of painting and
paper hanging.

Two or three years ago, Mrs. Garesch had a "stroke"; her speech is
a little thick, and her lips twist to one side as she talks. Mrs. Garesch
spent several weeks in the hospital, and doctor and hospital bills, she
says, were an "awful burden" on Mr. Garesch.

The Gareschs have 10 children, 3 of them married with homes and families of their own. One daughter died when she was only 3 months old. Mr. Garesch says that "the burial lot" is the only thing which he managed to keep through the depression. "The depression hit" the Garesch family "at the worst time," for the children were just growing up. Mae, 26 years old, Howie, 24, and Dorothy, 18, who was graduated from high school in 1937, have all been unemployed. Howie's first job was with the Dubuque Bakery, where he earned only $5 a week. Mr. Garesch feels that Howie's employer was in a position to pay higher wages and simply "took advantage of the depression." Since the spring of 1936, when Howie was laid off at the Dubuque Bakery, he has been working for the Joliet Baking Company, earning 50¢ an hour.

Mr. Garesch explains that none of the older boys has been interested in his trade of painting. Instead of another painter in the family, Mr. Garesch "has a machinist, a millwright, a butcher, and a baker." Only Waite, the 9-year-old fourth-grader, has shown any aptitude for painting. Early in the depression William quit school in the hope of finding work; since there was none to be had in Dubuque, he went to another Iowa town, where he is now regularly employed. He is married and getting along nicely; yet Mr. Garesch still regrets that William did not finish high school.

Mae had no work except as an enumerator for the 1930 Census of population from the time of her graduation from high school until last October, when she began work at a battery factory to which she had been referred by the State employment office. Mrs. Garesch bitterly resents the rudeness of persons to whom Mae went looking for work; on one occasion she was told even that her high school education was worthless. Mr. Garesch states patronizingly, "Mother thinks that just because they have high

school educations, they ought to be given jobs."

The Gareschs are a happy family, living in a small frame house,

weatherworn to a dingy gray. Furniture is battered, and the rugs are

threadbare; the rooms are not too tidy, but seem to have been lived in com-

fortably. Mr. Garesch explains that during depression years there have been

no replacements of household equipment, "as you can see," but the Gareschs

have tried to "keep a home" to which the children can bring their friends.

Howie has recently purchased a secondhand piano, which he plays entirely by

ear. He would like to take music lessons, but every music teacher with whom

he talks tells him that he is now too old to start in as a beginner. All

members of the family enjoy listening to the radio. Every fall Mr. Garesch

goes on a hunting trip with his sons; Waite enjoys the trips as much as the

older boys do.

Mr. Garesch, born in Germany, was brought to the United States

before he was 3 years old. His mother died not many years after coming to

this country, and Mr. Garesch never got along well with his father. Since

leaving hone at the age of 13, he has "never eaten a meal in his father's

house." At 13 he was "a grown man" and "a doubting Thomas," who, "like

Columbus, had to see for myself that the world was round." During the next

8 or 10 years, he traveled all over the world, earning his living by paint-

ing as he went, and paying his passage "across both waters" by working as

assistant cook.

Though traveling interfered with his schooling, Mr. Garesch was

always anxious to have a good education. At one time he hoped to go to

medical school, and it was agreed that he should help his younger sisters

with their schooling and that they in turn would put him through school.

His hopes ended when one of the sisters married as soon as she finished
school.

Ever since his marriage in 1903 Mr. Garesch has worked as a painter
and decorator in Dubuque. Before 1915 he was employed by various local
contractors; from 1915 until the early years of the depression he had his
own business.

When he was drafted for service in the World War, he sold the
business, but as the Armistice was signed before he was called he immediately
set up shop again. His downtown store was stocked with paints and wall
papers. Rugs and draperies he bought in Dubuque or Chicago department stores,
and he was given commissions on purchases for his customers. The business
was prosperous; during the twenties, his net income averaged from $3,500 to
$4,500 annually, and his gross business amounted to $20,000 or $30,000.

As early as 1930, however, Mr. Garesch's business was slack.
Interior decorating is, after all, he says, more or less of "a luxury trade."
During depressions, even the well-to-do let repairs go or decide to give such
work as must be done to unemployed relatives. A man says, "Oh! Jim can do
that," and, says Mr. Garesch, "Jim does it"--not very well, to be sure, but
still well enough to take the job away from Mr. Garesch. His last big
contract was for decorating a lodge building in 1930. Gradually, he let his
employees go, and by 1931 he had only one man working for him. Soon, he, too,
had to be laid off. Mr. Garesch's earnings reached their lowest ebb in 1933,
when he cleared exactly $122 during the calendar year.

Meanwhile, he was supplementing his meager income from his savings.
He converted such assets as he had into cash--his car, and most of his tools,
and his insurance policies. He now has only one small fraternal policy--
"just enough to bury me." Mr. Garesch states that the "only honest way"

of putting it is to say that the family spent "several thousand dollars"
aside from his earnings during the depression years. He "tried to keep his
credit good," but went in debt several hundred dollars, chiefly for rent,
which he is now attempting to pay.

When Mr. Garesch expresses regret that his savings went for current living expenses instead of for a home, Mrs. Garesch remarks philosophically that it's just as well that savings hadn't been invested in a home,
"or we'd have been on poor relief even sooner." Sharply Mr. Garesch tells
her, "We were never on poor relief." Mrs. Garesch merely shrugs her
shoulders. Making the best of an embarrassing situation, Mr. Garesch explains that the family did receive purely "temporary" assistance for about
2 months in 1934. When there was no food in the house, Mr. Garesch went
down to the relief office and explained his situation to the director of
relief, who said, "You should have come in sooner." Mr. Garesch believes
that accepting temporary aid is not at all comparable to being "on poor
relief."

According to Mr. Garesch the family managed satisfactorily on the
relief grants, as there was always a little supplementary income. Hastily,
he goes on to explain that the family could buy farm produce very cheaply.
When they visited a married son in a small Iowa town, they brought home with
them sacks of potatoes purchased for almost nothing. Once they bought a
whole pig for $5; "of course, $5 was a small fortune to us then, but the
pig was two fortunes." The Gareschs also supplemented relief grants by
gardening for the first time in their lives. The boys helped Mr. Garesch
work several vacant lots near the family's home which they were permitted
to use rent-free.

Mr. Garesch considers "the idea of relief that Roosevelt has

fathered" a very fine one. There have been some "abuses," as might be expected in any such extensive program, but for these "Roosevelt is not
responsible." For himself, Mr. Garesch thinks it better to help "two
cheaters" than to leave one person "in misery."

Mr. Garesch considers the depression entirely "man-made"—brought
on by stock market speculators who let the situation which they had helped to
create get out of control, and then "didn't know how to stop the ball's rol-
ling." Furthermore, the world has gone "money-crazy." "Greed for profits"
and impersonal business relationships have taken the place of the "neighbor-
liness and generosity" of Mr. Garesch's youth. Emphasis on money is partly
the result of "our educational system" which stresses preparation for jobs.
Two factors tending to increase unemployment are the "discarding of older
men" by industry and the reluctance of industries to "undertake programs for
expansion."

Mr. Garesch is hopeful about his own future prospects for work.
Last year was an unusually good one—"not in comparison with the twenties,
but in comparison with 1933." His earnings totaled $800 or $900. He expects
to have plenty of work during the coming spring and summer, though he earned
nothing in February. From now on, he anticipates working only with his hands;
profits from "salesmanship" are a thing of the past, for he has no shop and
he no longer buys decorative materials on a commission basis. But he is content with trying to earn a living, and he is glad that his earnings depend
on his own efforts and that his age is not so great a handicap as it might
be if he worked in a factory.

Employment Chronology for Mr. Garesch

Until 1915 – Painter

1915 – 1930 – Own interior decorating
            business

1930 – present – Self-employed painter
               and paper hanger; employment
               highly irregular.

PILSNER

Mr. Pilsner	40
Mrs. Pilsner	38
Mildred	13
Jimmie	11
Bobby	9
Tommy	7

Interviewing completed
February 3, 1938

Mr. Pilsner, 40 years old, is slight of build; his face is thin
and pale. He relates his unemployment and relief experiences matter-of-
factly and consistently. He was a spray painter at the Stevenson Company
from the time he left the farm in 1919 to the close of the Stevenson plant
in 1931—except for 3 years at the Dubuque Woodworking Company—but he was
unemployed for 3 years during the worst of the depression. Since his reemployment nearly 4 years ago by the Dubuque Woodworking Company the family
has gradually paid off debts and partially regained its predepression status.

Mrs. Pilsner is a pretty woman with black curly hair and dancing
black eyes. Mildred, 13, the oldest of the four children, is an enthusiastic
member of the Girl Reserves. Jimmie, 11, and Bobby, 9, take violin lessons
and hope to become members of the school orchestra. They practice in different parts of the house, creating a din with their cheap instruments.
Tommy, 7 years old, is a second-grader.

The Pilsners occupy their own home, a two-story frame house, badly
in need of paint and repair. The furniture and rugs, of excellent quality,
are reminders of more prosperous days. The home is comfortable, well-ordered
and immaculately clean.

Mr. Pilsner attended country school until he completed the eighth grade. Though he liked farm work, he was attracted by the wages paid mill-workers in town; so he left the farm when he was 22 to work at the Stevenson Company, where in those days a job could be had for the asking. Mr. Pilsner's entrance rate in the assembly department was 30¢ an hour, but within a short time he was placed on a piecework basis. After working on various machines, he was assigned in 1923 to the finishing department as a spray painter, usually earning $30 a week. By the time of his marriage in 1924, he had saved enough during his 5 years at Stevenson's to buy his present home, which had been owned by his mother.

About a year after the Pilsners were married they decided to borrow money on the home to go into the grocery business; the home was mortgaged with a building and loan association for $1,500. Mrs. Pilsner ran the store while Mr. Pilsner continued on his job at the Stevenson Company. The Pilsners found to their sorrow that the location of their business was extremely poor. Then, too, they extended too much credit and in consequence the business failed after 2 years. This venture the Pilsners now consider the worst mistake they ever made. It was difficult during the depression to keep up the monthly payments of $15 to the build-ing and loan, and only through the consideration of the loan company was the property saved from foreclosure, as taxes were not paid during 3 de-pression years. The building and loan company finally paid the taxes to save the property and added the amount of the taxes to the mortgage.

In 1926, during a slack season at the Stevenson plant, Mr. Pilsner got a job in the finishing department at the Dubuque Woodworking Company. For this work he was paid on a piecework basis, averaging 65¢ an hour. At Stevenson's he had averaged only 60¢ an hour. In 1929,

however, when his pay at the Dubuque Woodworking Company was reduced to a
straight hourly rate of 45¢, he quit to return to the Stevenson Company,
where he remained until the factory closed in December 1931.

The Pilsners had no savings at this time, as it had been necessary
to apply all surplus cash on the mortgage and on bills incurred in the
grocery store venture. Mr. Pilsner had two $1,000 insurance policies on
which he borrowed $80 before the policies were allowed to lapse. The
neighborhood grocer and butcher extended credit without question until
$130 was owed to the grocer and $50 to the butcher at the time the Pilsners
applied for relief early in 1933. During the summer and fall of 1932
Mr. Pilsner painted three houses and shingled a roof. His profits on these
jobs were small, as it was necessary to set a very low price in order to
get the work. Mrs. Pilsner took in some laundry work for which she, too,
was poorly paid. "A dollar now and then helped though to buy a pair of
shoes for the children." It seemed that one or another of the four children
was in need of shoes most of the time. Mrs. Pilsner had never realized
before how much money was needed "just for the children's school supplies."
While 10 or 15 cents a week for writing paper seems like a small item, it
was a big consideration when there was no regular income in the family.

Finally, by February 1933 all resources except credit had been
exhausted. Though the grocer and the butcher had not even mentioned the
Pilsner's mounting bills, Mr. Pilsner felt that it wasn't fair to expect
them to carry him when his prospects for steady work were daily growing
more remote. While many of the Pilsners' acquaintances had gone on relief,
the idea of relief was distasteful to the Pilsners, but they decided it was
better than to ask futher credit of their neighbors, who could ill afford
to extend it. The Pilsners had managed for more than a year before applying

for relief; they are proud of having waited longer than many other families.
Mrs. Pilsner talked with the school nurse about their situation and the
nurse called the director of relief before the Pilsners went to the office
to make application. Relief was granted about 3 days later. The Pilsners
feel that they were well-treated by the relief office. They did not object
to the investigation and questioning as they understood the purpose of this
procedure.

Mrs. Pilsner was able to manage nicely on the weekly grocery allowance after milk was received from the Milk Fund. Before that, however, she
had felt that the children's diet was inadequate. The big problem was fuel;
it was impossible in zero weather to get along on 1 ton of coal a month, but
Mr. Pilsner was often able to get some wood from the country just for the
cutting and hauling of it. Without a truck it would have been impossible
to keep an adequate supply of wood for all purposes, but the small loads
hauled in the car were enough to supplement the relief coal.

About 2 months after the Pilsners went on relief, Mr. Pilsner had
an opportunity to move his family to a 40-acre farm in the neighborhood
where he grew up. The Pilsners never considered not taking this farm as
they were so anxious to get off relief. They rented their Dubuque home for
$15 a month—the amount of the building and loan payments—and moved to the
country early in April 1933. During the year that they were on this farm
the Pilsners made their own way, but realized practically no profit. The
owner died and his sons took over the farm, making it necessary for the
Pilsners to move back to town in February 1934. They rented a place with
a huge garden space for $10 a month, $5 less than they received from the
renters in their own home. The large garden space, they thought, would
make it possible to raise produce for sale.

By May, however, before anything had been realized from the garden, they again had to apply for relief. The relief office allowed the family $7.50 a month for rent in addition to food. In June Mr. Pilsner was assigned to work relief at $28.80 a month. Until the end of March 1935, when he was called to work at the Dubuque Woodworking Company, he continued on work projects. He much preferred work to direct relief, and believes that most of the men take the project jobs seriously, putting into them just as much effort as they would on jobs in private industry. Mr. Pilsoner was employed first on road repair, then at the rock quarry, where he was working when the call came from the mill. The Pilsners had discontinued their telephone early in the depression, but he had given the number of a neighbor when he made application at the Dubuque Woodworking Company. The day the call came from the mill was a red-letter day in the Pilsner household. The whole family wanted to go to the rock quarry to tell Mr. Pilsen about the job. While he had been on work relief he had kept his application active at the State employment office and had often made the rounds of the factories. Up to 1935, however, there had been little activity in the factories.

Mr. Pilsner's entrance rate at the Dubuque Woodworking Company was 34¢ an hour, but with the several increases he has been granted he now earns 49¢. Last spring and summer several hundred men were employed at this mill, but he doubts whether half of them are now working. However, he feels quite safe in his job as he is one of the mill's most experienced spray painters.

Mr. Pilsoner takes no interest in the millworkers' union. He became disgusted with unions years ago when the street car men and railroad shop men, out on strike, tried to get the jobs of Stevenson men by offering to work for less money. He can see no principle or consistency in that sort of thing. He also feels that the officers of the unions are "more interested

in making easy money than in the cause of the working man." Mr. Pilsner
would not think of scabbing; he will walk out any time a strike is declared,
but he "will not join up with the union."

The system of old-age annuities under the Social Security program
is much fairer, in Mr. Pilsener's opinion, than the Iowa State pension system,
under which home-owners are "penalized." He believes that the limited buying
power of workers is largely responsible for unemployment. For example, he
would like to paint and repair his home, but he can't spare the money for the
materials. This, he believes, is true of most workers today— they can
afford to buy only the barest necessities.

Since Mr. Pilsner has been reemployed he has paid off the $50-
butcher bill and most of the $130- grocery bill by making small monthly pay-
ments. He has also caught up with payments on his taxes and the interest on
the mortgage, and he has taken out a small insurance policy. Mrs. Pilsner
believes, however, that it will take years for them to recover from their
depression experience, since no clothing or household supplies have been
purchased for so long that there is need now to replace many things. During
the summers she has been able to get ahead a little, but living expenses are
so much higher in the winter that there is nothing left 'after small payments
on debts have been made. Mr. Pilsner has recently gone on a 49-hour week for
the first time in almost a year; this should help materially, as there will
be almost $5 more in the weekly pay check. The Pilsners attend church
regularly and send the children to Sunday School. For recreation they
occasionally attend dances, play bridge, or go to movies. They are ambitious
for their children and hope to be able to give them good educational
advantages.

Mr. Pilsner has often thought that he would like to return to farming. In fact, if he had the money to **stock** a farm, he would move to a farm "in a minute." Without capital, however, he fears that this dream will never be realized, but he intends to "keep on dreaming just the same."

Employment Chronology for Mr. Pilsner

Until 1919 - On father's farm.

1919 - 1926   Spray painter, Stevenson Phonograph
              and Radio Company.

1926 - 1929   Spray painter, Dubuque Woodworking
              Company.

1929 - December
1931   Spray painter, Stevenson Phonograph
              and Radio Company.

December 1931 -
March 1935   Unemployed.

March 1935 -
present   Spray painter, Dubuque Woodworking
              Company.

<u>TAGLER</u>

Mr. Tagler   42
Mrs. Tagler 37
Junior   13

Interviewing completed
January 7, 1938

Carl Tagler, his wife Anna, and their 13 year-old son Junior live
in their own home in one of the older downtown residential sections of
Dubuque. Mr. Tagler's height, slightly under 6 feet, is accentuated by his
slenderness and by an unruly mop of black hair which tends to grow upward.
His small black mustache adds dignity to his somewhat youthful appearance;
though he is 42, he looks younger. Mr. Tagler has strong convictions which
he expresses with force and intelligence and at times with not a little show
of humor. His expressive brown eyes twinkle with amusement or burn with
scorn while he talks, depending on the topic under discussion. Though he
speaks with the utmost self-assurance, he frequently mispronounces words
which apparently have been added to his vocabulary through reading.

From 1910, when Mr. Tagler left school, until 1921 he had held a
variety of jobs. In 1921 he began work for the Dubuque Woodworking Company.
"I didn't want to settle down as a mill worker for the rest of my life, so
I quit my factory job, at the end of 7 years, to sell insurance." He had
marked success for 2 or 3 years, but by 1932 the lapses had made this job
utterly unprofitable. Except for work relief, he was unemployed for 2 years
until hired on his present job as driver for a dairy. Now as an officer of
the truck drivers' union and active in the recent strike of Dubuque truck
drivers, he has high hopes for unionism in the city.

To Anna, and her good management, Mr. Tagler attributes their
home ownership and present solvent financial state. Before their marriage,

16 years ago, she had accumulated savings from 5 years of "clerking in a store." Two weeks after they were married she suggested that their combined savings of $500 be used as a down payment on a $2,500 house. Mrs. Tagler had been horrified at the thought of paying $16 for only 2 weeks in furnished rooms; so she set out forthwith to look for a house. Their home, a two-story gray stucco, unpretentious in appearance from the outside, is attractively and adequately furnished. The mortgage was paid off in 1931, when Mr. Tagler received the first payment of his veteran's adjusted compensation; the bonus of 1936 was used for remodeling and repairs.

At 37, Anna Tagler is fair-haired, rosy-cheeked, and plump. Gracious and friendly of manner, she discusses the family's depression experiences with frankness and considerable objectivity. Her ancestors were among the early Bohemian settlers in Wisconsin, and from early childhood she had been well-trained in thriftiness; this training, she feels, has stood her in good stead in the management of her own home. Both parents are devoted to Junior, their only child.

Mr. Tagler, of German parentage, was born in a small Wisconsin town. He had to quit school to go to work after completing the second year of high school. He started to work for the town's only butcher. This job, however, came to a sudden end, after only a few weeks, when he was ordered to kill a calf. The calf licked Carl's hand, looked at him with "trusting, beseeching eyes," and Carl quit the job. For the next 4 years he was employed as office boy and clerk for the local hotel. He then worked for almost 2 years as a fireman on the railroad before a back strain forced him to quit. He had been hired on this job before he was 19 years old and the work proved to be a bit too strenuous for him. Through friends, Mr. Tagler was employed in Chicago by the street car company as a motorman. He had worked there only

6 months when he was drafted for service in the World War.

After 17 months of service, most of the time overseas, Mr. Tagler returned home expecting one of "those fine jobs the soldier boys were promised," but he was unable to find any kind of work for more than a month. He then came to Dubuque in April 1919 and was immediately employed by a creamery as ice cream maker; at the end of a year he was promoted to the position of shipping and receiving clerk. Soon after his marriage in 1921 he was employed as a benchman at the Dubuque woodworking mill where he remained for the next 7 years, earning from 40¢ to 48½¢ an hour. His work as benchman was less monotonous than many of the factory jobs. In fact he really enjoyed the work, but he says that he has always had the philosophy that only a fool is satisfied with things as they are. He gave up the factory job in 1928 to try his hand at selling insurance. For 2 years he averaged from $45 to $65 a week but early in the depression selling became increasingly difficult, and even more difficult was the collection of premiums; by the latter part of 1932 the job was utterly unprofitable.

In January 1933 he gave up insurance altogether and was idle for 10 months except for scattered odd jobs. In November he was employed as a non-relief worker on a CWA project at the rock quarry. Being unaccustomed to rough work, his hands were badly cut and bruised for several days, but he didn't mind the heavy work because it provided an interesting change. He continued on CWA projects, working at common labor and receiving $15 a week, until March 1934, when he was laid off during the general retrenchment period. Between January 1, 1933, and the beginning of CWA in the latter part of November, the Taglers had used up their savings of only a few hundred dollars and borrowed $300 on two of their three insurance policies. These two policies were then allowed to lapse. The one policy is still in force and another has been taken out since Mr. Tagler returned to work.

At the time of Mr. Tagler's lay-off from CWA, the family had no resources except a small amount Mrs. Tagler had managed to save from CWA pay checks. This was exhausted in about 6 weeks, and it was impossible for him to be placed on a work project without the certification of the relief office; he applied for relief in June 1934. In less than a week after he made application an investigator visited the home and the first grocery order was granted. He was not assigned to work relief, however, until November, and then his assignment was on a budget deficiency basis of $32 a month. From November 1934 to February 1935 he was employed at carpentry work at $1 an hour, making furniture for the lodge at Eagle Point Park and working only 8 hours a week. He supplemented his earnings by selling typewriters, cash registers, and adding machines. While he enjoyed the project employment and derived satisfaction from the knowledge that he wasn't "stacking up debts," he feels that some of the men did not appreciate this opportunity to work. Several of them loafed on the job; improper supervision, Mr. Tagler believes, was responsible for this. As the city was required to provide supervision for projects, it was necessary to assign minor officials in the city highway and other departments to supervise projects which should have had trained men with some executive ability.

While Mr. Tagler was unemployed, the family had cut out all un-necessary expenses. For example, they did not buy a license for the car they had owned for several years; neither did they buy new clothing except the necessary school clothes for Junior. Mrs. Tagler refused, however to reduce her food budget, as she considered adequate food the first requirement for good health. Though she considers herself an extremely economical cook, she believes she could not have managed on the relief grant, had Mr. Tagler been unable to supplement it with odd jobs of selling. She feels that the

allowances were too low; though some families which made special requests
fared better than the Taglers, who neither requested any additional items
nor questioned the amount they were allowed. The Taglers believe that some
families receive more than they require, while others go without. The
explanation of this, they believe, lies in the fact that the relief office
is understaffed and, in consequence, families are not visited often enough.

Mrs. Tagler was very much "embarrassed" over being on relief—so
much so that the relief worker, noticing her discomfort, had explained that
she should not feel humiliated since there were hundreds of families in the
same predicament. Just the same, she "never felt right about it." Mr. Tagler
on the other hand, looked on direct relief as an unpleasant but necessary
step toward getting an emergency work assignment; he considered work relief
only a temporary means of getting by until he could find private employment.

While employed on work relief, he visited the State employment offic
and local factories every week or so in search of private employment. Early
in 1935 the Dubuque Woodworking Company, for which he had previously worked,
telephoned him to report for employment. He worked as benchman for a week
before he was able to determine what his wage rate would be; on discovering
that he would receive only 31¢ an hour, he quit. Each benchman was expected t
examine and repair "about 400 window frames in an hour." He considered the
rate of pay for this highly speeded up work "outrageous."

In his search for work Mr. Tagler had talked with a dairy owner for
whom he had made ice cream once during a Fourth-of-July rush, when the
regular ice cream maker was ill. He again made contact with this dairy and
was employed as a driver in the middle of March 1935. He has remained on this
job to the present time and finds it interesting. As he has a wholesale route
and factory district, he has an opportunity "to meet new faces," and he enjoys

talking to the men around the factories. He is paid $15 a week, but his commissions average $9 to $11; so he considers that he earns considerably more than most of his millworker acquaintances. Mr. Tagler believes, however, that with the recent membership gains in the millworkers' union, the employers will be forced to concede to the union's demands in March, when the present agreement expires, or risk having the mills closed. The millworkers' union has just been reorganized and is now headed by "more aggressive leadership." "One mill owner has been told that if he fails to meet the union's demands they will affiliate with CIO."

In Mr. Tagler's opinion, the CIO does not represent collective bargaining, but rather a "steam roller method." He does not approve of violence and thinks that there "has been too much bloodshed in the CIO strikes"; if, however, the present millworkers' union fails, he feels sure that the CIO will be brought to Dubuque. He believes that some of the mills in Dubuque have resorted to unfair labor practices. "During layoffs," he says, "there are two union men let out to one nonunion man." Then, too, he feels that there was no justifiable reason for putting the men on short hours. One mill had been working three shifts when suddenly this mill began laying men off. A foreman told Mr. Tagler, "At this same time a pile of orders disappeared out of my desk without any explanation." Mr. Tagler does not know whether these were orders that could wait until the union could be "demoralized" or whether they were sent to one of the company's other plants. The unions in Dubuque have requested the National Labor Relations Board to make an investigation of labor conditions in the city.[1]/

Mr. Tagler believes that certain big mills tried to prevent too much unemployment and part-time work from showing up in the November unemployment census by calling back men who had been laid off and by increasing the hours of work during the week preceding the census. During that week, he

[1]/ The local press of Jan. 12, 1938, reported hearings held by the National Labor Relations Board.

says that he saw men at one mill who had not worked there for 2 or 3 months.
The victory of the truck drivers' union in their recent strike has added
vitality to unionism in Dubuque, according to Mr. Tagler. Six weeks ago the
truck drivers' union had a membership of only 50; now its membership has
reached 400. The only point not conceded by the employers was the demand
for a closed shop. The union has voted, however, to fine each member $1 a
day for every day that he works on a truck with a nonunion man. Mr. Tagler
believes that the "majority of working men are favorable to the present
administration," though many have "turned against the President because recovery has been too slow." In his opinion "too much emergency relief money
has been used to help farmers and not enough has been spent in the industrial
centers of the country." The much-discussed housing bill before Congress at
the time of the interview would actually aid working people if loans could
be made "directly to the people at 4 percent interest." If the loans are
made through the banks and finance companies, Mr. Tagler "doesn't doubt that
the interest will amount to 6 percent."

The Taglers never run bills; neither do they live beyond their
income. They are teaching their son the same thriftiness. Junior was
shocked when a schoolmate received a wrist watch for Christmas, for the
schoolmate's family was unable to pay for his school books. Junior had been
well-pleased with a sled his father had made for him, using old runners and
left-over bits of paint. Mr. Tagler is handy with tools; a kitchen cupboard
that he built is exhibited with pride by his wife. Back of the house he has
built a rock garden and fish pond; gayly painted trellises, weather vanes, and
bird houses add color and attractiveness to the garden. He considers that his
versatility gives him a certain feeling of independence and security; at least
he is dependent on no one industry for a livelihood, as is the case with some
workers.

The Taglers feel that they are completely on their feet again, none the worse off for their depression experiences. They are saving for Junior's education and for a rainy day. Mr. Tagler, now secure in a steady job, "wants to help bring about better working conditions for all workers in Dubuque"; this, he believes can be accomplished only through "strong, aggressive labor organization."

Employment Chronology for Mr. Tagler

1909 - 1913 Hotel office boy.

1914 - 1916 Railroad fireman.

March 1917 -
September 1917
              Street car motorman.

September 1917 -
February 1919
              U. S. Army.

April 1919 -
April 1921   Ice cream maker and shipping clerk,
              creamery.

May 1921 -
August 1928   Benchman, Dubuque Woodworking
              Company.

September 1928 -
January 1933 Insurance salesman.

January 1933 -
February 1935
              Unemployed except for emergency work.

March 1935 -
Present   Milk truck driver.

<u>CALMER</u>

Mr. Calmer   35
Mrs. Calmer   34
Bob   14
Billie   12
Pete   10
John   6
Anna   4
Dickie   2

Interviewing completed
March 9, 1938

          Frank Calmer, 35 years old, employed as a clerical worker for 8
years and in local factories for the better part of 9 years says, "I hate
to think of spending the rest of my life in a mill." Now employed at the
Mississippi Milling Company, where he had worked for 4 years previous to his
depression unemployment, Frank earns only enough for a "bare existence" for
his wife and six children. On two occasions since he was reemployed in
January 1935, he has been laid off for short periods, once during a strike
in 1935, and again during the taking of inventory in December 1937. Both
times he had to seek relief immediately. Though he is glad to have a job,
resents his present meager earnings and general insecurity. Before going
on relief in 1933, the Calmer family had run up a grocery bill of $265 and
a medical bill of $150. With Frank's present earnings of $14 a week, the
family is again running behind with bills.

          Frank Calmer, of German descent, is dark and striking in appear-
ance; his hair and eyes are quite black and his skin is olive. His physique
is slender and youthful. He talks freely, expressing his feelings with abando
and with considerable objectivity. Though he is critical of the modern industrial system and its inequalities, he is not bitter. Devoted to his wife

and children, he is doing all he can for their welfare.

Illness has complicated the family situation; 2-year-old Dickie
has been ill since his birth and Mrs. Calmer is leaving within a few days
for Iowa City, where she will undergo an operation at the State hospital.
Though the family physician to whom the Calmers still owe $150 offered to
take care of Mrs. Calmer, Frank felt that it was not right to impose on
this physician. Then, too, the hospital facilities in Iowa City are "far
superior to those in Dubuque." During Mrs. Calmer's absence from the home,
her mother will keep house for the family.

Four children attend school. Bob, 14, is in the ninth grade;
Billie, 12, is in the eighth grade; Pete, 10, is in the fifth grade; and
John, 6, is in the first grade. According to her brothers, 4-year-old Anna,
the only girl in the family, "thinks she can rule the roost." The children,
with the exception of the baby, are sturdy, healthy-looking youngsters.
The baby is pale and somewhat lifeless.

The Calmer family occupies a 5-room brick house, badly in need of
repair, which rents for $12 a month. The house is located half-way up a
hill in a rather poor residential neighborhood of rented houses. While
Frank had steady work about a year ago, he repapered the living room and
had started to paint the dining room and kitchen. When he was put on
short hours at the mill, he was unable to buy paint to complete the job.
He wonders now if he should have spent any money for this repair, but the
walls were so dingy and cheerless he could hardly bear to look at them. The
furnishings of the home are simple but adequate. Since Frank's reemployment a few replacements have been made; "after 15 years things just wear
out."

Frank Calmer, born on a farm near Dubuque, was one of 8 children.
At the age of 16 he got a job in town at the Iowa Foundry, where he worked
for 2 years at general labor. At the time he left this job, in 1920, he
was earning $23 a week. Frank considers it somewhat ironical that he earned
more on this "kid job" than he has earned during the past several years, :"but
of course that was during war times."

As he preferred clerical work, he quit the foundry job to work
for a coal company in the office and at collecting. Though his entrance
rate on this job was only $18 a week, he was receiving $24 when he left 8
years later. This pay he had considered too low; so he found employment
at the Mississippi Milling Company, where the pay was 60¢ an hour for a 54
hour week. On this job Frank worked on a door clamp. In May 1929 business
began to fall off, and in consequence the hours of work were reduced to 40
and the rate of pay cut 10 percent. By 1931 an additional pay cut of 10
percent and a further reduction in hours had brought Frank's earnings down
to $8 a week; so he quit to take a job as an attendant in a service station
at $60 a month. After 2 months this rate was reduced to $40, and finally
to $30. As Frank felt that he could not support his family on this wage,
he quit to look for a better job. Almost immediately he found work with
another oil station at $60, but as soon as the heavy summer business was
over, Frank was laid off. This was in the fall of 1933, "the worst part of
the depression in Dubuque."

Though Frank diligently searched for work he could find nothing,
and finally applied for relief in January 1934. In the meantime, the family
had been living on credit, which he had no difficulty in getting as he had
always paid his bills promptly. Now Frank thinks his credit was "too good,"

and he wishes the grocer had not carried him so long, as he sees little
chance of paying this bill of more than $200 from his present earnings.
While he was on full time he had paid $50, at the rate of $2 a month, but
since last July, when hours were reduced, he has paid nothing on back bills.

Frank did not like the idea of relief and found it very embarrassing at first, but he soon got used to it. "When you have hungry children
to feed, it is easy to cast your pride aside." He has no "kick to make"
against the relief office. He feels that he was fairly treated at all times.
It is his opinion that big families received more consideration than small
families. At any rate, the men he has heard complain most are men with
small families. On a few occasions, Frank had to "put up a fight" for certain things, but an investigation was always made and the requests granted.
"After all, those investigators had to be convinced of a family's needs."

The Calmers received direct relief for about 1 month before Frank
was assigned to the CWA airport project in February 1934. He had worked on
this project only 2 months when CWA was discontinued. For 2 months during
the summer of 1934, he was employed on the lock and dam project. From
October 1934, until his return to the Mississippi Milling Company on January
7, 1935, he worked at cutting meat for the canning project and was paid on
a budget deficiency basis. Frank liked CWA and PWA work best because he
received more money; he preferred "cash work relief" on a budget deficiency
basis to direct relief. He found that by shopping around at different
stores and by taking advantage of "specials," he could buy food much more
economically.

Frank enjoyed project work, and he feels that men work just as
hard on these jobs as on jobs in private industry—except for a very small

percentage "who would loaf anywhere." For that matter, Frank believes that a few people "actually get a kick out of being on relief," but they are the ones "who never did much work anyway." Frank "can't see" this attitude. He has never minded hard work and doesn't like the idea of being dependent on anybody.

He was one of the first men taken on in 1935 at the Mississippi Milling Company when business began to pick up. He had kept in touch with the superintendent, who told him when to apply. He had always worked on a piecework basis at the mill, and since his return he has averaged from 40¢ to 50¢ an hour. The mill was quite busy until last July, when "things began to go dead," and Frank's hours were cut to 35 a week. He finds his work as benchman interesting, "but factory work is factory work; it don't get you anywhere." A 75-year-old employee works with him. At the end of the day this old man staggers out of the factory, but he can't afford to quit since he has nothing saved from his lifetime in the factory. When Frank looks at these old men who still hang on, he thinks that the old-age pension system under the Social Security legislation is a fine thing. In Frank's opinion the modern factory is not very different from old-time slavery "except that there is no blacksnake." He feels that most of the foremen and even the superintendent in the mills are "just figureheads" and no different from the workers; in fact, they sympathize with the workers. "It's the big fellows in the office who are hard-boiled." "The workers spend their lives making a lot of money for these big shots and get nothing out of it for themselves--not even a decent living."

Frank had belonged to the millworkers' union until after the 1935 strike, when he became "disgusted" and allowed his membership to lapse.

He is convinced that the union will not accomplish anything for mill-workers
in Dubuque. He felt that it was not right to continue to take the money
from his family to pay dues to an "utterly ineffective organization."
He believes in unionization and knows that it has been effective elsewhere,
but Dubuque woodworking mills he considers hopeless. The CIO tactics, he
considers "too radical; after all, you can't blow up a man's building
because he won't give you something." Green, on the other hand, "has been
a little too easy-going."

Frank blames machinery for widespread unemployment, and he sees no
reason why wages should not be raised and hours of work reduced. Inasmuch
as production has been speeded up by these machines, and employers' profits
greatly increased, the employers should be willing to shorten hours and
increase the rate of pay, "but they won't until they are forced by law."

Frank is favorable to all recent social legislation, but feels
that taxation is a little too heavy. The Social Security Act is, in his
opinion, "the finest law ever enacted." He is afraid, however, that the
Social Security program may not last. If something happens to this program
after workers have contributed from their meager earnings "it will be a great
shame." He also considers the Works Program very much worthwhile. Relief
has, in his opinion, been satisfactory and the Federal Government should
continue to help. The Social Security program will take some of the burden
and gradually reduce the amounts needed for direct relief.

Since Frank returned to work in 1935, he has earned a little less
than $900 a year; "you can imagine how far $75 a month goes with a family of
eight." With $1,200 a year, Frank believes he could manage satisfactorily
and lay by a little for emergencies. His present earnings barely meet current expenses. A layoff means that the family must go on relief immediately.

Frank believes that most of the workers had to have assitance from the relief office during the December layoff. For that matter, however, many mill-workers who have large families have had to have supplementary aid, even while employed.

If Frank had his way he would have a service station of his own. He found service station work very interesting, and "I'd like being my own boss." He liked clerical work, too, but not so well as his filling station experience. "Anything, though, would be better than working in a factory the rest of my life on a hand-to-mouth wage."

Employment Chronology for Mr. Calmer

1918 - 1920	Laborer, Iowa Foundry
1920 - 1928	Office clerk and collection agent, coal company
1928 - 1931	Machine operator, Mississippi Milling Company
1932 - 8 months	Attendant, service station
November 1933 - January 1935	Unemployed except for emergency work
January 1935 - present	Machine operator and benchman, Mississippi Milling Company

DICHTER

Mr. Dichter	53
Mrs. Dichter	43
Jack	22
Emerich	20
Henry	11

Interviewing completed
February 4, 1938

Since 1918 Bill Dichter, 53 years old, has worked with some
regularity as a freight locomotive fireman, first as an "extra," later
on a regular run. He has been accustomed to fill in with jobs in the
local factories or with construction work when work is slack on the
road. For a few months during the winter of 1933 and again in 1934, so
few jobs were to be had in any line of work that the Dichter family found
it necessary to depend on relief grants.

For about 19 years, from the time he was 14 years old until he
began work as a fireman, Bill had gone from job to job and from place to
place with great frequency and with little foresight. He has had more
jobs than he can remember. Dates of employment, hours, and wages are
indifferent matters to Bill; he recounts the high spots of his work history
as a series of adventures, mildly interesting, but not at all unusual.

Bill is a bulky, vigorous-looking man. His ruddy cheeks are
deeply wrinkled. Moreoften than not he has his teeth clamped together on
his pipe or on a cigar so that he talks through his teeth in a gruff voice
which remains as expressionless as his face. Bill repeats, word for word,
lengthy conversations, accounts of which are liberally sprinkled with
"I says" and "he says." He uses slang expressions with abandon, his
special favorites being "by golly" and "doggone."

Mrs. Dichter has evidently taken more responsibility than Bill
for the management of the home and the budgeting. Her interest centers in
the home and family. She "keeps to herself" most of the time, and has
very few friends in Dubuque, where the family has lived for the past 20
years.

The Dichters have three sons, all still at home: Jack, 22;
Emerich, 20: and Henry, 11, a fifth-grade pupil.

Jack has never had "what you could call a steady job." After
graduation from high school 3 years ago, he tried his hand at selling
vacuum cleaners on a commission basis for a while, but found the job a
thankless one. He also set out on one occasion with a crew of fellows
selling contracts for school printing on a commission basis. But on the
second day out when he learned that boys who did not do satisfactory work
were likely to be left "stranded" by the boss, Jack hitchhiked the 90-odd
miles back to Dubuque. He has had several odd jobs in East Dubuque. Last
summer he worked for a few months for the Dubuque Wood-working Company in
three different departments. The various transfers were arranged at his
request--he found none of the jobs very satisfactory.

Jack was laid off when there was a general reduction in force;
this he attributes to "labor trouble." The men had demanded so much in
the way of pay increases and reduction of hours that the wood-working
company "had no choice" but to transfer outstanding orders to other factories
so as to "weaken the union."

Jack's present unemployment is apparently of little concern to
him or to his parents, though his father grumbles that the State, in levy-
ing income taxes, does not take enough account of the fact that he must

support a "24-year-old son."   But Mrs. Dichter feels that the family
"has taken care of Jack this long, and can take care of him a little
longer."   When she comments on the younger boy's regular work, she is
quick to add that Jack is "more interested in drawing."   She is rather
proud of his work; so is Jack. He delights in showing his oils and water-
colors, his crayon drawings, and pen and ink sketches. In addition to the
regular high school art courses, Jack has taken as many night courses as
have been offered in art. His pen and ink sketch, "Desolation," took
first prize in a high school exhibit at the public library.

Since his graduation from high school in 1936, Emerich has
worked regularly in the tool room of the Iowa Foundry.

Bill Dichter's father came to America from Germany to avoid being
drafted for service in the Franco-Prussian War. He settled near Milwaukee,
where he married, farmed, and reared his family. Bill's mother died when
he was 9 years old. When Bill was 14 his father remarried, and Bill left
the family farm. From this time until he was 21, Bill lived and worked
on several different farms, all near Milwaukee. He next did construction
work in Milwaukee for a while; then he partially completed a machine shop
apprenticeship, which was interrupted by a strike.

Instead of waiting for the strike to be settled, Bill got a job
on bridge construction work which took him to South Dakota. When the
job was completed at the end of several months, the workmen were offered
transportation to any point desired. Bill chose to go to Kansas City,
where he applied for work through a private employment office and paid
his fee of $1.50. He was sent to a sugar-beet factory in a small Colorado
town. "A company-run boarding house", he says, "staked me to my grub

until my first payday." Here he worked "slacking line" on an 11-hour
night shift until an explosion of the line resulted in his being rather
badly scalded. He knew he wouldn't be able to work for some 2 weeks, and
since he was "about ready to quit that job anyhow" he drew his $85 out of
the bank and went to Denver.

On his first day in Denver he was just walking down the street
when he met a fellow who offered him a job on an "extra gang" doing railroad maintenance work in Kansas. Bill stayed with this work for the 3
or 4 weeks required to complete the job; then he returned to Denver.
Immediately, he met a fellow who asked if he wanted a job. Bill answered,
"Not particularly. I just got done working." Still, he listened to the
details. The fellow needed a hand on his fruit ranch; "wanted to pay
$30 a month, board, room, and washing." Bill was still considering this
job when he met a fellow he knew, and "forgetting all about that other
fellow, by golly we went and joined the Navy."

For 4 months Bill was stationed on "what the sailors called
Goat Island" in San Francisco Bay. He then made "one trip South"— to
Mexico, Central America, and the still uncompleted Panama Canal—on the
cruiser Boston, "the one that took part with Dewey in the battle of Manila."
Next, Bill was stationed some miles from Seattle. He then made a trip on
the Nebraska—"she was the one that made the trip around the Horn to fight
in the battle of San Diego." Still later, Bill was assigned to the Albany,
and to the flagship of "the torpedo boat destroyers." He was "mustered out
January 8, 1911," and returned to Milwaukee. Bill had planned to reenlist
in the Navy within a 4-month interval so that he might claim a bonus of
$100, which "looked appealing to me, but then I met my wife through my step-
sister. We got to going together, and by golly I forgot about reenlisting."

Bill now got a job as a packer for a wholesale grocery firm, where he earned $11 a week for 2 years. "That was good work, nice clean work, but nothing to it, had no future to it. I knew fellows, there for 20-25 years, got the same as I did---oh, $2-$3 a week more, maybe, but that didn't amount to nothing. But when Christmas time came around, that guy was pretty doggone good. He gave all the fellows 5-dollar gold pieces and cigars and groceries, except the fellows who had been there 10 years. They got 10-dollar gold pieces, and the brand of cigars was a little better, too, for that matter. *** Everybody liked to work for that outfit; those fellows sure were stickers."

But Bill was less of a "sticker." He had been married while he worked for the grocery firm, which he now left to go to a Milwaukee power company. Here he was "straw boss" of a gang of five men assembling trucks for streetcars. Bill worked 10 hours a day was paid a bonus in addition to the hourly rate, but "danged if I know what the hourly rate was." "Well, finally I got tired of that." A speed-up system had been inaugurated, and "one gang got to beating out another. *** They got to assembling them doggone cars in 15-16 hours, where it used to take 20 hours." The boss complained when any gang was a little slow, even though delays had obviously been occasioned by waits for materials or mistakes made by other gangs. The bonus was frequently not forthcoming. "I got so doggone disgusted, I says to that fellow, I says, 'I'm quitting,' I says; 'I'm going over and get my time card,' I says." He had been with the power company for "a year or so."

Bill now drove a team for a coal concern, did odd jobs of moving and some driving for an express company. But in 1914 "things got

tough" in Milwaukee.   The family had difficulty in managing even though
Mrs. Dichter had taken a job doing housework at $3 a week to supplement
Bill's irregular earnings.   "The reports were out that 35,000 people
were on the streets" in Milwaukee.   Hoping to get a job elsewhere, Bill
went to the State employment office, where he was introduced to a farmer
who needed a hand.   "They had a room there where you could talk things
over"; so Bill and the farmer talked things over, and Bill got the job.
He was given a house rent-free, fuel, a garden plot, and 2 quarts of milk
a day in addition to the pay of $35 a month.   The Dichters left this
farm only when it changed hands in March 1917.   From March until June 1917,
the family lived on another farm; Bill left when the farmer owed him $85
which he had no hope of getting.

          According to Mrs. Dichter, it was she who urged that Bill "get
a good steady job with some future to it."   Consequently, in 1917 Mr. and
Mrs. Dichter with their one child, "Sonny," came to Dubuque, where Bill
planned to look for work on the railroad.   On their arrival here, Bill
left Mrs. Dichter and "Sonny" in the railroad station while he went out
to see the town and to find living quarters.   He soon returned with the
announcement that he was to start work the next morning as laborer on a
construction job.   Mrs. Dichter was amused and a little dismayed to learn
that Bill had got a job before the family knew where they would spend the
night.   But they quickly arranged to move into furnished rooms.

          After completion of the construction job, Bill worked briefly
in the Dubuque railroad shops, and for the Midwestern Foundry Company.
During a strike at the Midwestern Foundry, he got a job at the Julien

Foundry. He was called out from time to time, while working at the foundry,
to make extra runs as freight locomotive fireman.   Finally, he was called
away from the plant so frequently that it was necessary for him to give up
the foundry job.

Bill first worked as railroad fireman in 1918.   While he was
on the "extra list" as a fireman, he was also irregularly employed in the
car department and on maintenance work.   By transferring frequently from
one job to another he was able to earn reasonably adequate wages.   One
winter he worked in the railroad coal sheds at night and made occasional
runs during the day.   At other times when work was slack on the road he
drove coal trucks in winter and ice trucks in summer.   During the winter
of 1919 "or somewheres around in there anyhow," he occasionally cleaned
cars.   "Around 1920" he "probably thinks it is" Bill carried bricks for
6 weeks or so for a firm of contractors.

Bill has little idea what his earnings on the railroad totaled
for any given year or averaged over a period of years.   "The extra list
always was a feast or a famine.   They held you down to a maxium," and
there was a "minium," too, though the men's earnings did not always reach
this theoretical minimum.   Some years, Bill earned as much as $1,200 or
$1,500, and "one year in there somewheres I made out a federal income tax."
Several years ago he was put on a regular run from Dubuque to Rockford,
Ill.   The run is called out at different times on different days and
canceled when there is little freight.   Bill's pay is determined on the
basis of mileage, and the mileage rate depends on the type of engine used.
A run of 100 miles is considered a day's work, and 32 days constitute a
full month's work.   On rare occasions, Bill has completed a day's work (a
run of 100 miles) in 1 1/2 hours.   If Bill put in the full time of 32 days,
with the "highest paid engine," he would earn about $200 a month.

During 1932, 1933, and 1934, he made very few runs. He was, however, called out at least once every 6 months; otherwise, it would have been necessary to have a physical reexamination. During the past 2 or 3 years, his work has been fairly regular. In 1936 his earnings exceeded $2,500; so he "went through the formality" of filing a Federal income tax return "to keep on the good side of Uncle Sam," though it was not necessary for him to pay a tax.

Since Bill's work was still fairly steady in 1931, he did not anticipate more than purely temporary "hard times." And so it was that the family "made a wrong move" by going from a four-room house renting for $16 month to a six-room house renting for $25. Since the family was not able to meet the rent in 1932, they moved to a house renting for $20. Finding that this rental, too, was beyond his resources, Bill arranged in 1933 for another move, this time to a house where he could make his own terms with the landlord.

The family now paid $14 a month for a four-room frame house which had once rented for $25. Even so, the Dichters got behind in the rent as Bill's 2-week pay checks sometimes amounted to no more than $5. Nor could the grocer and butcher and doctor bills all be met, even though the family obtained $600 by cashing in some insurance policies and borrowing on others. Bill gave up his insurance with the railroad brotherhood, which had increased his union dues by $2.60 a month. The policy provided for a $1,000 death benefit and a monthly payment of $50 in case of disability. Bill regrets losing this policy, especially as he is now too old to secure a new policy with such liberal terms.

In the hope of getting his coal without putting up any cash, and of receiving also "a little differential in cash," Bill applied to

a coal company for the work of unloading coal cars.   After some delay he
and Jack were finally permitted to unload two cars.   For this job they were
given $13 and 1 ton of coal.   During the winter of 1932-33, Bill and Jack
unloaded 13 cars of coal.   "This goes to show," Bill thinks, "that odd jobs
can be picked up, even in bad times."

However, such odd jobs were not enough.   In February 1933 the
Dichters applied for relief, which was granted without any special difficulty
or delay.   The relief workers were invariably "awful nice" to the family,
and raised no questions about the family's need for relief nor about their
expenditures, with the exception of the telephone bills.   When Bill explained that he must have the telephone to receive calls for work and that
the pay for only one run would cover telephone bills for a year, the matter
was quickly "dropped."   The family's chief difficulty had been with the
neighbors, who took pains to report each of Bill's runs to the relief office.
Such complaints did not affect the granting of relief, as Bill had always
reported his earnings.   Though on relief themselves, the neighbors felt that
"a railroader" should not require relief.

While on relief the family received grocery orders, surplus commodities, and four "rent slips" for $7.50 each.   Mrs. Dichter states that
the family "got along all right" on the relief grants—"and we had our cake,
too, but nothing was ever left over from one week's order to the next."
Mrs. Dichter baked inexpensive cakes as well as bread from the flour that
was provided, and "knew how to use the salt pork."   She says that she "never
went hungry during the thirties, but there were times when she didn't have
enough to eat during the depression 1914-15.

Bill was assigned to work relief projects for only short periods;
he worked for 1 week at the stone quarry, and for a few days on road repair.
He was paid only in grocery orders.

In July 1933 Bill "got in 11 days of work" for the railroad; so
he requested that relief be canceled. He explained that he had been
"humilated" by the necessity of applying for relief in the first place and
had never liked "that way of living." He adds, "By golly, it was a relief
to get away from having to go down there (to the relief office) all the
time." When Bill asked to be taken off the relief rolls, the director
of relief "says to me, she says, 'I am amazed. Here,' she says, 'all these
other people are trying,' she says, 'to get on relief,' she says, 'and you
are asking to be taken off,' she says."

Bill managed fairly well during the summer of 1933, when he
made runs with some frequency, had a few "pickup" jobs. He put in a
garden on land secured rent-free from a Mr. Higgen on condition that Bill
should work Mr. Higgen's garden as well as his own. Mr. Higgen also furnished some of the seeds and plants. The gardening was fairly successful,
even though Bill had "too much help in the harvest" and not enough with the
planting, hoeing, and weeding.

By January 1934 Bill's work had become so slack that it was
necessary to reapply for relief. Bill understood that the investigators
had to "check up" on his work and his pay, but after some delay, he
"got desperate" and made another trip to the relief office. The day of
Bill's second visit to the office, a worker called at the home and left
a grocery order. From then on, the family kept getting "all kinds of
slips."

Since the Dichters have been managing altogether on their own
resources, they have paid up bills amounting to some $300. At one time
the family had owed $125 in back rent to one landlord and $108 to another.

They now owe only $30 on one rent bill; "when this $30 is paid," Mrs. Dichter says, "I can hold up my head." In November 1937 the Dichters moved to a six-room half of a double house, more conveniently located and in better repair than their last home and renting for $6 a month more.

Bill Dichter does not bother with much theorizing or philosophizing about problems of a general nature. He says, "all I know is the stuff I see in the papers," and he doesn't pay too much attention to that. He dislikes "radicals" and "Bolsheviks" and the CIO and Hitlerism. He thinks that Hitler has made "a big mistake" in his treatment of Jews and Catholics. "Even if the Jews do control capital," he says, "the greatest professors in the United States and Germany are Jews, and there is no greater professor than Einstein." Since everybody accepts the religion "his mother teaches him," Bill sees no great difference between Jews and Gentiles, Catholics and Protestants.

Bill now considers his voting for Roosevelt in 1936 "the biggest mistake he ever made." He got the impression from the "company magazine" that corporation surplus taxation is responsible for the current business recession; the railroad has recently used to meet the "surplus tax" money which would otherwise have been paid into a "benefit fund" for employees.

Bill approves of his brotherhood, which has secured wage increases without "allowing any sit-down strikes," of the Railroad Retirement pension system, and of unemployment insurance for "railroaders." Beyond that, he does not go in speculating about general problems. For that matter, he doesn't spend much time thinking about his own past or present or future, either. He takes things as they come.

Employment Chronology for Mr. Dichter

1898 – 1905 –	Farm hand.
1905 – 1907 –	Construction worker, machine shop apprentice and section hand.
1907 – January 1911 –	U. S. Navy.
January 1911 – 1914	Packer, wholesale grocery firm "Straw boss" of assembly gang, power company; truck driver.
1914 – June 1917	Farm hand.
June 1917 – 1918	Laborer, construction companies helper, Midwestern Foundry Company and Julien Foundry.
1918 – present	Railroad locomotive fireman.
Winters 1932, 1933, and 1934	Unemployed most of the time.

Mr. Gaether	47
Mrs. Gaether	46
John	20
Mary	18
Lorna	14
Clara	9
Mrs. Bremer	68

Interviewing completed
February 22, 1938

Robert Gaether has been a carpenter all of his working life, except for 10 years of farming. For 8 years prior to the depression he had been employed by one contractor for whom he now works, having been reemployed in the spring of 1936. Though Mr. Gaether had worked no more than 1 or 2 months a year between 1931 and 1935, relief was not received until August 1935.

Mr. Gaether is 47 years old. His personality is pleasing and forceful. Though he speaks with a slight German accent, he expresses himself with clarity and intelligence. He has a youthful face and smiles easily.

Mrs. Gaether, somewhat deaf, takes little part in the conversation though she listens intently and occasionally adds a pertinent comment. She, too, is pleasant—attractive in appearance and refined in speech and manner.

The Gaethers, with their four children and Mrs. Gaether's 68-year-old mother, live in their own home in one of the sparsely settled neighborhoods in the north end. Mr. Gaether likes the location, for it is "just like living in the country," though they have all the advantages of town. The home, a seven-room red brick bungalow, is attractive and in excellent repair; the furnishings are adequate and in good taste. The radio plays an important part in the recreational life of the family. They all gather in the living room for favorite programs. Sometimes they find it difficult to make a choice, for the younger members of the family prefer swing music, while Mr. Gaether likes to listen to symphony concerts, news reports, and speeches. John, 20

years old, has been unemployed during the past 7 months. After dropping out
of school in 1935, his junior year in high school, because of the family's
needs, he sold vacuum cleaners on a commission basis for several months. His
earnings averaged about $9 a month. He then worked for a butcher for nearly
2 years at from $3.50 to $4 a week, but he was laid off when the butcher
decided that he could get along without a helper. Lorna, 14, who has never
been strong, attends school only irregularly; Mary, 18, is a senior in high
school, and Clara, 9, is in the fourth grade. Family ties are strong and the
Gaethers seem to have a happy home life.

Mr. Gaether, born on a farm near Dubuque, completed the eighth
grade and then helped his father with the farm work until, at the age of 18,
he decided to learn carpentry. He worked at this trade for 5 years. Then,
after his marriage in 1914 he rented a farm near Dubuque. For a few years
farming was profitable; but as rents increased and farm prices decreased, it
became more difficult to make a living. After 10 years Mr. Gaether moved his
family to town and returned to carpentry, which he had continued to follow to
some extent while he was on the farm. Immediately after coming to Dubuque,
he was hired by a contractor for whom he has worked ever since, except for a
period during the depression when he was employed on emergency work projects.
For 6 years Mr. Gaether was employed as a foreman by this contractor. Some
years he worked practically the entire year, but usually he lost about 3
months during the winter as "200 days constitute a good year's work in the
carpentry trade." His annual earnings ranged from $1,200 to $1,800, but they
seldom went above $1,500. Because of his profits from the farm and from
carpentry work during the good years, he was able to save $1,000; this he
invested as a down payment on the home in 1926. The home was purchased
through a building and loan company; the monthly payments were $10, of which
$4.50 was interest.

Mr. Gaether had kept busy during 1929, but building began to fall
off early in 1931; in 1932 and 1933 he averaged no more than 1 or 2 months
work during the year. He had $350 in savings which were used to supplement
earnings, and he borrowed on his insurance policies to pay the premiums
amounting to $54 a year. These policies are still in force. Prices were
low; meat could be purchased for as little as 6¢ a pound. The Gaethers had a
fine garden and always canned enough produce to see them through the year.
So the family was able to manage on Mr. Gaether's small income. However,
Mrs. Gaether adds, "we just about starved ourselves." Mr. Gaether agrees that
even though meat was only 6¢ a pound, they had it no oftener than once a week.
The loan company was considerate, permitting him to pay only the interest of
$4.50 a month. He was determined not to lose their home. "So no matter how
short we were we managed to keep up the monthly payments." After 7 months
without any income he applied for relief in March 1933, only to be rejected.
He had hated to ask for help but he worried because the children were not
getting enough to eat. He accepted the rejection without question. For the
next 6 or 8 weeks, and until he was able to pick up some odd jobs, the family
lived on practically nothing. With the odd jobs he picked up during the
summer of 1933, he managed until he was employed irregularly, during 1934-35,
on some of the building jobs provided by Federal Housing loans. For this work
he was paid 80¢ an hour.

In August 1935, after 2 months without any income, Mr. Gaether again
applied for relief. By this time he knew of a number of families on relief
which had not been nearly so hard up as his family; so he went to the relief
office prepared to "argue it out." This time Mr. Gaether "had sense enough"
to take "someone" with him to verify his needs. Relief was granted immediately.
After 3 months on direct relief, Mr. Gaether was assigned to the lock and dam

project, where he was paid $1.20 an hour and worked 30 hours a week. He was
very happy on this job, since it was the only steady work he had had in almos
4 years. The family had found it difficult to manage on direct relief and ha
not liked it; the weekly pay check of $36 from the project "seemed like a lot
of money."

After 6 months on this project Mr. Gaether left, in May, to work du
ing the summer months for his "old boss." He returned to the dam project on
November 1. During the summer he had been paid the regular union scale of
$1 an hour for a 40-hour week.

On his return to the dam Mr. Gaether was employed as a foreman at
$45 a week, with considerable responsibility. The Government engineers were
"unusually strict about specifications"; some of the men were "pretty poor
carpenters," making it necessary for Mr. Gaether to exercise close supervisio
The depression, in his opinion, "created a lot of carpenters and painters
because the rate of pay for this work was so much higher than for common
labor." Some men who registered as carpenters with the employment office
"had never even used a hammer." Mr. Gaether feels that the poor workmanship
of these "would-be carpenters" has reflected unfavorably on the trade. The
contractor for the lock and dam project wanted to transfer Mr. Gaether to
another job in Illinois in May 1937, as general foreman at a higher rate than
the $45 he was receiving in Dubuque. The day after he was asked to go to
Illinois, his "old boss" called him; Mr. Gaether never once considered
staying on the project job, even though it paid more than he would receive in
private industry. Since November 1937 he has worked steadily for his old
employer, except for a 2 weeks' layoff in January. He feels that only a few
men loaf on the project jobs with the excuse that it is "just relief after
all." In his opinion a good workman works just as hard on projects as he
works on any job in private industry; "the man who loafs on projects will loa
on any job."

Mr. Gaether has been a member of the carpenters' union for some 14 years. He is conservative in his views, and he is thoroughly "fed up" with the fight between the CIO and the A.F. of L. Being a little disgusted with both leaders, he believes that both Lewis and Green are at fault--there are always "two sides to every fight." Most agitation and trouble starts with a "few incompetents" in a labor group, in Mr. Gaether's opinion; locals are often swayed by "mass psychology" to take steps that are harmful to labor unions as a whole. Until the small business men and working men in Dubuque "stand together, working conditions will not improve." A few manufacturers "control" the Chamber of Commerce and the banks; the small business man is afraid to "buck them," and in consequence these manufacturers continue "to hold the balance of power." Cedar Rapids was in much the same predicament as Dubuque when Cedar Rapids business men "took a stand with the working men against the ruling manufacturers" and organized the Junior Chamber of Commerce. "As a result, new industries moved into Cedar Rapids and the town has been on the up-grade ever since."

Mr. Gaether feels that many factors have contributed to widespread unemployment, and that "one man's guess is as good as another's." There is no doubt in his mind that all of the recent social legislation has helped to bring about better economic conditions. "If the old-age pension and unemployment insurance do not bring security to the working man, nothing will." Mr. Gaether fears only that these laws may be changed in some way by Congress. He adds, "The President has done all he can; one man can't do everything." Mr. Gaether approves of the recent farm legislation though he knows that many working men are opposed to it. He knows from experience "what a hard road" the farmer has traveled. While Mr. Gaether enjoyed farming, he likes the carpentry trade better. He thinks it is a great mistake for farmers to move to town expecting to find work unless they have a trade.

While there is little building in Dubuque now, Mr. Gaether hopes
that conditions will improve within the next month or so. Most of the employed carpenters are working on repair jobs. There is enough needed repair
work in Dubuque to keep all of the carpenters busy indefinitely, if people
only had the money to spend. Though Mr. Gaether knows that he will have work
so long as there is carpentry work to be had in Dubuque, he dreads another
period of unemployment. The family no longer has savings, as all money above
that required for living expenses has been used to pay the back payments to th
building and loan company as well as the back taxes. No household furnishings
or clothing had been bought during the 4 years he was out of work. Since his
reemployment he has purchased clothing only for the children attending school.
Mr. Gaether feels sure that should he lose his job now, the family would have
to ask for assistance within a month. If he can only work steadily, however,
he expects to start a savings account again within a short time.

Employment Chronology for Mr. Gaether

1908 - 1913	Carpenter.
1914 - 1924	Farmer.
1924 - 1931	Foreman carpenter, Knight Contracting Company.
1931 - December 1935	Unemployed except for odd jobs and emergency work.
May 1936 - October 1936	Carpenter, Knight Contracting Company.
November 1936 - May 1937	Foreman, PWA project.
May 1937 - present	Carpenter, Knight Contracting Company.

FOGEL

Mr. Fogel	47
Mrs. Fogel	43
Ira	21
May	19
Agnes	18
Leonard	16
Bobby	10
Don	7
Betty	2

Interviewing completed
December 20, 1937

George Fogel, 47 years old, is a rugged, muscular man with gray hair
and large clear blue eyes. He has a pleasing personality and talks intelligently and with self-confidence about his work and the family's depression
experiences.

Except for his grease-stained hands he looks like a self-assured
business man instead of a mechanic. Actually, he has worked as an auto
mechanic for 24 years, operating his own garage for 14 years; at present he
ranks as one of the best auto mechanics in Dubuque. Mr. Fogel is proud of
his family and home. Though his income has been uncertain during recent years
and it has been necessary for the family to adjust itself to a lowered plane
of living, he has insisted upon maintaining a cheerful, comfortable home life.
His chief concern is that the older children are not finding suitable employment opportunities.

Mrs. Fogel, 43 years old, looks much older. She is a buxom person
with a full bosom and large hips. She has short gray hair and dark brown eyes.
Her family is her universe; she speaks of their 7 children, all at home, with
pride and affection. She is an intelligent mother and seems to have a re-
markable understanding of the personality and problems of each child, speaking
with equal affection of the first-born, 21 years old, and the last-born 2-years
old. She has continued to study with the older children as they have gone

through high school and now proudly holds her own with them in any kind of discussion even though she completed only the eighth grade in country school.

Since graduation from high school the 21-year-old Ira has worked only irregularly, and at present averages 1 day a week. He is interested in psychology and would like to work with boys. May, 19, and Agnes, 18, were graduated from high school last year, both in the commercial course. May is now unemployed; Agnes, valedictorian of her class and voted by the student body the "ideal girl," works as a domestic earning $4 a week. Primarily because he prefers tinkering with tools to studying, Leonard, 16, has not progressed beyond the eighth grade. His father considers him a "born craftsman" and regrets that the family cannot afford to send him to a trade school. Bobby, 10 years old, is in the fourth grade, and 7-year-old Don, is a second grader. Betty, 2 years old, is the family's darling. She probably suffers from too much attention, as she is a nervous,high-strung little thing. According to Mrs. Fogel, "a more welcome baby was never born."

Mr. Fogel farmed with his father, near Dubuque, until he was 23 years old. After his father had bought one of the earliest Ford car models, the task of keeping the car in repair fell to George, who considers himself a born mechanic. As neighboring farmers acquired automobiles, George was called on whenever auto repair was needed; during his last few years on the farm a goodly share of his time was spent as an auto mechanic.

When Mr. Fogel was married in 1913, he started a garage of his own in Valley, Iowa, which he continued to operate and expand during the next 14 years. After 4 or 5 years he added an automobile agency to the garage and, from time to time, new equipment was purchased. Valley was a prosperous little farm town of 1,700 people. Just preceding the World War, farm land was very high priced, and as it was expected to go even higher, many Valley farmers invested all of their wealth in land, on which heavy mortgages were

carried by the local banks. During this period of prosperity, a piano
factory and two lumber mills were built in Valley. As local business men were
expected to show their civic spirit by investing in the new companies' bonds,
Mr. Fogel invested $600 in the piano factory bonds. Shortly after the war
the price of land dropped, thus ending the era of prosperity and expansion in
Valley.

In 1924 two of the town's three banks failed, followed almost
immediately by the piano and lumber companies. The third bank, which held
a $3,200 mortgage on Mr. Fogel's home and a $1,200 mortgage on the garage
also failed; in consequence he lost both his home and business. Mr. Fogel
had usually averaged $3,600 a year from his business and had already paid
$5,000 on his home. Because of the increase in bank failures, he had decided
that insurance was a safer investment than a bank deposit. His savings were
therefore invested in 20-year endowment policies with an insurance company
which later changed hands several times.

In 1927 the family carried insurance amounting to $14,000. As
premiums on all but one policy were paid up for 3 or 4 years, Mr. Fogel cashed
the one policy on which the premium was due for $350 and did nothing about the
others, thinking that there would be plenty of time to make adjustments later.
During the turmoil of the next 4 or 5 years the Fogels neglected to check up
on the regulations governing these policies, and after a 6-months lapse the
insurance company, without consulting Mr. Fogel, converted the four policies
to one $3,000 extended policy maturing in 1945. Mr. Fogel admits that he was
ignorant about insurance at that time. He adds, "I never dreamed that I
would not be able to demand cash and get it when I wanted it." He feels that
the insurance company took advantage of his ignorance and gave him a "rotten
deal," but there was nothing to be done as the original company no longer
existed.

After the bank failed in 1927 Mr. Fogel came to Dubuque immediately
and was employed by the Iowa Garage as a mechanic for 3 years at $45 a week.
The car agency which he had operated in Valley was actually a branch of the
Iowa Garage. The bank examiner allowed him to place on sale in Dubuque the
cars that were on hand in Valley at the time of the bank crash. Mr. Fogel
considers that the bank gave him a square deal, and he has no hard feelings
toward its owners.

The Iowa Garage lost heavily in the stock market crash of 1929-
1930, so early in 1931 Mr. Fogel's salary was discontinued and he was paid
only for the actual time he worked on cars. During bad weather business was
dull and Mr. Fogel's earnings were too uncertain; so he took a job at a
garage in a Wisconsin town near Dubuque, telling the Iowa Garage owners that
he would return only when they could pay him a regular weekly salary. He
worked for 2 years in Wisconsin and received $35 a week. During the bank
moratorium in 1933 the Wisconsin garage "went under" as the garage owners
were also the owners of the bank and all of their money was tied up indefinitely.

Mr. Fogel returned to Dubuque and soon found work as an auto
mechanic with the Capital Garage at $90 a month. With the coming of NRA and
the reduction in hours of work, the company placed him on an hourly rate; when
he began picking up repair jobs on his own in order to make up the difference
in his pay check, the company objected and let him go. Within a week he got a
job at the rock quarry operating the air compressor at $30 a week. This job
lasted 6 months; the quarry then closed the latter part of November 1934.

Mr. Fogel was unemployed until May 1, 1935, when he started to work
in the repair shop of an oil station. During his best weeks at the oil station
he averaged $22, but he usually made no more than $18. After 2 months on this

job he was asked to return to the Iowa Garage at $30 a week. He has continued
with this company to the present time, working 55 hours a week. The garage
employees are talking about organizing a union, but Mr. Fogel feels that such
organization will get them nowhere. If the hourly rate is increased, the
company will see to it that the men earn no more by the week than they now
receive.

During the first 2 months that Mr. Fogel was unemployed, he went to
all the people he knew "drumming up" repair jobs. Many of these people were
not able to pay cash, but he accepted service and commodities in exchange for
his work. A dentist, for example, in exchange for a general overhauling job
on his car, "fixed up" the Fogel family's teeth. Fuel and food were also
received in payment for car repair jobs. After 2 months, however, he had
exhausted the possibilities for this type of exchange and found fewer and
fewer odd jobs of repair. The last repair job of this type had been on a
truck in exchange for a load of wood. The truck was so large it was necessary
for Mr. Fogel to leave the garage door open, though the temperature was 10
below zero. Although his fingers were frozen on this job, he did not receive
the promised load of wood.

The family owed the grocer $150 and the landlord $80. By this time
Mr. Fogel was desperate, but he had never considered going on relief until the
grocer suggested it one day. Mr. Fogel had reached the point "where nothing
much mattered"; he had exhausted every resource and found himself "up against
a stone wall." He reacted to the suggestion of relief as "a drowning man
grabs at anything within reach to save himself." Mr. Fogel made application
for relief; an investigator visited the family the following day and had a
grocery order delivered the same day.

The Fogels were on direct relief 10 weeks, receiving $14 for each 2-week period. Mrs. Fogel had a difficult time feeding a family of eight on $1 a day. The six children were in school; as they were short on clothing, Mrs. Fogel washed three times a week. Ira walked 2 miles to high school that winter and had no overshoes. Mrs. Fogel fights back tears as she tells of this; it was a particularly bad winter, but Ira missed school only 1 day and that absence was due to illness.

When Mr. Fogel went to work in May 1936, relief was discontinued before he had received his first pay check, and it was again necessary to ask the grocer for credit. After Ira was graduated from high school, the relief worker "did stop by 1 day to suggest that he register for CCC camp." Mrs. Fogel appreciated this because it helped out the family budget.

Ira was at CCC camp from September to April, and he liked it very much. After he returned home, he got a job at a saw mill, but when he had worked less than a week, his hand was caught in a saw. Had he not been wearing a stiff leather glove, he would have lost three fingers on his right hand. His first worry was "What will mother say?" As soon as the hand was healed, Ira returned to the saw mill against his mother's wishes and worked 6 months, receiving 30¢ an hour. In the fall, when the saw mill closed, Ira got a job remodeling the stock room at the Iowa Garage. This job lasted 3 months and the pay was $12 a week. Then Ira was unemployed for 6 months and until June 1, 1937, when he was employed as a pressman at the Highland Paper Box Company where he still works. The work has been highly irregular for 6 weeks; he has averaged only 1 day a week for the past 3 weeks. Ira is an ardent reader and plans to study psychology in night school after the holidays when the family "quiets down."

Had it not been for the little employment Ira has had, Mr. Fogel
doubts if the family would have "got by" on his small earnings before he got
his present regular job. The Fogels have paid "a little" on back debts, but
$300 still remains to be paid. Mr. Fogel thinks it would have been better
had they gone on relief sooner instead of getting so deeply in debt. "The
pity of it is we won't be able to get credit again." The Fogels' one New
Year's resolution is to try to get out of debt, but Mrs. Fogel doesn't see how
they can lower their standards much more—"all we have is electricity, a radio,
and an old car." Mr. Fogel fears that the Nation will suffer as a result of
the general lowering of living standards. He believes that the morale of
young people is greatly affected when a family lowers its plane of living too
much.

The Fogels follow a very strict budget and buy economically; yet
they have little left from the pay check when current bills are paid. Mrs.
Fogel estimates that she spends $5 a week less for food than was spent in
1930, as she now purchases an inferior quality. The six-room frame house is
rented for $20 a month, but there is no hot water heater or bath tub. An
ordinary wash tub is used for baths and the water is heated on the kerosene
stove in the kitchen. "Maybe you think it is a small job to keep a family
of nine clean this way." Mrs. Fogel is surprised that they have managed as
well as they have, and she is sure that "one half don't know how the other
half live." The entire house is heated by an oil burner and circulating
heater which Mr. Fogel installed at a very small cost. If he can find a
cheap second-hand bath tub, he plans to install it and also a hot water heater,
which he can rig up at little expense.

A nearby vacant lot, rented by the Fogels for gardening every
summer, has yielded large quantities of vegetables to be canned for winter use.
Mr. Fogel thinks this has helped greatly to keep down their expenses in the

winter. Mr. and Mrs. Fogel are not only thrifty, but they show unusual
ingenuity in making the most of the resources at hand. Mrs. Fogel does all
her own baking and is handy at sewing, cutting down, and making over garments
time after time. She thinks the only thing she and Mr. Fogel have not tried
during the depression is paper hanging, and they would have tried even that
had not new paper cost money. Paint received in exchange for an auto repair
job was used for freshening up the interior of the house.

Mr. Fogel has made most of the children's Christmas toys for
several years. Last year he made a Ferris wheel, which revolves very
realistically by means of a motor from an old electric fan. The prize toy,
however, is a merry-go-round on which the horses move up and down and the
lights flicker as the merry-go-round goes round and round. This, too, is
operated by a small motor originally intended for quite another purpose. The
only materials purchased for the making of these toys were small nails which
cost only 10¢. Mrs. Fogel and May make all kinds of Christmas candies,
cookies, and popcorn balls. Last fall the whole family went on a nutting
expedition and gathered 2 bushels of black walnuts.

The disparity in the ages of the Fogel children presents no barriers
to family unity. There is an unusual degree of congeniality in the family and
no evidence of jealousy or discord. The neighbors are amazed at the way the
Fogels enjoy "doing things together." The 21-year-old son and the grown
daughters prefer a family weiner roast or picnic any day to the more
sophisticated type of recreation. "The nine of us pile into the old clonk
and away we go."

As Mr. Fogel works 55 hours a week and some weeks even more, he
has little time for reading. He is not particularly concerned about the
present business depression, as he considers it "just a scare." He has not

thought much about the reason for widespread unemployment, but doubts if
conditions will materially improve until there is an increase in the purchasing
power of the workers. He considers wages in Dubuque "much too low," but he
does not share the belief of many Dubuque citizens that the city "faces a
hopelessly dark future." While conditions have improved for the man with a
skilled trade, he feels that the young, inexperienced worker faces a serious
situation in respect to employment opportunities. He is much concerned because
Ira has no regular employment, and the two girls have never had a chance to
show their skill at stenography though they passed the 100-word-a-minute test
in dictation.

      Mr. Fogel is heartily in favor of the recent social security legis-
lation, but he considers the waiting period for unemployment insurance too
long unless there is an appreciable increase in the wages of workers. The
"majority of workers" would not have funds to carry them for more than a week,
as all resources have been used up during the depression and the weekly pay
check barely pays current expenses.

      Mr. Fogel feels quite secure in his present job and believes that
his pay will be increased before long as the company is again prospering. He
overheard his boss boast that Mr. Fogel is the best mechanic in Dubuque. In a
recent test given to mechanics at the garage he rated 99 percent. He knows that
he is building up a good reputation in Dubuque because most of the garage's
regular customers invariably request that he do their work. If business conditions continue to improve for another year he would like to go in business
for himself again if he can find a partner to put up the capital.

Employment Chronology for Mr. Fogel

Until 1913 –   On father's farm.

1913 – November
1927   Operated own garage and car agency.

November 1927 –
February 1931   Auto mechanic, Iowa Garage.

February 1931 –
April 1933   Auto mechanic, Wisconsin garage.

April 1933 –
June 1934   Auto mechanic, Capital Garage.

July 1934 –
November 1934   Air compressor operator, rock quarry.

December 1, 1934
April 30, 1935   Unemployed.

May 1, 1935 –
June 30, 1935   Auto mechanic, service station.

July 1, 1935   Auto mechanic, Iowa Garage.
present

BY THEIR OWN BOOTSTRAPS

PAINTER

Mr. Painter	28
Mrs. Painter	27
Junior	8
Jean	4

Interviewing completed
December 9, 1937

John Painter is colorless in appearance. His hair is blond
and smooth and his eyes pale behind gold-rimmed spectacles. He speaks
slowly in a flat monotone, expresses opinions carefully and thoughtfully
and with some assurance. While he talks, he looks down at his stubby-
fingered hands and toys with his knuckles. In his blue denimcoveralls,
he looks the part of a stolid, painstaking workman, older than his 28
years; he is one of the Midwestern Foundry Company's department superintendents. Though Mr. Painter's work history covers a period of only
10 years, including 2 years of unemployment, he has worked for four firms,
in each of which he has had a variety of jobs. Starting as a machine
operator on a piecework basis, he has slowly worked up to his present
salaried position.

John Painter's high school course included some machine shop
work. Though he believes that practical experience is more valuable than
formal education, he has tried since graduation from high school to get as
much additional education as possible, despite the difficulty of studying
after he has put in a full day at the shop. Just now, he is taking a
correspondence course in mechanical drawing; he has made his own drawing
board, and spends most of his evenings working over it.

Before high school graduation, John had worked for two summers
in the Iowa Foundry. After commencement he was again employed in the

machine shop for some 3 months. He operated lathes and other machines, 10 hours a day, on a piecework basis; earnings averaged about $20 a week. The work was somewhat distasteful to him for more reasons than one: his jobs were highly routine and monotonous; the hours were long and the work heavy; his foreman was somewhat overdemanding and missed no chance of telling John 'how dumb he was. One day when the foreman, in attempting to reset the machine, dropped a monkey-wrench, thus stripping the gears, John had an opportunity too good to miss: he lost no time in telling the foreman how dumb he was. From then on, John's relationship with his foreman was still more strained and unsatisfactory.

In the fall of 1927 John left the Iowa Foundry to go to the Midwestern Foundry Company, where he worked for less than 1 year. Here, again, he put in 10 hours a day. He now earned $18 a week at metal work. Once he had an attack of metal-poisoning which the doctor checked just in time to save him. Besides constantly fearing poisoning, John was annoyed by the fact that his hands must be always damp, and consequently raw and chapped. About a week after he was frightened by the poisoning, he slipped on the wet floor and fell with one hand across a live wire. His fingers were burned to the bone. This was the last straw; he quit the job the next day. Still, in some respects he had liked the work at Midwestern better than his work with the Iowa Foundry; he got along better with his foreman, and it was partly because of his earlier experience at Midwestern that he was taken back in the summer of 1934.

From the Midwestern Foundry Company John went to a wholesale grocery firm, where, from June 1928 until January 1929, he did clerical work which consisted largely of figuring the salesmen's commissions. Though his earnings--$50 a month---were lower than they had been at the foundry, he hoped that there would be more opportunity for advancement in this line of work. Actually, there was almost no such opportunity. Through this experience he learned that he should consult the older workers in any concern if he wants to know what chance there is to "get ahead."

It was while he worked for the grocery firm that John Painter was married to a plump, pretty girl about his own age. She presents a contrast to her husband in many ways: her appearance is not so neat as John's; wisps of her curly brown hair escape to blow across her cheeks; in her own words, she is less orderly and painstaking than her husband, though she has been a reasonably competent housekeeper and mother.

Just after their marriage John and Mary Painter went to Chicago, where they stayed with John's brother, who had an "excellent job." John knew that he had neither the training nor the experience for work equivalent to his brother's, but he hoped that the brother might help him to get some sort of work in Chicago, where jobs were more plentiful, wages higher, and opportunities for promotion more numerous than in Dubuque. John went immediately to the State employment office, where he was given a list of jobs for which he might apply, although the interviewer indicated that none of the jobs---factory work, mostly---would be just what John wanted. He chose to go first to the factory nearest the home; this happened to be a company manufacturing steam shovels and other heavy machinery. He was hired immediately, for "jobs were easy to get, then." He worked first in the factory, $9\frac{1}{4}$ hours a day, at 60¢ an hour. Soon he was transferred to the rate-setting and production department, where he was engaged in determining piecework rates, mapping out wage incentive plans, and figuring amounts of bonuses. For this work, he received a monthly salary of $150.

While the Painters lived in Chicago, they established their own household, rented an apartment, bought $800 worth of furniture, and had their first child, Junior, now 8 years old. In April 1932 John paid the final installment on the furniture; he thinks he "got a break" in that he was not laid off until 3 months after this last payment was made. The men had known for some time that orders had fallen off, the company's stock was going down, and, in consequence, production would have to be curtailed. They knew "something would happen"; they could not anticipate what.

John had worried for so long a time that it was "almost a relief" to be laid off and to begin making specific plans for a readjustment. The Painters had come to Dubuque for a brief vacation with John's parents when one of the men telephoned that there would be no job for John on his return to Chicago. Mary thought it "nice of him" to let them know as quickly as possible of the sweeping layoffs; otherwise, the family "might have spent a little more on the vacation." Luckily, John knew a man who was driving to Chicago with a load of furniture the following day; he went along, packed all his household goods, and was back in Dubuque with his furniture on the second morning. In this way he was able to arrange for the moving at a cost of only $25.

John made no attempt to look for other work in Chicago, as he was certain that no jobs were available. The factory where he had worked had laid off 1,500 men, about half of the total force, within a single week. All the shop workers were now put on an hourly rate basis in order to simplify office work; there was thus no further need for a rate-setting division. Work at other plants had been similarly curtailed. Because of the many obligations which the family had had to meet and emergency expenses during

illnesses, John had not been able to save any money; he had invested only
in an insurance policy, which was now allowed to lapse.

The Painters would "hate to live through 2 more years" like those
of 1933 and 1934, when John was unemployed.   They do not want even to recal
their experiences in the depths of the depression.   "There is no use talking
about it now," but John's unemployment even made for disagreements and
"fights" with Mary's parents, who thought that anyone who wanted work could
get a job; therefore, John must not want work.   Mary's sympathies were with
John, though she explains that "that was just the way my father looked at
things."   Having been a farmer all his life, he had no conception of
industrial employment or unemployment.

The Painters stayed with John's parents for a while, though Mary
spent the greater part of the 3 years immediately following John's loss of
employment on her father's farm near Dubuque.   John remained in his parents'
home, where his furniture was stored, except for occasional visits to the
farm.   He helped to pay his way on the farm by doing all kinds of jobs.
During one visit he built a couple of chimneys.   Mary is proud of John's
"handiness" and ability to learn any job quickly; she was doubly appreciativ
of his work on the farm, for she realized that "he did hate farm work so."

In Dubuque John picked up what odd jobs he could find, and he
also went to the various factories in search of work.   Jobseeking was
especially difficult in that the factories would not take applications, but
hired, if at all, from among the men waiting at the plant when openings occurred.   John worked for two trucking companies, did odd jobs of automobile
repair work, and helped with preparations for automobile shows—building
booths and installing public address systems.   The longest time he put in at

any one job between July 1932 and August 1934, when he was taken on at
Midwestern, was the 3 or 4 weeks spent in preparation for an auto show.
He thinks that his earnings for the entire 2-year period totaled no more
than $100. Mary Painter states that his earnings were barely enough to
purchase shoes for the family and a very few absolutely necessary articles
of clothing. She was "fortunate" in being able to sew well enough to make
over old clothing for herself and the two children.

The second child, a girl, now 4 years old, was born while Mary
Painter remained on the farm. Though Mary's pregnancy made the family
situation especially difficult and worrisome, she comments placidly that
"children don't always come just when you want them, but afterwards, you're
always glad you have them." John and Mary were unhappy over their necessary
separation; almost every year of their married life, it seems that they have
"happened to spend more time apart than together." After her mother's
death, Mary kept house for her father and a younger brother. She feels
that she was not a burden to her father as she "paid her way" by doing the
housework.

After many fruitless attempts to find work, John finally cornered
a man at Midwestern and persuaded him to take an application. He left at
the plant the telephone number of a friend through whom he could always be
reached. One day in the summer of 1934 John was mending fences on the farm
when his friend drove up and shouted to him, "You have a job!" Thinking
that the fellow was joking about the fence repair work which John "hated so,"
he made some casual reply. But the friend assured him that he had a real
job; a telephone call had come through from Midwestern, where John was to
report for work the following day. He promptly returned to town, but Mary
remained on the farm until he had bought some new household equipment and

planned to take care of the family in a home of their own.   Some of the
family's furniture was in use in the home of John's parents, who "needed it
as badly as we did," so that John could not bear to reclaim all of it.

At Midwestern John worked in the machine shop during the mornings, and in the pouring-off room, where he "almost roasted to death," durir
the afternoons. He was paid 23¢ an hour for 9½ hours a day. With his earnings, he purchased, among other things, a living room rug, the family's bes*
rug having been left with John's parents, and a coal range. In Chicago Mary
had cooked with gas, but the Painters feared now that they would be unable *
meet gas bills and so considered the coal stove more practical. John tried,
as far as possible, to "surprise" Mary. When he was ready for her return to
Dubuque, he moved her and the children into a "flat," the second story of a
frame house in a rather sparsely-settled section of the city.

Meanwhile, John had been granted a pay increase as a direct
result of NRA. When the act was put into effect, hours were reduced to 8 a
day, and John's pay was increased to 35¢ an hour. By now, he was working
full time in the machine shop, instead of dividing his days between machine
shop and pouring-off room; this arrangement he found much more satisfactory.

After the NRA was invalidated, hours and wage scales remained
the same. John's earnings were increased gradually as he was transferred fr
one job to another. He was first made a timekeeper, then went to the tool
room, and still later was promoted to the job as department superintendent,
on a purely temporary basis, while the regular superintendent substituted fr
a foreman who was away from the plant for some months. During these few mo:
he "made some innovations" which met with the approval of the management. (
the return of the foreman, John was put in charge of the tool room, at 45¢ a
hour.

A little more than 2 years ago the foreman left the plant permanently; the department superintendent was again transferred, and John was formally promoted to the job as superintendent. At the end of the first year his monthly salary was increased from $90 to $100; at the end of the second year he was granted another $10 increase.

John is thoroughly interested in his work; his sole dissatisfaction is with the meagerness of his pay. If he "could get a $10 raise every year for the next 10 years," he would be content, but he fears that he has already reached the top because of the generally "low wages in the Dubuque factories." Mary points out that "the best of them don't get much here." John finds it especially disconcerting to be making less at Midwestern than he earned at the Chicago plant, where his responsibility was not nearly so great.

Within the limitations set by John's income, the family manages excellently. John believes that running a home is as important, and requires as much planning, as running a business. He has tried to plan well for the family: "the first thing he did after he got back at Midwestern" was to take out insurance policies for all four members of the family. This may have been "a mistake," as an insurance agent has recently indicated that it is most practical to have only the wage earner insured. Still, if anything were to happen to another member of the family, he does not know how he could meet funeral expenses, for he has been unable to save any money.

There is always some extra expense to be met: last winter, Mary and both children had serious illnesses; since the doctor advised all three to have tonsilectomies before another winter, John spent $100 for operations during the past summer. Again, John has taken some little responsibility for his parents, though he has not been able to contribute regularly to their

support. In 1933 Mr. Painter, senior, was laid off by the newspaper for
which he had worked as a printer for 19 years. After receiving relief for
a time, he was assigned to a WPA project, but was transferred in March 1936,
when he reached the age of 65, to county relief rolls and the waiting list for
an old age pension. Since he and his wife, both of whom are eligible,"
"couldn't even apply for pensions until his Iowa State pension tax was paid,"
John Painter made the $14 payment. John also carries an insurance policy
for his mother.

Last fall the Painters moved to a five-room bungalow, a fairly
new and attractive house, which they were able to rent for $17 a month, with
the understanding that the landlord would not be responsible for repairs.
Having lived in "flats" during most of her married life, Mary had been anxious
to "get to herself," even though she had always been "fortunate in having
very nice neighbors" in apartment houses. Mary has added to the household
equipment by making a number of tidy and attractive rag rugs from old clothing; and she is now working on draperies for the living room windows. She
has continued to make the children's clothing. The sewing machine is
chronically laden with clothes to be mended.

Junior and Jean are hearty, rowdy, red-headed youngsters. Junior
feels his superiority to Jean, who attends kindergarten in the afternoons
and "can print only two or three numbers," while he is able to execute
elaborate and properly-labeled drawings of Tom Mix and Speed Gibson and can
make paper airplanes which sail unpiloted through the hoops of the living-
room chandelier.

John Painter looks forward to the day when he can leave Dubuque;
he might by this time have found a better job elsewhere, were it not for "this

now depression," which he attributed to the fact that business men were mark-
ing time until they learned whether the wage and hour bill would be passed
and corporation taxes reduced. Of course, he finds many advantages in working
for Midwestern, a "one-family concern": when he was out because of a 3-weeks
illness last winter, he was not docked for time lost; last summer, he was
given a 1-week vacation with pay; he is permitted to use his own initiative
without unnecessary supervision. The head of the firm is a "fair employer":
he has kept the plant in operation during some slack periods when there was
scarcely enough work to keep the men busy, and even though "he has enough
money that he wouldn't need to speak to common men he is friendly and democratic."
However, on the other hand, John finds, "The family is making money, but doesn't
know where it's coming from"; though the factory workers actually "make the
profits," the salesmen are paid at higher rates than foremen and superintendents.

John sees very little future for Dubuque industries in general.
Though the foundries will probably keep going for a long time, the sash and
door factories are following "a short-sighted policy," John believes, in not
branching out into production of equipment for steel construction, which will
eventually eliminate the demand for wooden sashes and doors.

There is some conflict between John's recognition of the fact that
he is "a workingman and should be on the side of the workingman," and his
business class philosophy. For he has seen the industrial picture from
"two sides"—the side of labor and the side of management. This conflict is
evidenced again and again as John elaborates on his general philosophy and
his feeling about specific industrial and governmental problems. As a workman
he feels that his contributions have been neither properly recognized nor
adequately recompensed; as a superintendent he sees with some clarity the
problems of business and management.

John is opposed to unionism in general and particularly to the CIO, for he sees in John L. Lewis a potential "dictator" to labor and management alike, "and the capitalists aren't going to stand for that." At Midwestern the "trouble-makers" during strikes have usually been "irresponsible" workmen, many of them earning at Midwestern more than they had ever earned elsewhere; yet they still complained. On the other hand, John has found that he "can't argue" about his salary, for "one man can do nothing" and "you would never get superintendents unionized"—not, of course, that he would approve of such organization.

The men do not always "appreciate what is being done for them"; for himself, John is "grateful" for his employment even though he is "underpaid." He is not particularly interested in wage and hour legislation, as it would in no way affect him; yet, he resents what he considers to be a fact—that more attention has been given by Congress to increasing farm income than to increasing salaries of industrial workers.

John looks at Government as a business enterprise. He would approve extreme centralization, even to the point of erasing State lines to avoid complications arising from differences in laws from State to State and the expense of supporting 48 separate legislatures. Men experienced in business are those who should be entrusted with Government positions. John does not believe in party politics; he would like to cast his vote on a ballot which lists experience and qualifications of "Mr. X" instead of name and party.

Recent legislation which John most heartily approves is the Social Security Act, though he considers it unnecessarily complicated. The Midwestern Foundry employs extra men full time to make out reports for the Social Security Board. John would be willing to pay "even a higher tax" if the act were revised so as to allow for flat-rate pensions to all persons over 60 years of age, and to impose a flat tax on total pay rolls without regard to individual earnings. He thinks that the relief program, as well as WPA, should be federally administered.

But none of this is of much importance in John's scheme of things. Quiet, acquiescent, happy in his home and with his family, he is chiefly interested in having a job as satisfying as his present one, but with a higher rate of pay and a "chance for advancement."

Employment Chronology for Mr. Painter

Summers, 1925, 1926, and 1927	— Machine operator, Iowa Foundry.
Fall 1927 – June 1928	Metal worker, Midwestern Foundry Company.
June 1928 – January 1929	Clerical worker, wholesale grocery firm.
January 1929 – July 1932	Factory and clerical worker.
July 1932 – August 1934	Unemployed.
August 1934 – present	Machine shop helper, timekeeper, and department superintendent, Midwestern Foundry Company.

Mr. Milter   25
Mrs. Milter   23

Interviewing completed
February 28, 1938

        Paul Milter, 25 years old, had hoped to become a lawyer, but
through lack of funds he was forced to drop out of college at the end of
his junior year. Always interested in athletics, Paul played on the high
school football and basketball teams and made the college football squad
at the beginning of his sophomore year. Since he was 14 years old, he had
been able to get "man-sized" jobs during summer vacations because of his
physique. He is more than 6 feet tall, slender, and extremely muscular.
His features are unusually fine, and his personality is excellent. He
expresses himself without reserve and tries to be objective in his thinking.
Since dropping out of college in 1933, Paul has experienced two periods of
unemployment of a few months duration. Though he had held responsible and
well-paid jobs, none had lasted longer than a few months until he was employed as an estimator by the Dubuque Woodworking Company in January 1936.
He is not altogether satisfied with his present meagerly-paid job. He has
not abandoned the idea of returning to college, though he has given up all
hope of ever completing a legal course; now he thinks he would like to
become an accountant.

        Paul and his wife, to whom he was married about $1\frac{1}{2}$ years ago, oc-
cupy an attractive, small, furnished apartment in a big house, formerly the
home of one of Dubuque's rich families; this home was turned into an apartment house some years ago. The hardwood floors and a tile fireplace give
the apartment an air of distinction. For their two rooms the Milters pay

$26.50 a month. Mrs. Milter, pretty and friendly, has continued to work as
a stenographer for a contractor since her marriage. The Milters are buying
household furnishings, one piece at a time; this way they hope to be able to
acquire complete furnishings without going in debt.

The Milters are an active couple. They visit back and forth with
many friends and Paul teaches a Sunday School class, coaches athletics,
belongs to a club of young professional men, and hopes to run for election
to the school board. Through his contacts with the youngsters, Paul has
become interested in initiating some much needed reforms in the school
system; he believes that membership on the school board is the best means
to this end. Paul has all the self-assurance in the world, and he does
not doubt that some day he will make his mark.

The summer that Paul was 14 he got a job as a section hand by giving
his age as 18. On this job he was paid 40¢ an hour. The following two summers, he worked as a cement puddler on a road construction job. Lifting
the large shovels of cement proved to be tiring work, but Paul was elated
over his earnings; he was paid 60¢ an hour, and as he often worked 14 or
16 hours a day his earnings ran as high as $200 a month. During the sum-
mer of 1930 Paul was almost as much interested in building himself up for
the football team on entering college in the fall as in earning enough
money to pay his expenses. He compromised by getting a job as a herder
on a Montana ranch. During the summer of 1931 he worked as a trouble
shooter for a power company, and in 1932, when he was only 19, he was
employed for 4 months by a hydro-electrical construction company. On this
job he worked at various tasks; for several weeks he did acetylene torch
welding and was paid from $1.80 to $3 an hour. Though he had left school
early to take this job and had entered about 10 days late in the fall, he

came out at the end of the year with the second highest average in his class.
Paul had cleared nearly $500 during this summer's work, but it did not see
him through the year. At the beginning of his sophomore year he had made
the regular football team, but he had been injured in his first big game of
the season. His knee kept bothering him, and finally, in his junior year,
he went to a specialist who advised an operation. This operation ate into
Paul's savings so that it was necessary for him to borrow money to finish the
school year. During the summer of 1933 he rode freight trains to the Pacific
Coast and down South in search of work, but invariably found his nonresident
status a handicap. He feels, however, that he learned a great deal on these
trips even though he was thrown in the "hoosegow" a couple of times as a
"suspicious looking character."

Upon his return to Dubuque Paul was very much discouraged. Through
a friend he was sent to a CCC camp for 6 months as mess sergeant at $45 a
month. After he returned home from camp he was unemployed for 2 or 3 months.
He was hired in April 1934 to superintend a rock quarry acquired by a Wisconsin contractor who had expected to get a big construction contract. On
this job Paul was paid $250 a month, and he was allowed gas and oil for his
car. He had complete responsibility for the quarry; several hundred men
were hired to work on day and night shifts. Unfortunately for Paul the contractor lost the expected contract by overbidding; the quarry was closed in
January 1935. Soon after this, Paul was hired on a road construction job
near Dubuque. He had worked only 3 months when a load of rock fell on him
one day. As a result of this accident he was in the hospital for 10 weeks.

As Paul felt none too strong after this experience, he thought it
best to avoid heavy work. For about 3 months he worked for a national ad-
vertising company, but he did not realize much from his efforts. Again he

found himself unemployed in September 1935. After some 4 months of unemployment he was feeling quite desperate, when one day he met a friend from
the Dubuque Woodworking Company who offered him a job in the mill.

Though Paul had always sworn that he would never work for a Dubuque mill, he gladly accepted the offer, reasoning that "a job is a job
whether you like it or not." For 3 months he was permitted to work in various departments in the mill; then he was transferred to the office. Though
he carries considerable responsibility, he said that he is earning less than
on any job since he was a youngster. He seems to be somewhat embarrassed
over his salary, and does not volunteer details as to the amount. Furthermore, Paul feels that this mill offers little opportunity for advancement;
he is particularly discouraged when he looks at fellow office workers who
have made no advancement during 20 years with the company. Though somewhat
critical of his employers, Paul also is loyal to them to a certain extent.
He likes the people with whom he works, and enjoys the work itself, but he
would not want to settle down to it for very long. He looks on his present
job more as a "depression stopgap." The experience, he thinks, is valuable
and may lead to something better. Paul has always found "figures easy" and
thoroughly enjoys accounting. Now he would like to become an accountant.
He has thought of trying to get a job in Chicago, where he could attend
Chicago University night classes.

Paul thinks that Dubuque is very backward in many ways. He criti-
cizes the Chamber of Commerce for not offering inducements to companies, such
as the Goodrich Tire, to settle in Dubuque, but blames the business men rather
than the manufacturers for this failure.

Paul feels very bitter about the job preference given to veterans.

In his opinion "those fellows" have had long enough to get on their feet.
He adds, "why should they be given preference now, 20 years after the war?"
In Paul's search for jobs he found the policy of giving preference to veteran
and the rules pertaining to residence status most annoying. Time after time
he was turned down for one or the other of these reasons. Paul feels that
"it is high time someone took an interest in helping the young fellow to get
a start.

Paul is much opposed to relief as it is now administered. For one
thing, "too much money is being spent, and also, it has a tendency to make
bums out of people." The time has arrived for States to take care of their
own relief problems without the help of the Federal Government. The Social
Security program should now make this possible. Paul knows that some families were actually up against it and had to have help. So long as people
know, however, that the "Government won't let them starve, they don't make
as much effort to take care of themselves as they would if there was no
Government help available." Paul feels that some of the recent legislation
is quite worthwhile, but in his opinion, "too many laws have been passed."
"People would be better off if all laws were erased and the country started
all over again with just the Ten Commandments--and perhaps a few six-
shooters."

Seriously, Paul thinks the Social Security legislation is a good
thing, but he can't see that it will offer much security to Dubuque workers
who receive low pay and work only irregularly. In spite of Social Security,
Paul predicts that the county will have to bury many of these workers. Paul
has no confidence in labor organization; he sees in it "too much exploitation
of ignorant workers by leaders whose chief interest is money." Then, too,

Paul feels that "you can't beat the bosses"; they always have a way out. For example, a millworkers' strike in Dubuque would not prevent the Dubuque Woodworking Company from getting out orders, as this company owns several branches in other cities. In case of labor trouble in one mill, orders are transferred to another.

Paul considers insurance the safest and surest way to save; since his marriage he has taken out a $5,000 double indemnity policy. He expects to start on a 30-year annuity as soon as he has finished buying furniture. Paul's uncle, an insurance man for many years, has advised Paul as to the best insurance plan. Though Paul and his wife both receive low salaries, their combined income has made it possible for them to get along without too much skimping. Last summer they spent their vacations with Mrs. Milter's aunt, who has a summer home in Wisconsin, and this summer they plan to take a nice trip if they can arrange to take vacations at the same time. Paul realizes that he is still "just a youngster," but he is anxious to get established in a job that offers some opportunity for advancement.

Employment Chronology for Mr. Milter

1926 – 1932 –	**Summer work** only: section hand, cement puddler, cattle herder, trouble shooter, acetylene torch welder.
July 1933 – January 1934	Mess sergeant, CCC Camp.
January 1934 – March 1934	Unemployed
April 1934 – January 1935	Superintendent, rock quarry
February 1935 – May 1935	Laborer, road construction.
June 1935 – August 1935	Solicitor, national advertising campaign.
September 1935 – January 1936	Unemployed

January 1936 – Present – **Office clerk,** Dubuque Woodworking Company

                    Mr. Gantzler   37
                    Mrs. Gantzler   35
                    Ruth   11
                    Arlene   3

Interviewing completed
December 31, 1937

        Mr. and Mrs. Gantzler feel that many persons receiving relief might

have avoided, or at least postponed, making application for assistance if they

had planned as carefully as the Gantzlers planned and saved as much as Mr.

Gantzler saved from his not unusually high earnings. They are proud of having

managed while Mr. Gantzler was unemployed without running so much as a grocery

bill and without requesting any assistance.

        The Gantzlers' five-room frame house, freshly painted, comfortably

furnished, and altogether attractive was planned and built by Mr. Gantzler

soon after he lost his job when the Stevenson Phonograph and Radio Company

closed at the end of 1931.

        During $2\frac{1}{2}$ years of almost total unemployment, the Gantzler family

lived entirely on savings accumulated during the 10 years that Mr. Gantzler

had worked for Stevenson's, and invested $2,300, likewise from savings, in

materials for the building of the house. Though unemployed, Mr. Gantzler was

far from unoccupied; besides building the house and a garage, he did extensive

gardening in vacant lots which he was permitted to use rent-free, sawed and

hauled the wood which was the family's only fuel, and worked for 4 months

without pay on the farm owned by his father.

        Both Mr. and Mrs. Gantzler are friendly, poised, and intelligent.

He is tall, broad-shouldered, and husky-looking except for his unusually pale

and heavily lined face. Ruth, 11 years old, and Arlene, almost 3, are

attractive and bright youngsters. Ruth, a sixth-grader, is a member of a junior Girl Scout troup whose activities she describes with enthusiasm.

Until 1921, when he began work for the Stevenson plant, Mr. Gantz-ler had never had a regular, full-time, paid job. He had worked on his father's 90-acre farm not far from Dubuque, and he had had several short-term jobs in town while he continued to live on the farm. Among many and varied jobs on the farm, Mr. Gantzler had done some bits of carpentry work, which he enjoyed more than the day-by-day tasks of farming.

When he was 21 years old Mr. Gantzler started to work in the ship-ping room at Stevenson's. He earned 35¢ an hour for 9 hours a day. At the end of about a year, he was transferred to the fitting department, where his work consisted of putting hinges and doors on the phonograph cabinets. In this department he was paid on a piecework basis. Though earnings varied with the alternation of rush and slack seasons, Mr. Gantzler's earnings for each pay period averaged about twice as much as his more consistent earnings in the shipping room. The work was fairly regular; he lost few whole days because of lack of work before December 1930 although occasionally he did not put in full days. On the other hand, during the busy season before Christmas he sometimes worked until 9 p.m.

Until Mr. Gantzler, in the course of general conversation, chanced to refer to the temporary unemployment of 1931, Mr. Gantzler had forgotten to mention it. The 5 months of unemployment from December 1930 until May 13, 1931, had been dwarfed in his recollection by the years from the beginning of 1932 until he was reemployed in July, 1934. During the 5-months period in 1931 when the Stevenson plant was temporarily shut down, the family managed without assistance. Within this same period Mr. Gantzler had an emergency operation. His doctor had told him he might return to work on the 15th of May. As chance would have it the plant reopened and Mr. Gantzler was recalled to work on the 13th; thinking that 2 days could make little difference one way or the other, he went. Looking back on this experience, Mr. and Mrs. Gantzler find it amusing that the operation fitted in so nicely with the layoff.

After returning to work, Mr. Gantzler continued at the same job until the plant closed permanently in December 1931. While he worked at Stevenson's the Gantzlers lived near the plant in a five-room house renting for $20 a month. Three of his brothers, regularly employed, made their home with the family and paid board and room. The only other family income was Mrs. Gantzler's small and irregular earnings; she occasionally "helped out" in a nearby restaurant during the lunch hour. Her work ended soon after the Stevenson closing.

During 10 years of employment Mr. Gantzler had saved several thousand dollars. He had anticipated building his own home and had invested his funds in savings accounts. By December 1931 he had accounts in each of four Dubuque banks. Early in 1932 two of the banks were closed, thus tying up more than $2,000 of Mr. Gantzler's savings.

Fearing that the other banks might be no more secure than those that had failed, Mr. Gantzler determined to withdraw all of the remaining funds. He felt that he might just as well begin the building of the house while he was not otherwise occupied. Perhaps he would not have done so if he had not anticipated being back at work within a year at the outside limit. But now he has no reason to regret the investment in the home, easily worth double the amount of actual cash expended.

Mr. Gantzler bought the lot in the spring of 1932. During the following summer he worked most of the time on the three-car garage which was later used for storage of building materials. Mr. Gantzler built the garage with his brothers in mind, for it was taken for granted that they would continue to live with the family. As it happened, however, no one of the three has lived in the new house: one has died; one is now in a sanitorium: the third brother is working and living elsewhere. The garage spaces are now rented.

September had come before Mr. Gantzler actually began work on the house. Mrs. Gantzler takes special pride in telling how her husband built a house when he was only 31 years old though he had had little experience with carpentry. Mr. Gantzler says deprecatingly that "anyone who can read blueprints can build a house." He himself worked from two sets of blueprints, combining the best features of the two plans into one which he felt would be most practical for his family's home.

In February 1933 the Gantzlers moved into the house though only the subflooring had been laid; only storm windows had been put in; walls remained unfinished; and inside doors had not been hung. Mrs. Gantzler cooked on a wood stove in the basement for several weeks before gas was installed.

Mrs. Gantzler helped with much of the finishing work. She stained and varnished woodwork and helped with the finishing of the floors and the papering. The only work which the Gantzlers did not themselves undertake was the plastering. Since Mr. Gantzler has had regular employment, he has continued to do odd jobs about the house when he has had time to spare.

When Mr. Gantzler speaks of picking up odd jobs whenever possible while he had no full-time employment, Mrs. Gantzler reminds him that he hadn't even an odd job which netted him any cash between December 1931 and July 1934, when he began work for the county in a nearby stone quarry. He had helped his father, and instead of paying poll taxes in cash had done some county road work. The supervisor, impressed with the quality of Mr. Gantzler's work

and with his dependability, had stated that there was no reason why he should
not be given a regular job. It was this road work which later led to his employment in the stone quarry.

Meanwhile, the family had been living on savings. Occasionally the
Gantlers received installments on deposits in the closed banks, usually about
5 percent of a total account at one time; these dividends "came in handy." To
date they have received about 50 percent of the total deposits; $1,000 is still
tied up, and not all of this amount will be forthcoming. The Gantzlers estimate
that expenditures were cut in half after the loss of Mr. Gantzler's job. Except
for a very few essential items, clothing was eliminated from the budget. The
hauling of wood eliminated expenditures for fuel, and garden produce supplemented the staples which still had to be purchased. Mr. Gantzler usually raised
enough potatoes to last throughout the year.

In July 1934 Mr. Gantzler began work in the stone quarry. This work
was not much to his liking. He was unaccustomed to such heavy physical labor,
and in 2 weeks he sweated off 17 pounds. The pay of $19 a week was scarcely
adequate, though "better than nothing."

The work involved some dangers. In January 1935 another worker,
slinging broken rock from one side of the quarry to the other, let fall a
rock which hit Mr. Gantzler on the head and broke the skin of his scalp in
several places. Thus, only about 1 month before the family's second child
was born, Mr. Gantzler spent a couple of days in the hospital—his doctor
and hospital bills were paid by the county. Mr. Gantzler also lost many days
of work—and of pay—because of bad weather. And even in good weather the
quarry was damp and uncomfortable.

Nevertheless, during the 10 months or so that Mr. Gantzler worked
in the quarry he had not thought very seriously of trying to get other work.
So far as he knew, none was to be had. The Dubuque factories had closed
their employment offices and hung out signs, "No Men Wanted." Even odd
jobs were at a premium. Mr. Gantzler had kept an application on file at the
State employment office from the time it opened, but was not referred to any
job. He had rather hoped to be assigned to some work project, but did not
want to seek employment by way of the relief office. Though Mrs. Gantzler
did without "luxuries" which other women had, she "feels good now" to know
that she never had to ask for help.

Finally, in March 1935 Mrs. Gantzler persuaded her husband to try,
at least, to have applications filed at the local woodworking mills. He was
still without hope of getting work but promised to go to the factories "just
to please her." Now Mr. Gantzler thinks that he may have "made a mistake"
in not applying earlier, for just a week later he was called to work by the
Dubuque Woodworking Company, where he has continued, except for brief layoffs
up to the present time.

For almost 3 years Mr. Gantzler has been employed as an assembler.
He began work at 44¢ an hour for 8 hours a day. On the average of every 6
months he has been granted a wage increase, and he now earns 56¢ an hour.
Mrs. Gantzler is proud that he has been one of the few men to receive raises
at fairly regular intervals.

Though Mr. Gantzler's earnings are still not so high as when he
worked as a fitter at Stevenson's, he is reasonably well satisfied. Mrs.
Gantzler has heard many persons indicate that the woodworking company is "no
better than a sweatshop," but Mr. Gantzler has never found it so. In additic

to the regular wage, he usually receives a bonus. Since the bonus plan had
not been mentioned when he began work, the first bonus check was like " a
present." He has continued to regard the bonus as just a little unexpected
extra pay.

In spite of his satisfaction with his job, Mr. Gantzler has been
worried over the "business recession," the wholesale layoffs at the woodworking
company during the taking of inventory, and the prospect of slack work until
spring. The layoff during inventory-taking is of least concern; he expects
to return to work within a few days, and has taken advantage of the free time
to pour a cement flooring in the basement. Though his hours may be shortened
during the coming slack season, Mr. Gantzler anticipates having fairly regular
employment.

Mr. Gantzler thinks that the local woodworking mills will have increased business if the housing legislation goes through. But he believes
that this stimulus will not be enough. What is needed is a "more permanent"
stimulation of business activity through an increase in wages, and thus an
increase in purchasing power, and through the shortening of hours of work to
spread employment. Mr. Gantzler believes that wage increases and the shortening of the work-week to "25 or 30 hours" could be accomplished only by legislation. Managements cannot be depended upon to grant wage increases sufficient to guarantee enough purchasing power "to keep the wheels of industry
turning." He thinks that unions will accomplish little as long as they
continue to "bicker over jurisdictions." He was once a member of the millworkers' union but dropped his membership when he began to feel that it was
not strong enough to secure any real gains for the workers.

Mr. Gantzler has heard many workers attribute extensive unemployment

to the displacement of men by machines, but he believes that machines should,
and can, increase rather than decrease employment. He does believe, however,
that farm machinery has displaced workers to some extent, for he knows of
farms that once supported as many as three families but now are worked with
the help of machinery by one family. Though Mr. Gantzler would not want to
see physical labor substituted for work done by machines, he does think that
farm holdings should be "limited by law to 160 acres." Such acreage could
be worked by one family; machines might be used to secure maximum production,
but no one farmer would be in a position to displace many men by introducing
more machinery.

The "business recession" Mr. Gantzler lays at the door of "Wall
Street." The "depression" he considers largely an aftermath of the World
War and of overspeculation in "foreign stocks." On the other hand, he states
that the depression of the thirties really began in 1914 but was postponed by
the "war boom."

Though Mr. Gantzler states emphatically that certain reforms are
needed to minimize unemployment and to strengthen job security, he feels
that his own family requires no guarantee of security--for he is self-confid
and proud of his achievements.

Employment Chronology for Mr. Gantzler

Until 1921	-- On father's farm.
1921 - December 1931	-- Fitter, Stevenson Radio and Phonograph Company
December 1931 - July 1934	-- Unemployed
July 1934 - March 1935	-- Laborer, stone quarry.
March 1935 - present	-- Assembler, Dubuque Woodworki Company

Mr. Dalfurst   36
Mrs. Dalfurst   35

Interviewing completed
February 1, 1938

Mr. Dalfurst, 36 years old, is a rugged, muscular man, accustomed
to heavy work. Since leaving the farm 16 years ago, he has worked at road
construction and river dredging, spending 9 years with one Dubuque employer.
Though he had never earned more than $1,000 a year since 1923, he had $500
in savings and owned a car when he became unemployed in the fall of 1931.
Unemployed for more than 2 years, Mr. Dalfurst never received relief and is
strongly opposed to direct relief, which he believes encourages shiftlessness.
He expresses opinions with a display of strong feeling and not a little
prejudice. His vocabulary is somewhat limited and his grammar is poor.

Mrs. Dalfurst, a year younger than her husband, shares his prejudices,
but she expresses her views with considerably more objectivity and consistency.
Though of slight build, she, too, is physically strong and doesn't mind hard
work. During the fall of 1932 she helped her husband on various farms around
Dubuque, husking over 2,000 bushels of corn and receiving, in payment, a pig,
a quarter of beef, and various other farm produce. Mrs. Dalfurst lived in
Texas until her marriage in 1923. She had worked 4 years for one employer,
embossing stationery by hand.

The Dalfursts have no children. The two of them live in three
rooms over a store in the north-end residential section, for which they pay
$14 a month. The rooms, simply furnished, are heated by a large coal stove
in the living room. A fox terrier dog and a half-grown red fox, found in the
woods when he was only a few weeks old, vie with each other for attention and
keep the rugs and bed in a state of wild disorder.

Mr. Dalfurst attended country school until he had completed the eighth grade, when he was about 17 but "never really learned much as the teachers usually knew little more than the pupils." Mr. Dalfurst's mother often had to work out "examples the teacher couldn't do." Having grown tired of farm work, Mr. Dalfurst, at 19, got a job in town with a road construction contractor. For the next 3 years he worked with road gangs in the Dakotas and in Oklahoma and Texas. He was married in Texas in 1923. They returned to Dubuque and Mr. Dalfurst was employed by a sand and gravel company, where he remained until this concern "went under" in the fall of 1931. This company dredged up and down the Mississippi River for sand and gravel to be sold to building contractors. Mr. Dalfurst was paid 50¢ an hour and usually averaged from $100 to $120 a month for about 9 months out of the year. During 3 months in the winter the crew was laid off.

In spite of the winter layoff the Dalfursts always managed to save nearly $100 each year. When Mr. Dalfurst was thrown out of work in 1931, they did not want to draw too heavily on their savings of $500. In fact, this money was used only for rent during the first year of unemployment, as Mr. Dalfurst found odd jobs to pay for food and insurance premiums. Mrs. Dalfurst was also able to earn a few dollars by sewing for people in the neighborhood. In 1932 the Dalfursts just missed losing their money in a bank that closed; Mr. Dalfurst drew out their balance only 2 days before the bank failed.

During 1932-1933 Mr. Dalfurst worked at anything he could find. For several months he cut posts at $1 a day. This was back-breaking work and the pay was low, but he was glad to have the job. When no work was to be had in town he hired out by the day on farms. As they were paid in kind for most of the farm work the Dalfursts were able to fill their cellar with a winter's supply of food. During the summer of 1932 Mrs. Dalfurst canned

500 quarts of vegetables and fruit, and each winter Mr. Dalfurst butchered a hog.

When it became increasingly difficult to find even odd jobs in the spring of 1933, Mr. Dalfurst tried to get on a work relief project. It was necessary to make application through the relief office, as Mr. Dalfurst did in May, though he considered that he was applying only for work. He resented all the questions, but was glad to be assigned to a job without delay. A week after he started on this job, however, he injured his ankle and was unable to work for some time. Later he was notified to report on another job. Discovering, at the end of the first day, that this work was to be on a budget deficiency basis, he quit. "We didn't need no food; I wanted work."

Mr. Dalfurst was anxious to get on the lock and dam project, as he understood river work and knew that the contractor wanted to hire him, but the State employment office men said they had to give preference to men with dependents and to war veterans. Mr. Dalfurst is quite bitter toward the relief setup and the employment office, for he feels that there is "too much red tape." In his opinion the Works Program should have been kept separate from the relief program. In fact, he is opposed to direct relief in principle as "it makes people dependent and shiftless." He sees no reason why people should "expect the Government to give them groceries." A neighbor of the Dalfursts was on relief and received a mattress, comforters, sheets, towels, and other supplies, in addition to food and clothing. This neighbor had worked steadily at good pay for 19 years. Since he had no children or other dependents except his wife the Dalfursts see no reason why this family should not have had adequate savings if the Dalfursts were able to save $500 and buy a car in 8 years, with only 9 months work a year.

Mrs. Dalfurst had always replaced bedding and towels "a few at a time," and she can see no reason for people's needing help with such articles.

The Dalfursts struggled along on his earnings from odd jobs, supplemented by savings, and Mrs. Dalfurst's few dollars from sewing until Mr. Dalfurst was reemployed in March 1934. During the last year of unemployment the Dalfursts "lived so short" Mrs. Dalfurst "wants to forget about it." Now they are glad that they did not go in debt or allow insurance policies to lapse. Mr. Dalfurst regrets though that all of their savings are gone; with his present low earnings he doubts that they will ever get ahead again. Since 1934 he has worked for the Northern Sand and Gravel Company. This company owns a good-sized steamboat, a dredge, and several barges. With this employer Mr. Dalfurst is paid on a monthly basis, at the rate of $70; during the winter months equipment is renovated and the hours are reasonable, but during the busy season the men often work 16 hours a day and at times 7 days a week. If the stevedores' union "should come in, this sort of thing would be stopped." At the present time, however, the men are not organized and dare not complain about working conditions. Neither are they covered by Social Security legislation, as the work is classified as "marine service." In the case of illness, the men receive free hospitalization in the marine hospital; this, Mr. Dalfurst believes, is the only advantage, and as he is never ill he receives "no benefit."

Mr. Dalfurst was so dissatisfied with his low pay that he went to Texas last fall in an attempt to find a better job. Mrs. Dalfurst's people had written about a possibility of security work with the park board in their city. He would have got the job except for one park board member, who held out against Mr. Dalfurst because he was "an outsider." Mr. Dalfurst's em-

ployer in Dubuque had told him that his job here would be open if the Texas
prospect did not "pan out." The trip did not cost a great deal; the Dalfursts
drove their car and stayed with Mrs. Dalfurst's people. The two of them,
with the fox terrier and the pet fox, made the trip in a coupe. The Dalfursts
were surprised "to find that Texas cities had not been hard hit by the depression." They were also impressed by the lower cost of living in Texas.
They dreaded to return to Dubuque, but Mr. Dalfurst thought it best not to
take a chance on losing his old job, and there was nothing definite in sight
down there.

Mr. and Mrs. Dalfurst were considered quite "old-fashioned" by her
relatives, as neither of them appreve of women's smoking or drinking. Mr.
Dalfurst was shocked at seeing "15-year-old girls smoking cigarettes." The
Dalfursts never go to dances or beer taverns as do many of their friends.
This, they believe, is the reason they had $500 ahead to see them through
Mr. Dalfurst's unemployment. They enjoy fishing and hunting, and in warm
weather picnics with friends. Nearly every Sunday, they take "the dog, a
gun, and the fox and strike out for the country."

Mr. Dalfurst is opposed to war and would be willing to fight only
if American soil were invaded: "Wars are usually made by rich men, to be
fought by poor men." He believes that unemployment is a product of a machine
age, and there "ain't much chance of preventing it." Mr. Dalfurst blames the
Chamber of Commerce for low wages and poor working conditions in Dubuque, and he
believes that "there ain't much chance of doing anything about that either."

Mr. Dalfurst is glad to have a year-round job, but he is not satisfied with the pay. Though the Dalfursts had been accustomed to a small income,
they had always been able to lay by at least $5 a month; now they can just

make ends meet, and there is nothing but the insurance to fall back on in
case of an emergency.

Employment Chronology for Mr. Dalfurst

Until 1921   – On father's farm.

1921 – 1923   – Laborer, road construction.

1923 – Nov. 1931   – Dredging, sand and gravel company.

November 1931 – March
29, 1934   – Unemployed except for odd jobs.

March 30, 1934   –
present   Laborer, Midwestern Sand and
                          Gravel Company

RENICK

Mr. Renick	42
Mrs. Renick	40
Peggy	12
John	10
Rose	8
Anna	6
Jackie	3

Interviewing completed
February 9, 1938

The Renicks, with their five children, occupy their own four-room bungalow at the very end of a residential street in the north part of town. The bungalow is well-kept and quite attractive, though much too small for the growing family. The seven of them fill the small living room where the big stove is located. Four of the children, 12, 10, 8, and 6, attend school. The youngest is a lively towheaded boy of 3.

Joseph Renick, 42 years old, tall and muscular, makes an excellent appearance. Though his formal education did not extend beyond the eighth grade, he is well informed and highly intelligent; well poised and gracious; and exceedingly forthright in manner. He had worked for the Stevenson Phonograph and Radio Company for 2 years and then for the Key City Lumber Company from 1924 until thrown out of work by the depression in 1934. Though he had no work in private industry for nearly 2 years he was employed most of the time on emergency work projects on a nonrelief basis. Two and a half years ago he was called back to the Key City Lumber Company where he is still employed.

Monica Renick, 40 years old is short and round. Jolly and friendly, she talks freely of the family's difficulties in making ends meet on a limited budget. She makes all of the children's clothes, does her own baking, and cans from 400 to 500 quarts of garden produce every summer. Last summer she found time to paint the exterior of the house;

and she shocked some of her conservative neighbors as she climbed about on
the ladder in overalls. Mr. and Mrs. Renick did most of the work on the
house when it was built 8 years ago. Mr. Renick dug the foundation and
helped with the carpentry. Mrs. Renick did all of the inside painting and
varnishing. The home was purchased through a building and loan company for
$3,000, monthly payments amounting to $24. The Renicks owned the lot which
has a 420-foot front and a depth of 1,400 feet, providing ample garden
space.

As a youngster Mr. Renick had, for 3 years, walked 2 1/2 miles
from his mother's farm to school in Dubuque. After completing the eighth
grade, he worked on the farm until drafted for service in the army in 1918.
He had been in training camp only 5 months when the Armistice was signed.
After returning home he worked on a farm and ranch in South Dakota for 3
years. The first year he was paid $100 a month. At that time corn was
selling for $1.10 a bushel in South Dakota and cattle brought an equally
high price. As prices dropped Mr. Renick's wages were reduced accordingly;
he received only $80 the third year he worked on this ranch.

From 1922 to 1924 Mr. Renick worked at the Stevenson plant, the
last 2 years in the finishing department. He finished phonographs by hand
and was paid 80¢ an hour. The work, however, was not steady; from September
to Christmas this department was very busy, but the rest of the time the
work was somewhat uncertain, depending on orders. Though he enjoyed work
at Stevenson's, he was anxious to find a steady job, after his marriage in
1924. During a slack season at Stevenson's in 1925, he was employed by the
Key City Lumber Company where he continued to work until January 1934.
This company handles all kinds of building materials, and in the winter,

coal and coke. Mr. Renick was the last man hired, and, in consequence, the first to be let out when this company found it necessary to reduce its force. For 6 years Mr. Renick was paid at the rate of 40¢ an hour for a 60-hour week. During the last 2 years, however, he received a weekly rate of $28, and there was almost no limit to the number of hours and no pay for overtime.

Almost immediately after Mr. Renick's layoff from this job, he was placed on the lock and dam project at common labor by the public employment office. He worked on this project for 13 months, receiving 50¢ an hour for a 30-hour week. He had been unemployed only a month after his lay off from the project when the employment office placed him on a paving job which lasted 4 months. When this work was completed, Mr. Renick was unemployed for 2 months. There had been considerable illness in the family: Mrs. Renick had had an operation and had also given birth to a child; one of the children had had a tonsilectomy. Medical bills amounted to more than $200. The family also owed a grocery bill of $50, and payments to the building and loan company were several months in arrears. Fifty dollars had been borrowed on an insurance policy to apply on hospital bills. The Renicks decided they would have to ask for relief, as much as they disliked the idea. Mr. Renick had exactly 45¢ left the day he went to the relief office to make application. He was given a blank to fill out and bring back to the relief office the following day. While he and Mrs. Renick were "laboring" over this blank, Mr. Renick was called to a neighbor's telephone to be told that he should come to work at the Key City Lumber Company the next morning. After the telephone conversation, he joyfully announced to his wife, "We don't have to fill out that blank; I go back

to work tomorrow." The Renicks feel that fate was unusually kind to
them, as they both had felt so depressed over having to ask for help.

After his return to the Key City Lumber Company, Mr. Renick
was paid 50¢ an hour until the recent strike, when the rate was increased
to 55¢. He now averages $26.40, as the hours have been reduced to 48.
Most of the time he drives a truck, but at present he is working in the
yard. The work of continuously loading trucks is very heavy. He prefers
driving a truck because he is then responsible for unloading only his
own truck. The work is very dirty, especially when he handles coal.
Mrs. Renick has to wash his work clothes three or four times before they
are reasonably clean.

Since Mr. Renick's return to work the family has caught up with
some of its bills, though $100 is still owed on the medical bill.
Mr. Renick's veterans' bonus of $127 was used to make small payments to
different creditors. Now two of the children need tonsilectomies, and
Mrs. Renick needs to have her teeth pulled as she is suffering from
rheumatism. She is trying to save the cost of the plates this winter but
has not been very successful. Mr. Renick recently strained his back and
was unable to work for a week; this set them back again. The building and
loan company has been very considerate, allowing them to pay only the interest of $10 while Mr. Renick was out of work. Now they are paying $15
though they should pay $24. Mrs. Renick estimates that food costs
approximately $50 a month as all of the children eat heartily. Mrs. Renick
uses 100 pounds of flour a month for baking. School clothing for the
children is a problem, but she makes garments over many times. By dyeing
two old dresses she recently made the 12-year-old daughter a very "good-
looking" snow suit. She put in 2 days on this suit but "it looked as

good as any in the stores when it was finished." School tuition for the
four children amounts to $1.70 a month. The Sisters don't expect payment
from unemployed families, but Mr. Renick has always been very conscientious
about paying the tuition if at all possible, for he knows the school needs it

Mr. Renick blames the Chamber of Commerce for low wages in
Dubuque. "Once, he says, "while I was employed at Stevenson's, the Chamber
of Commerce tried to get the plant superintendent to lower wage rates, but
the superintendent told the Chamber of Commerce to jump in the river." The
men who sponsored the establishment of a river terminal in Dubuque were
"directly responsible for the railroad shops moving out of Dubuque." This
terminal has never employed many men. Mr. Renick also blames the Chamber
of Commerce and "a handful of employers" for the fight against unions. Some
of the older men in the manufacturing plants "will never join the union."
Mrs. Renick's father, now 75 years old, began work at the Mississippi
Milling Company when he was 16 years old and is still employed there. He
sides with the employers and would never consider joining the union.
Mr. Renick has belonged to the truck drivers' local since October. At one
time the teamsters had a good union in Dubuque, but "the treasurer ab-
sconded with the funds" and embittered many workers against organization.
The present truck drivers' union is run in a "strictly businesslike fashion,
and the treasurer is bonded. Mr. Renick believes that the unbusiness-
like nature of many of the early "wildcat" unions in Dubuque has been
responsible for some of the prejudice on the part of workers against labor
organization. Mr. Renick "would hate to see the CIO come to Dubuque," as
he believes it is "too radical." This radicalism is caused, he believes,
by "the large proportion of foreigners in the CIO."

Mr. Renick sees little difference in the present business recession and the depression of 1930, except that banks are not closing now. "The capitalists," in Mr. Renick's opinion, "are responsible for the present recession, just as they were responsible for the 1930 depression. Big business tried to run the country but made a mess of it; President Roosevelt tries to straighten out the mess and they are bucking him." Much of the recent legislation has been "fine for the working man, but the industrialists won't stand for some of the laws that cost too much; the depression will continue until the industrialists are pulled into line."

Mr. Renick believes that the Federal Government has done more than its share in respect to unemployment relief and the States should now assume more responsibility. The administration of relief, in his opinion, is particularly difficult because of the tendency of some people to misrepresent their needs. "It is very bad for people to stay on relief too long, as it is apt to make them lazy and dependent. For that matter, though, idleness makes a man develop habits of laziness."

While Mr. Renick was unemployed, he read current magazines at the public library and borrowed books to read at home. Since he has been working, however, he gets home late during the winter and never has time to go to the library; in the summer he spends all of his spare time in the garden. The Renicks are very proud of a cabinet radio, given to them recently by a relative. Mrs. Renick and the children listen to the music and stories, but Mr. Renick enjoys most the discussion of current events. Twelve-year-old Peggy plays cards with her sisters, Rose and Anna, 8 and 6, or reads them stories. The Renicks seldom go to movies except when Shirley Temple is at the 16¢ neighborhood theater. Ten-year-old John never tires

of his grandfather's stories of his boyhood in Dubuque when Indians roamed
the section of town where the Renicks now live.   Fifty years ago this part
of Dubuque was unsettled.   The grandparents have a nice home next door to
the Renicks.   Three-year-old Jackie insists on saying his prayers in the
living room by the big stove.   During a pause in his "Now I lay me down
to sleep", his mother inquires if he has finished praying.   To the family's
delight, he answers, "No, I am jus' tinking."   The Renicks are anxious to
send the children through high school, if possible, and believe they can
manage it unless Mr. Renick should again become unemployed.   The children
are well behaved though unrepressed; Mr. and Mrs. Renick seem to be very
companionable with the children, and the home life is gay and happy.

Employment Chronology for Mr. Renick

Until 1918   - On father's farm.

June 1918   -
November 1918 U. S. Army.

1919 - 1922   South Dakota ranch work.

1922 - 1925   Finishing phonograph cabinets,
                Stevenson Company.

1925 - January
1934   Truck driver and yardman, Key
                City Lumber Company.

February 1934 -
October 1935   Unemployed except for 16 months
                on emergency work projects.

October 1935 -
Present   Truck driver and yardman,
                Key City Lumber Company.

<u>HITSON</u>

Mr. Hitson   48
Mrs. Hitson   47

Interviewing completed
February 9, 1938

Mr. Hitson is a little man, scrawny and weary. His pale face
is rutted with wrinkles, and his eyelids are raw and red-rimmed, irritated
by the sawdust in the woodworking mill where he works as sanding machine
operator. He is somewhat taciturn, and speaks, when at all, in a dull-
toned voice.

What the Hitsons want now more than anything else is economic
security, but they think that they are "too old" to find any real security.
Both Mr. and Mrs. Hitson are "nearly 50." After having been unemployed
for the better part of 5 years, Mr. Hitson got a job with the Dubuque Woodworking Company about a year ago. But short hours, temporary layoffs,
wages inadequate to purchase even "the necessary things of life," and
permanent layoffs of men who are not much older than Mr. Hitson but yet are
considered by the management "too old" to work, all have contributed to
Mr. Hitson's feeling of insecurity on his present job.

The Hitsons managed through the depression years without assistance, though Mr. Hitson did work for several months on the Dubuque lock
and dam project. At first, they had thought that they would be able to
manage without any great difficulty, for "who knew it would last so long?"
Some 9 years ago when Mr. Hitson, laid off at the Dubuque railroad shops,
began work for an engineering firm, going from city to city building power
plants, the Hitsons sold their furniture. "And here we are." They are
now living in two furnished rooms, comfortable and light and airy. But

there are many disadvantages: coal for the heating stove in the bed-living room must be carried from the basement up the two flights of stairs; cooking must be done on a two-burner gas hot-plate in the make-shift kitchen. The Hitsons feel that living in furnished rooms is simply not the same as having a house of their own, but they have "no choice."

Still, they don't really mind living in furnished rooms. They explain, "all we want is a steady job and money enough to buy the necessary things of life, and that doesn't seem like much to ask." Yet, it is evidently "too much to ask." Mrs. Hitson feels that there is no longer any "security," especially for people of her age and of Mr. Hitson's. "Everything is for younger people. The depression was supposed to bring people closer together, but it has only made them hard. Everybody wants to grab what he can get—to heck with the other fellow." Mr. Hitson says disconsolately, "A fellow doesn't know what to do—you can't be sure of nothing any more."

Mrs. Hitson has thought many times, "Life isn't worth living— and it isn't, it really isn't when you can't get the necessary things of life."

The Hitsons do not want very high wages or a great deal of money, or many luxuries. Mr. Hitson wouldn't care about having a car even if he had "a million dollars," but they would like to have enough money to pay the current rent and grocery bills without worrying about how to meet the next ones, and to have the dental and medical care which they both need.

Mr. Hitson has lived almost all of his life in Dubuque. He was 1 of 10 children of a plumber's assistant, who never made very high wages; so it was necessary for Mr. Hitson to begin work when he had completed grade

school. He began work in a Dubuque woodworking mill where his earnings
were 16¢ an hour. Next, he drove a delivery wagon for a grocery store. It
was in 1908—or was it 1912? he can't be sure of dates—that he started work
in the railroad shops as one of four men on a wheel-press crew. His earliest
earnings were 16¢ an hour; his highest earnings in the shops, 65¢ an hour.

During the years he worked in the shops, he saw significant
changes in methods of production—the substitution of iron and steel for the
wood earlier used almost exclusively in the making and repairing of cars
and the displacement of men by machines. The work of pressing the wheels on
to their axles could soon be done by a crew of two men instead of four, and
the two men could now accomplish, with the aid of machinery, about twice as
much work as previously. Similar changes have taken place in all industries,
Mr. Hitson believes. Though there have been increases in rates of pay, he
believes that they have not kept up with increases in the productivity of
labor; "the factories must be getting the profits." Though he would not go
so far as to say that the introduction of labor-saving machinery has been
the sole cause of unemployment, he does consider it the main cause.

After his layoff from the railroad shops in the spring of 1928,
Mr. Hitson was unemployed for several months before he was hired by the
engineering firm, for which he did "all kinds of work"—many types of carpentry—at 75¢ an hour, a step up from his shop earnings of 65¢ an hour.
He worked for some months in Dubuque, and then he was transferred to New
Jersey, where he spent 8 months on the construction of another plant. Since
it was anticipated that the work would be permanent, though involving
frequent moves from place to place, the Hitsons sold their furniture before
leaving Dubuque. They wish now that they had not done so, but still, if

the furniture had been stored, storage charges might have been so high that
they could never have reclaimed it. Mrs. Hitson did store two boxes of
odds and ends, mostly gifts for which she had a sentimental attachment; she
reclaimed the boxes only last summer, and the storage charges were more than
the things were worth in cash.

After the couple had been in New Jersey for 8 months, Mr. Hitson
was sent to Indianapolis, where he and his wife were still living when the
engineering firm failed in 1931. In the meantime, they had transferred
their savings of about $2,000 to an Indianapolis bank from a Dubuque bank,
which, as it happened, remained open through the depression. Shortly before Mr. Hitson lost his job, he had lent $1,000 to Mrs. Hitson's brother,
who had at one time been quite well-to-do, but now feared that he would lose
his business. His business has since failed; he has had a stroke; and he
has a family of children to support. The Hitsons do not "regret" having
lent this money to the brother, nor do they regret having helped Mrs. Hitson's
sister, even though they know that none of the money can ever be repaid.

Not long after Mr. Hitson lost his job, the Indianapolis bank in
which he had most of his savings failed; not one cent was ever paid to
depositors. Thus, in 1931, Mr. Hitson was left without regular employment
and almost entirely without resources. At the same time, Mrs. Hitson's
father, living alone, was quite ill; so she went to him, while Mr. Hitson,
knowing that there was no hope of his finding other work in Indianapolis,
returned to Dubuque. Mrs. Hitson stayed with her father until his death
3 years later; then rejoined her husband in Dubuque.

The Hitsons managed by picking up what odd jobs they could and
by running bills when they couldn't possibly pay cash. They don't ask for
credit unless it is absolutely necessary—"bills are too hard to pay."

Mr. Hitson wishes that he had kept track of the number of days he worked during the 5 years of almost total unemployment; it couldn't have been many, and there were never more than 2 or 3 consecutive days of work except on the lock and dam project.

A few days as a construction worker; a few days as a cement worker; slightly more regular work, averaging perhaps 1 day a week, perhaps less, as assistant to a plumber—this is the story of Mr. Hitson's work from the spring of 1931 until July of 1934, when he was first placed through the State employment office on the locks project. He worked on this job until November of the same year as a carpenter, earning 80¢ an hour. The difference in his rate of pay and that of the carpenters earning $1.20 an hour was that he did not furnish his own tools. Mr. Hitson was unemployed from November 1934 until almost a year later, when he was again assigned, likewise on a nonrelief basis, to work on the dam.

Both Mr. and Mrs. Hitson worked at whatever odd jobs they could find to do. They weren't "particular" as to the type of job; Mrs. Hitson recalls one occasion when Mr. Hitson worked all day and all night shoveling snow from railroad tracks, and came home, after 24 hours of work outdoors in very cold weather, with the perspiration frozen through shirt and overcoat. Mrs. Hitson clerked occasionally as an extra in a department store, but her earnings were neither high nor regular. The Hitsons laugh at the idea of making any estimate of expenditures during depression years; all they know is that they lived on as little as possible—less than many others would have thought absolutely necessary. They asked for credit as they had to, and paid up most of their bills as they went along, and as Mr. Hitson got bits of work.

The Hitsons never really considered applying for relief, though they knew many persons in no worse circumstances than theirs who did get assistance, and many persons who thought them "foolish" for not making application for relief. Mr. Hitson is rather less critical of the relief setup than is Mrs. Hitson, who believes that there was some "graft" and unsound discrimination in the administration of relief. Mrs. Hitson feels, too, that persons on relief have had many things which nonreliefers have not had; for example, she knows of families who have had extensive dental and medical care, such as the Hitsons have not been able to afford even now that Mr. Hitson's work is fairly regular.

Mr. Hitson, on the other hand, feels that relief clients haven't had such an easy time of it; certainly he would have "hated standing in line down at the relief office, and eating the canned beef" that was distributed to relief clients. Accepting relief would seem like "begging" or "panhand-ling" to Mr. Hitson, and Mrs. Hitson couldn't ever have "felt right about it." Mr. Hitson believes that it becomes easier and easier for a man to depend on relief grants alone, just as it becomes easier and easier for a street-corner beggar to ask for money. Mr. Hitson says, "Of course, people can't be left to starve, and relief has been necessary, but I think that it would have been better to put everyone to work."

Mr. Hitson's age, his nonrelief status, and his "lack of political pull," as he says, "were all against me when I tried to find work." He believes that the State employment office has been more anxious to place relief clients, and thus reduce relief rolls, than to find jobs for others, though the employment office was to some extent instrumental in having him placed at the Dubuque Woodworking Company. His application had been hanging fire for more than 2 years before he was finally taken on about a year ago.

Several times he was called to the plant without being given a job; the employment office men told him that the company hesitated to hire a man "so old."

Finally, he was called in and asked to operate a sanding machine under the direction of an old employee until he had learned the job. He learned to operate the machine effectively in less than half a day and was given the job. Not long afterwards, the man under whom he had first worked was discharged. Mr. Hitson feels that he displaced this man, still capable of handling the job, and that within a few more years he in turn, regardless of his ability or physical strength, will be replaced by a younger man.

In the meantime, Mr. Hitson is earning too little to be able to save anything or even to have a reasonable degree of "security." Theoretically he works an 8-hour day, at 40¢ an hour, plus a bonus which amounts to very little. He hasn't been able to find out just how the bonus is figured, except that it is based on the amount of work accomplished by the department rather than by the individual; frequently there are "deductions" which remain unexplained. He has had bonuses of as little as 0.2 of 1 percent; his highest bonus payment was 4¢ on the dollar.

Mr. Hitson has always accomplished more than the set task, and has sometimes done as much as "12 hours' work" in the 8-hour day. But he receives neither pay nor credit for this extra work. When the time comes for him to be laid off because of age, he believes that the management will take no accounts of how much he may still be able to accomplish in an hour or a day. He has seen older men laid off for no reason, or for "inadequate reasons," too many times not to know what is in store for him.

The woodworking company, like other Dubuque factories, is "hard on the unions," which it tries to "break" in any way possible. Dubuque has never been "a union town." Recently, the NRA and the "Wagner bill" have given impetus to organization and some protection to the unions, but the factory unions are still not very strong. Mr. Hitson has been a union man all of his working life: he belonged first to the carmen's union, and is now a member of the millworkers' union, affiliated with the AFL, which Mr. Hitson favors over the CIO, for there is "such a thing as going too far." Members of the CIO unions he considers "labor agitators"; the predominance of "foreigners" in the CIO accounts for its "radicalism."

The irregularity of Mr. Hitson's work has added to his feeling of insecurity and to the family's difficulty in managing. From September to December 1937 he worked only 3 days a week and earned from $9 to $10. During the December inventory-taking, he was out altogether for several weeks. As it happened, during this time Mrs. Hitson had 2 weeks of work in a Dubuque department store at $11.50 a week. Though her "sales were better than those of many of the younger clerks," she knew that there was no chance of her being given regular work "at her age."

Mrs. Hitson has had various other small jobs since Mr. Hitson began work for the woodworking company. Last fall, she kept a 4-year old boy during the day for 3 weeks. She went for him in the morning and brought him home with her, gave him his lunch, and took him to his home again in the late afternoon. For the 3 weeks she was paid $5. Mrs. Hitson wishes she could get a job, "at anything at all," but she, like Mr. Hitson, is "too old" to find jobs readily.

Since the first week in January, he has been working regularly 5 days a week, but he does not know when he may be put on short hours or

laid off altogether. He does not mind his work though the job is extremely
monotonous. Mrs. Hitson thinks that his ill-health may be due partly to
the nervous tension under which he works.

Mr. Hitson believes that there must be wage and hour legislation to spread employment and to raise wages. He could manage to live on
$18 a week fairly comfortably but not on $14 or $15 when $20 a month must
go for rent. Hourly wage-rates he considers less important than total
wages; what he would really like to see is legislation guaranteeing an
"annual living wage," but he thinks that this will probably come only far
in the future. Though he expresses mild approval of the Social Security
Act, he says that he is more concerned about what will happen to him between the ages of 50 and 65 than about how he will manage after he is 65.

Mr. Hitson believes that America will inevitably be involved
in war with Japan, though perhaps not very soon, for Japan will not be content with "conquering China and the Philippines." He would be willing
"to let Japan have the Philippines" but not to let her invade the United
States. He himself had enough of fighting while he served overseas in the
World War. He thinks that the United States will not again declare war
except in the event of threatened invasion. While he was unemployed,
Mr. Hitson received two soldiers' bonuses, but he called them "creditors'
bonuses" rather than "soldiers' bonuses," for they were owed before they
were received, and he immediately paid them on debts.

He sees little hope for any immediate improvement in the industrial situation in Dubuque, but assumes that Dubuque is no worse off
than many other cities. In Mr. Hitson's opinion, one reason for Mrs. Hitson's not liking Dubuque is that she hasn't had money to spend for recreation

during the past several years. Mrs. Hitson insists that she would not
mind staying at home day after day, and night after night, if she had money
enough to live comfortably, and some certainty of the future. She reads a
great deal—"too much perhaps"—and always has on hand a great stack of
books from the public library, Mrs. Hitson says, "I don't know what people
would have done during the depression without the free libraries." Reading at least gives the Hitsons some way of spending their free time and
something to think about, aside from their insecurity and their many un-
certainties.

Employment Chronology for Mr. Hitson

Before 1912	— Millworker, woodworking company Driver of delivery wagon, grocery store.
1912 (?) — Spring 1928	— Wheel press crewman, railroad shops.
Fall 1928 — Spring 1931	— Carpenter, engineering firm.
Spring 1931 — January 1937	— Unemployed, except for emergency work.
January 1937 — present	— Sanding machine operator, Dubuque Woodworking Company.

<u>GIEST</u>

Mr. Giest   49
Mrs. Giest   43
Alice   24

Interviewing completed
January 18, 1938

     Mr. Giest, at 49 years of age, might easily pass for 40. He is
tall and well-built. His red wavy hair is only slightly gray, and his face
has few lines. Cordial and spontaneous, he talks intelligently and objectively of his work and depression experiences. The family is outstanding for its thrift and general stability, but Mr. Giest speaks modestly
of his savings, investments, and ability to find work. Mr. Giest, a
mechanic for 32 years, earning on an average of $30 a week, had $3,000 in
savings and owned his home, clear of indebtedness, when the Stevenson plant
closed the latter part of 1931. He had worked at Stevenson's for 15 years.
During the 9 months that he was unemployed, he used only $900 of his savings,
though a daughter, the only child, was kept in college during this time.
Having been steadily employed for the past 5 years, Mr. Giest finds it
difficult to understand why so many men are still unemployed. He is also
appalled at the number of Stevenson workers who went on relief a few months
after the factory closed, though they had earned higher wages than he.
These men bought expensive cars and "lived high" when Mr. Giest drove a
10-year-old car and didn't even have a telephone. Now Mr. Giest feels that
it is somewhat ironical that they should expect the public to take care of
them. He is sympathetic, however, toward families who are in need through
no fault of their own.

     Mrs. Giest, a very pretty woman in her early forties, is highly
intelligent, but somewhat brusque in manner and not as friendly or hospitable
as her husband. She is also less tolerant of all people on relief than

is her husband.   Alice, the 24-year-old daughter, who was graduated from
college 2 years ago is now a teacher.

The Giests own half of a double two-story frame house in a better
type working-class neighborhood.   The house was originally owned by two
uncles of Mrs. Giest.   The Giests purchased their half of the house thinking that the other half would stay in the family, but a real estate company
now owns it; this half of the property is not kept in good condition.   The
contrast between Mr. Giest's half, painted and in excellent repair, and the
unpainted half owned by the real estate company gives the building a somewhat grotesque appearance.   At the rear of his home Mr. Giest has built
a bird bath and rose arbors.   He owns the large adjoining lot and "expects
some day to make money on it."   The interior of the home is beautifully
furnished with new furniture, rugs, and a few good antiques.

Mr. Giest, of German parentage, was born in Dubuque.   The grandfather brought his family to the United States just 6 months before Mr.
Giest's father would have been drafted for compulsory military service.
Mr. Giest's grandfather and his father were skilled mechanics; the father
was an expert carriage maker for many years.

After Mr. Giest was graduated from high school at the age of 17,
he began his apprenticeship as a mechanic in a small factory no longer in
existence.   After 4 years with this firm he worked for 4 years at the
Iowa Foundry before he decided to see something of the country.   At that
time, there was a scarcity of mechanics on a big construction job in the
South.   Mr. Giest went south, and worked in Alabama, Mississippi, and
Texas; he returned to Dubuque at the end of a year.   The trip had been
profitable as well as educational, as he had not been idle except while

traveling from one point to another. After working on a job in Mississippi for a few weeks without pay he decided he might get "gypped," so he moved on to a job in another town. When the employer had asked where he should send Mr. Giest's pay check, Mr. Giest gave his mother's address in Dubuque, thinking that the employer was just stalling. However, when he reached home some time later he was surprised to find a check for $130.

After returning to Dubuque, Mr. Giest worked at the railroad shops for about 3 years, overhauling engines. In 1916 he was hired in the maintenance department at the Stevenson Company, where he worked for the next 15 years at installing and repairing machinery and at setting up all sorts of machine work until the close of the plant in 1931. During the last 5 or 6 years at Stevenson's, Mr. Giest was also chauffeur for one of the "bosses" after regular factory hours. For this work he was paid his regular factory rate of 60¢ an hour, but usually received tips in addition to his pay. One month he drew $316, but he had worked almost day and night. He usually averaged no more than $30 or $35 a week. At one time, Stevenson men earned as much as $16 a day on piece work, though $12 was supposed to be the limit. The foreman and even some of the polishers lived at the best hotel, "spending their high earnings lavishly." A few months after the plant closed, Mr. Giest was driving by the rock quarry one day and saw a former Stevenson gang foreman working on the rock pile, one of the first relief projects in Dubuque. Mr. Giest says, "At first I couldn't believe my eyes; the very thought of this man being on relief made me sick."

Though he had never earned high wages, he and his wife had saved systematically. After the home had been paid for in 1919, they invested $20 a month in the building and loan association for several years until they had $2,000 by 1927. At that time a friend suggested that the Giests invest in public utilities stock. A few hundred dollars of building and loan savings were invested in this stock, some of which was sold at nearly 100 percent profit in 1929. Until 1929 Mr. Giest had driven his 10-year-old car and had had a telephone for only a year or so, and then only because he often received night calls from the mill. His first thought had always been "to lay something by for a rainy day," before spending money for nonessentials. He had never even considered marriage until he had $600 in the bank. In 1929, however, the family was quite prosperous; his home and an extra lot were owned clear; he had savings amounting to several thousand dollars and a steady income from his job. A new car was purchased, and, in 1930, a cabinet radio which retailed at $159; Mr. Giest, however, got a discount of 20 percent through the factory. In 1931 the daughter was sent to college. When the Stevenson Company closed the latter part of 1931, the Giests considered taking the daughter out of college, as Mr. Giest had no idea how long he would be unemployed. It was decided, however, that the parents would practice very strict economy at home and allow Alice to continue in college. Now they consider this a wise decision as Alice has a very good teaching position. During the 9 months Mr. Giest was unemployed, he and Mrs. Giest lived very frugally.

In October 1932 he was employed by the Billings Company, where he has worked to the present time. This company contracts for all types of machinery repair and overhauling. Mr. Giest is paid at the rate of 60¢ an hour, but receives pay only for the time he actually works. For 2 or 3 weeks since he started this job he has received as little as $8, but he usually earns from $30 to $35 a week and has earned as much as $45 for especially busy weeks. The Billings Company had the contract for over-

hauling the machinery at a brewery after beer was legalized. The machinery
in this brewery had been idle for 16 years; Mr. Giest, with several other
men, worked at this job for more than a year. The Billings Company has
also had much of the repair work for the local lock and dam machinery.
Though Mr. Giest has had offers of other jobs since he has been working for
his present employer, he has not considered making a change, because he
likes the variety of the work he is now doing. Then, too, the work is
mostly highly skilled. Mr. Giest apologizes for his appearance in his
work clothes. He usually waits until after 7 to change, because the shop
frequently calls him back for evening work.

Last year the Giests celebrated their 25th wedding anniversary
by investing in new living room and dining room furniture and rugs. These
furnishings cost $350, but they would have cost much more had not the
Giests paid cash. Mr. Giest wants the home to be attractive so that
"Alice won't be ashamed to entertain her friends at home." The Giests'
home in fact is "sort of an open house for Alice's crowd." Alice presented her parents with a very nice occasional chair as an anniversary
gift. Mr. Giest is very proud of an antique table, chair, and what-
not which belonged to his grandfather.

Mr. Giest continues to save at least $20 a month out of his
earnings. He is heartily in favor of the Social Security program, and he
figures that he will accumulate a sizable old age annuity before he reaches
the age of 65. Mr. Giest disagrees with a railroad neighbor who thinks
railroad men should receive a retirement pension of at least $125 a month
in order to get along; he argues that any man and his wife should live
comfortably on $75 a month.

Relief puzzles Mr. Giest somewhat. He knows there are a lot of
needy people who must be helped, but he also feels that relief offers
"an easy way of living for shiftless people." The people who occupy the
other half of the house are on relief. These people do not take care of
their part of the yard; this is a source of irritation for the Giests.
Mrs. Giest, much more caustic in her criticism than Mr. Giest, doubts if
many people have been made wiser by their depression experiences. She thinks
that most working class people will begin buying new cars and radios on the
installment plan just as soon as they get back to work.

Regardless of whether the responsibility for relief is assumed by
the Federal, State, or county governments, Mr. Giest knows that "the tax-
payers must pay the bills." He says, "Low wages paid in some of the Dubuque
factories make it impossible for men with big families to save anything for
an emergency;" in consequence, they are dependent on relief as soon as they
are laid off from a job. He doubts that the unions will be able to accomplish
much in Dubuque, as "the management of the biggest concerns are so set
against collective bargaining." Mr. Giest was a member of the mechanics'
union for over 15 years, having joined when he began work at the railroad
shops. He allowed his membership to lapse a year or two before the Stevenson
plant closed because the local union had become quite inactive. While
Mr. Giest does not believe that "the Chamber of Commerce has done as much
for Dubuque as its publicity would have you believe," he is a bit skeptical
of the rumors to the effect that they have brought pressure to keep certain
industries out. He has been told that there is a very good chance that a
large manufacturing concern will locate in Dubuque and occupy some of the
old Stevenson buildings.

Mr. Giest feels that business in general is greatly improved,
and he is not concerned about the talk of "a new depression." Even if
there is a new depression, he has no fears; he has weathered this depression, and he expects to be in a still better position to meet a second
one, should it come.

Employment Chronology for Mr. Giest

1904 – 1908	Apprentice mechanic.
1908 – 1912	Mechanic, Iowa Foundry.
1912 – 1913	Mechanic, construction jobs.
1913 – 1916	Mechanic, railroad shops.
1916 – Nov. 1931	Mechanic, Stevenson Company.
December 1931 September 1932	Unemployed.
October 1932 present	Mechanic, Billings Company.

<pre>
Mr. Hausmet   52
Mrs. Hausmet   45
Emil   20
</pre>

Interviewing completed
March 22, 1938

Mr. Hausmet had never done factory work until he came from Germany
to Dubuque 14 years ago in search of greater economic security for his wife
and son. He had been employed for 8 years as a sales representative in
Germany. After he had worked for nearly 8 years at the Dubuque Woodworking
Company he quit in 1930, when the piecework system was discontinued, to take
a job at the Stevenson Company. He had worked there for only 1 year when
the plant closed. Though Mr. Hausmet was unemployed for the next 4 years,
until his reemployment at the Dubuque Woodworking Company in March 1935,
the Hausmet family of three managed to eke out a living by baking and selling
coffee cakes. The family has had no assistance of any kind, and it has never
run into debt except for their passage to America. This ability to manage
in the face of hardship is thus explained: "We are German people; we are
accustomed to taking care of ourselves." The Hausmets are appalled at the
willingness of so many Americans to depend on the Government for support.

The Hausmets with their 20-year-old-son, Emil, occupy the upstairs
rooms of a house once the home of a prosperous Dubuque family. The building,
located at the foot of a wooded hill in a sparsely settled residential neighborhood in the north end, is surrounded by a spacious, well-shaded lawn.
Though the house is old, it is in good repair. The Hausmets pay only $15
a month for their four rooms, but have the responsibility for keeping them
papered and painted. They have occupied this home for most of the time since

their arrival in Dubuque 14 years ago.

Mr. Hausmet is 52 years old, though he looks much younger. Of medium build, he is neat and well groomed. His appearance and manner are those of the professional or white-collar worker. Though he knew no English at the time of his arrival in this country, he now speaks correct and fluent English with very little German accent. He discusses his experiences frankly and spontaneously, but with no show of emotion. His 4 years in the World War (2 years of which were spent in front-line German trenches) the postwar hardships in Germany, his depression experiences in America, and the family's present struggle to make ends meet are described matter-of-factly and with a certain detachment. Though he would like a "better position," he is making the best of his present situation; he considers life "too short to spend much time worrying about the morrow."

Mrs. Hausmet, a fiery-tempered, black-eyed woman in her early forties, is of slight build. She openly rebukes Mr. Hausmet for his calm acceptance of his situation. She seems to resent his ability to sleep 9 hours, and his enjoyment of his pipe and the evening paper. Mrs. Hausmet, highly nervous, sleeps little, and apparently feels that she works much harder than Mr. Hausmet. In fact, she is somewhat scornful of his work in the facto He is apparently undisturbed by her criticisms; he explains that she is not very well, and that the hardships of many years perhaps have had their effect Five days after her marriage to Mr. Hausmet in 1914, he was called into the Army, and she scarcely saw him again for 4 years; the postwar period in Germany had also been difficult. Though the predepression years in America had been fairly prosperous, Mrs. Hausmet had missed her family and found the adjustment difficult; now the insecurity of Mr. Hausmet's work and the low income place an additional strain on her.

Both Mr. and Mrs. Hausmet take pride in their son Emil, who they hope will become a professor upon the completion of his college work. Emil has never had any marks but A's on his report cards since he learned English in a Dubuque kindergarten. Last year he won a full fellowship at a junior college; he is now earning his expenses by assisting two professors with German translations of certain published materials. Emil is a tall, fair lad with considerable personality. Though he is proud of his German heritage he never wants to live in Germany again.

After Mr. Hausmet left school at 17, he worked as an office boy for a newspaper for 3 years. As he desired to improve his education through travel before serving the required 3 years in the Army, he went to South America where he was employed as a clerk in a store for 1 year. This gave him an opportunity to learn Spanish, which he thought would be an advantage in securing a better job. After returning to Germany and serving 3 years in the Army, he got a job as sales representative for office machines in eastern Europe, Turkey, Greece, and Syria. He had worked successfully at this job for 4 years when he was called for service soon after war was declared in 1914. He fought in the front-line trenches for the next 2 years and until he was wounded and sent to a hospital for 5 months. For the remainder of the war he was in the quartermaster corps. The war to Mr. Hausmet was "a job to be done efficiently." As to the horrors of warfare he is absolutely calloused.

At the close of the war Mr. Hausmet was reemployed by the concern for which he had worked prior to the war, but the job was unprofitable. With the fall of the German mark, business became demoralized and the Hausmets were on the verge of starvation when Mr. Hausmet's uncle sent money for the

family's passage to America in 1923. For a few months after their arrival
they had lived with this uncle on a farm near Dubuque. Though Mr. Hausmet
knew not one word of English, he was employed by the Dubuque Woodworking
Company 2 days after his arrival in Dubuque. He had no difficulties as
the foreman and many of the workmen spoke German. Both Mr. and Mrs. Hausmet
attended English classes at night school, and Mr. Hausmet had no difficulty
in getting his citizenship papers. After having worked in the packing room
at the mill for 3 years he was put on a machine. His entrance rate was 25¢
an hour, but after he was placed on a piecework basis operating a machine,
he earned from $4 to $5 a day. When the bonus system was introduced early
in 1930, and piecework was discontinued, Mr. Hausmet quit to take a job at
the Stevenson plant. Here he earned from $4 to $5 a day operating a machine
on a piecework basis. He had worked only a year, however, when the plant clo

For the next 4 years, until March 1935 when he was hired at the
woodworking mill, Mr. Hausmet was unemployed except for peddling the coffee
cakes baked by his wife. The Hausmets made a profit of 6¢ on each coffee cal
and sold from 200 to 250 cakes a week. The baking was done on an ordinary
cook stove. Mrs. Hausmet worked almost night and day, and Mr. Hausmet never
stopped his peddling until the last cake had been sold. He considers himself
a good salesman, and he believes that his careful routing and utilization of
sales methods contributed to the success of the enterprise.

Though the coffee cake venture was successful, Mr. Hausmet was
anxious to get a regular job, as he felt that the baking was too hard on
his wife. He had kept his registration active at the State employment offic
and made frequent visits to the factories. When he was finally reemployed
at the Dubuque Woodworking Mill 3 years ago he was paid only 30¢ an hour;

having been granted several raises, he now receives 45¢ an hour but works only 35 hours a week. Mr. Hausmet considers his present income inadequate to meet the family's needs. Though Emil is earning his tuition and board at college, Mr. Hausmet has had to buy Emil's clothing and help some with books and incidental expenses. Mr. and Mrs. Hausmet have bought no new clothing for themselves during the past 7 years, so they now need many things. The family had had no savings at the time Mr. Hausmet became unemployed, because the uncle's loan had been repaid. Since returning to work Mr. Hausmet has been unable to save anything from his earnings.

During the Christmas layoff at the mill he joined a publishing house crew and canvassed rural Illinois and Iowa. On this job he averaged $15 a week but had some expense for the upkeep of his car. Although he earned little, he liked the work, for he enjoyed talking with farmers. Most of the time subscriptions to publications were paid for in part with poultry or farm produce. "A 5-pound hen would just about pay for 1 year's subscription" to a weekly magazine. Mr. Hausmet usually had his car loaded with chickens, eggs, and vegetables, which he traded at the nearest market for cash. Mr. Hausmet feels that the farmers in Iowa and Illinois are quite prosperous, though they usually complain of hard times. It is difficult for him to understand the extensive Government aid to farmers. To him it is "unbelievable" that farmers should be paid for not planting certain crops. "The worst thing the American Government has done" in Mr. Hausmet's opinion "was the giving of direct relief." The Works Program he considers a fine thing. "But," he continues, "the giving of food with nothing in return is unbelievably stupid. As a result many families have come to look to the Government for the living."

Mr. Hausmet is none too well satisfied with his present job at the mill; though he has been put back on a piecework basis, it is impossible to raise his earnings substantially no matter how hard he works. "The more you produce, the more they require of you." On a piecework basis the men are not paid for the time lost when a machine breaks down or for time spent in collecting materials from the stock rooms. Mr. Hausmet has little confidence in the union as a means of improving working conditions. After his return to work in 1935, he joined the millworkers' union, but he dropped his membership after attending one union meeting. He disapproved of the way the meeting was conducted, especially the committees' decision "to call a strike without first giving the members a chance to express themselves." After 4 years of unemployment Mr. Hausmet was "against a strike." Then, too, the way some of the officers "walked around importantly, smoking cigars" irritated Mr. Hausmet. He felt that they would do nothing for "a poor man out on strike." He refused to pay dues after the first month.

Mr. Hausmet blames machinery, the speeding-up system, and the low purchasing power of workers for widespread unemployment. "If the working man had more money to spend, business in general would be improved. On the other hand," he added, "people who have money are holding on to it; they are afraid of the future."

The Hausmets express a somewhat strong nationalistic feeling; they admire Hitler and believe that people in Germany are at least as well off economically as people in America. Had it not been for Emil's attitude, the Hausmets probably would have considered returning to Germany, even though Mr. Hausmet had become a naturalized American citizen. The Hausmets were shocked to find so many poor people in this country; they had thought "all Americans were rich." In Germany people would not be allowed to live in "filthy hovels" such as Mr. Hausmet has seen in this country. They approve of Hitler's annexation of Austria and believe that the Austrian people will now have greater economic security.

Mr. Hausmet feels that he is handicapped by not having a trade; he is too old to try to change his employment now. Though he derives no great pleasure from his work as a factory hand, he is well content to make the best of it. He only hopes that conditions will improve to the extent that he can earn enough to meet his family's needs more adequately.

Employment Chronology for Mr. Hausmet

1903 - 1906	Office boy.
1906 - 1907	Sales clerk.
1907 - 1910	German Army.
1910 - 1914	Sales representative of office machines.
1914 - 1918	German army.
1919 - 1923	Sales representative of office machines.
1923 - 1930	Machine operator, Dubuque Woodworking Company.
1930 - 1931	Machine operator, Stevenson Phonograph and Radio Company.
1931 - 1935	Peddled coffee cakes.
1935 - present	Machine operator, Dubuque Woodworking Company.

<u>HAENER</u>

<u>At home</u>

Mr. Haener	65
Mrs. Haener	62
Foster	27
Mary	25
Rita	23
Harry	21
Bob	19
Frank	16
Viola	14

<u>Married and out of the home</u>

Jim	31
Florence	29

Interviewing completed
February 24, 1938

     Though Mr. Haener is approaching his 65th year, he has found his age no handicap in the carpentry trade; he expects to continue work for at least 8 or 10 years. In his own words, "Some men are old at 50 and others are young at 80." A carpenter for more than 50 years and employed by the same Dubuque contractor for 20 years, Mr. Haener, though unemployed for the better part of 4 years during the depression, managed on savings and odd jobs to take care of his family of nine without any outside assistance. No member of his family has ever been on direct relief or emergency work.

     Mr. Haener's grandparents, of mixed German and French stock, emigrated to America from Alsace-Lorraine soon after their marriage. They settled in Dubuque where Mr. Haener's father was born just 100 years ago this month. Mr. Haener, senior, lived to be 95, and Charles Haener thinks that he "will live just as long."

Mr. Haener is a man of unusual charm and intelligence. Though educated haphazardly in country schools "where there were no grades, and no one ever graduated," he is able to discuss almost any general topic with spontaneity and understanding. Though he speaks with a slight German accent and occasionally uses the German word order in the phrasing of sentences, his vocabulary is exceptionally good; he vivaciously expresses opinions without reserve and with little show of prejudice. He is of medium stature; his complexion, eyes, and hair are dark. His hair, worn longer on one side than on the other, is brushed so that the bald spot on top of his head is almost completely covered; his black mustache is slightly graying.

Both Mr. and Mrs. Haener are greatly concerned about their two unemployed sons: Bob, 19, never employed since his graduation from high school a year ago, and Harry, 21, employed for a year after graduation at the Dubuque Woodworking Company, but unemployed since last July. The Haeners have nine children, seven of whom are living at home. Viola, the youngest, is in the eighth grade, and Frank, 16, is a sophomore in high school. The three who are now working—Mary, employed at a "dime store"; Rita, clerking in a furniture store; and Foster, working at the Mississippi Milling Company—were all unemployed and dependent on their father during at least 3 years of the depression. A married son is the manager of a chain store in Chicago, and a married daughter lives in the north end of Dubuque.

The Haeners' large two-story brick house is located in a residential neighborhood on the fringe of the north-end commercial district. The home, bought in 1907 with money Mr. Haener had saved from 8 years of contracting, has never been mortgaged. The living room and dining room are comfortably furnished with the type of heavy furniture in vogue 20 or 30 years ago. The top of the player piano and the living room walls are adorned with photographs of the children and grandchildren; among them are baptismal, graduation, and wedding photographs of the children, and likenesses of the several grand-children.

Viola and Frank prepare their lessons at the huge round dining table where Foster reads the paper and Mrs. Haener darns socks. Rita, attractively and fashionably dressed, goes to the movie with her boy friend; and Mary hurries off to night school where she is studying stenography. Mr. Haener is glad that his children have had educational advantages; seven were graduated from high school, and the two still in school will at least complete the high school course and perhaps go to college.

Mr. Haener, born on a farm near Dubuque, decided when he was 14, that he wanted to be a carpenter; he applied to a contractor who was build-ing a barn in the neighborhood; he was put to work and was paid 75¢ a day. Since that time he "has stuck" to carpentry. For several years he worked with the contractor who gave him his first job; then he contracted for him-self for 8 years. He moved to Dubuque in 1906. From 1910 to 1930 Mr. Haener worked for one contractor and was usually paid at a higher rate than the union scale of $1 an hour. This contractor planned jobs so that the men worked almost the year around, except for time lost during inclement weather. The men were always paid for legal holidays whether they worked or not. Mr. Haener's annual earnings average from $2,000 to $2,200. He remembers filling out an income tax blank at the Post Office once several years ago, while all nine children were at home. A rather "cocky" official was sure that Mr. Haener would have to pay the Government a tax until he remembered to ask the number of dependents. When Mr. Haener answered "nine children and a wife,"

the official disgustedly threw the income tax blank in the wastepaper
basket.

After having used all of his savings to purchase the home in
1907, Mr. Haener again had savings amounting to $3,000 by 1917. At that
time South Dakota land was considered a good investment; so he invested
the $3,000 in a quarter section. Within a few years he could have sold
this land for $6,000, but held on to it thinking that the price would go
even higher. Now he realizes from it only $100 or so a year above the taxes,
but as he says, "At least I still have it." He philosophically reasons that
had he sold the land he would probably have lost the money in a bank failure.

Mr. Haener had had steady work up to 1930. During 1930 and 1931,
however, his earnings were cut in half, and from 1932 to 1936, he earned no
more than $400 a year. In 1930 he had $2,000 in savings available to draw
on. About $500 was tied up in a closed bank and another $1,500 was loaned
out on mortgages. From 1931 to 1935 no other members of the family were
working. Foster had been an assistant manager of a dime store in another
city, but not finding the work to his liking, had returned to Dubuque in
1927, and had worked at the Stevenson Company until it closed in 1931. He
was at home, unemployed, until the summer of 1935, when he was hired at the
Mississippi Milling Company. Mary and Rita were graduated from high school
in 1933, but they found no work until a year ago. The other children were
still attending school.

For 9 or 10 months for each of 4 years Mr. Haener had no work;
frequently during this time he became a little frightened when he realized
that there were nine people depending on him. The $2,000 he knew would not
last forever; he did not want to call in his loans as the interest had been
paid up, and he knew it would be practically impossible for his debtors to

raise the cash to cover the loans at that time. Strict economy was prac-
ticed by all members of the household; money was spent only for necessities. Mr. Haener feels, however, that there was little change during
this time in the family's plane of living in respect to food, as the family had always lived economically; each summer, garden produce was canned;
potatoes to last through the season were bought from a farmer, and a pig was
usually butchered as soon as the weather was sufficiently cold. Food costs
were low during these depression years, and the fact that no lunch pails
had to be packed also helped to keep down expenses. While this seems like
a small item, Mr. Haener feels that over a long period of time it would make
quite a difference, as a more expensive type of food is usually required for
a lunch box. Then, too, when men work they naturally eat more. There is
no doubt in Mr. Haener's mind that his wife's thrift and careful management
through all the years of their married life had made it possible for the
family to save money.

While Mr. Haener was unemployed, it never occurred to him to try to
get on any of the emergency work projects, though he had friends who worked
steadily for a year or more at "good wages" on the lock and dam project.
Mr. Haener had found a contractor who had a few small jobs throughout the
depression years; this contractor for whom he now works always used Mr.
Haener when there was work to be had. During 1936 he worked 50 percent
of the time, and since the beginning of 1937 his work has been fairly steady.

Had it not been for their savings, Mr. Haener knows that he would
have had to seek help between 1932 and 1936. He knows, too, that a great
many families were desperate and had to have assistance, and "it was only
right" that relief was made available to them. On the other hand, the

Works Program, in his opinion, has been "too much of a drag on the Government." He has known men who refused to leave WPA projects to take carpentry jobs in private industry, because they feared they could not get back on WPA when the carpentry jobs were completed. Mr. Haener feels that they should have been willing to take the risk. "Those Civil Service Camps (CCC camps) for the boys were very much worth-while," in Mr. Haener's opinion. He wouldn't mind having his two unemployed sons spend some time in a camp, as it would keep them from developing bad habits through too much idleness, but he knows that his sons would not be eligible for admission to camp because of the combined family income. Mr. Haener says that he is sorry for the youngsters who are not given a chance to "prove their worth"; he feels that the inexperienced youth is at an even greater disadvantage than the man in his sixties, as the young man has few contacts on which to capitalize."

"I didn't think much of those Supreme Court justices," says Mr. Haener, "for stopping the NRA, one of the finest pieces of legislation ever passed." While he gladly contributes 2 percent of his pay check to the Social Security fund, he doubts if it will benefit him personally. He seems to fear that it may even work against his plan to continue working after he is 65. Should he retire at 65, he estimates that he would draw no more than $10 a month, "and I·couldn't support my family on that."

Mr. Haener has been a union man for years and deplores the split in the labor movement. "The CIO is a bit too radical, but Green," he feels, "has been too easy-going." Mr. Haener is anxious to see the wage and hour bill passed in a form that will "satisfy those Supreme Court justices." He feels that economic conditions have greatly improved during the past 2

years, and that "these improvements will continue if big business will only
cooperate with the government." Mr. Haener hopes that America will not
become involved in another war, as it would help no one, except perhaps
"a few business men." At least three of his sons would be subject to service and he would hate to see them go to war. Mr. Haener fears that Hitler's
tactics will inevitably involve Europe in warfare. "Hitler, there is a man
I cannot care for--God he must think he is."

"The Chamber of Commerce is responsible for unemployment and poor
working conditions in Dubuque," in Mr. Haener's opinion. "No attempt has
been made to bring in industries to employ the men thrown out of work when
the railroad shops and the Stevenson plant closed."

Mr. Haener is not particularly worried about his own future, as
he knows he will have employment if there is any carpentry work to be had.
He knows, in fact, that he was kept busier than most Dubuque carpenters
throughout the depression. His chief concern is for his young sons, whom
he desires to see get ahead; he would like to teach one son the carpentry
trade, but union rules do not permit a contractor to have more than one apprentice, and Mr. Haener's employer already has one man learning the trade.
Mr. Haener approves of this method of limiting the number of new men in the
trade, as he believes that a great many carpenters are out of work now,
though most of them were busy during the summer months. The recent housing
legislation should mean a great deal to Dubuque, Mr. Haener believes; not
only the building trades but also the woodworking mills should benefit
materially from this program.

Employment Chronology for Mr. Haener

<u>1886 - present   -   carpenter.</u>

1898 - 1906   contract carpenter.

1910 - 1930   Star Contracting Company.

1930 - 1931   Worked 50 percent of the time.

1931 - 1935   Worked 3 months a year.

1936   Worked 50 percent of the time.

1937 - present Worked full time.

<u>FLUGEL</u>

<u>At home</u>

Mr. Flugel	65
Mrs. Flugel	63
Mary	27
John	26
Geraldine	23
Caroline	21
Paul	12

<u>Away from home</u>

Jeannette	18
Dorothy	29
Ellen	32
Lawrence	35

Interviewing completed
February 15, 1938

Mr. Flugel, a skilled carpenter, was unemployed from the time of
the Stevenson closing in 1931 until about 2 years ago, except for odd jobs
of carpentry. He has worked for about 8 months of each of the past 2 years
as a cemetery laborer. The family managed during the years of Mr. Fugel's
unemployment without going in debt or borrowing on insurance policies or the
home, and without lowering their plane of living to any great extent, for
they "always had girls working." "Otherwise," Mrs. Flugel says, "I don't
know what we would have done."

The taxes of $104 a year on the home are considerably lower than
the rent they would have to pay for any similar house; there is ample space
in the back yard for Mr. Flugel's garden; Mrs. Flugel cans vegetables from
the garden and fruits from an orchard of 13 trees. She and the girls do
their sewing. Mr. and Mrs. Flugel consider that they have always been
thrifty and economical; only a little more frugality was called for during
depression years.

Mr. Flugel is short and heavy-set; except for his white hair he would appear to be much younger than he is. He speaks vigorously and intelligently. Both Mr. and Mrs. Flugel are pleasant and friendly, and they talk rather freely.

Five of the Flugels' nine children are still at home. Paul, 12, is the only one still in school. Jeannette was graduated from high school in 1937 and is now living with a married sister. She has never had a job but hopes to do office work. Mary, who had done clerical work for 6 years before going back to school, was most anxious to have a college education. She is now living at home, attending college classes during the mornings, and teaching during the afternoons. Next year she hopes to have a full-time teaching job.

Geraldine and Caroline are both employed full time at office work. John has been working for the past year at a local battery factory. He left college at the end of his sophomore year, soon after Mr. Flugel lost his job at Stevenson's, because the family could not afford to keep him in school. He was unemployed for some time and spent about 8 months in a CCC camp. The income of $25 a month was a great help to the family, and John was glad enough to have something to do.

Mr. Flugel, one of nine children of a bookbinder, began work when he was 13 years old. His father had always provided well for the family, even though he earned only $12 a week for six 10-hour days. But he "wore a white collar" and "had a better trade" than Mr. Flugel's trade of carpentry. The children all began work early, and an education was considered of little importance.

Mr. Flugel's first job was "delivering bundles" for a grocery store. Later he worked for the same store as a clerk. He was always anxious

to learn a trade, and first tinkered with the idea of becoming a machinist.
The hope of learning this trade prompted him to go to work in a brass foundry
when he was about 15 years old. Finding that there was little chance of
getting ahead, he left at the end of 2 years and apprenticed himself to a
carpenter. For 5 years he did "outside work" as an apprentice, journeyman,
and master carpenter, and ended by knowing the trade thoroughly. He recalls
having worked as an apprentice from 4 until 6 and thinks that now few boys
of 16 would be able or willing to work such long hours.

Somehow or other along about 1895 Mr. Flugel "got the idea" of
doing "inside work"; so he found a job with a woodworking mill manufacturing
pews and altars. Mr. Flugel worked as carpenter and bench hand until the
plant shut down in 1918. His employment there had been steady except for an
11 months' strike and 6 months taken off to build a new home. In the beginning, he worked regularly 60 hours a week at 17½¢ an hour; hours stretched
out to 12 or 13 a day during the rush seasons just before Christmas. He can
remember the earliest agitation for Saturday afternoons off, and the reluctance with which many of the men relinquished their "right to work 5
extra hours" on Saturdays.

Mr. Flugel himself considered every decrease in weekly hours a
distinct advantage for the working men, for increases in hourly rates soon
brought weekly earnings up to previously established levels. Mr. Flugel's
wages were first increased to 20¢ an hour. In the early 1900's the men
struck for a 9-hour day and 25¢ an hour. The strike dragged out over a
period of 11 months before the men finally went back to work; the demand for
the 9-hour day had been granted, but with no increase in wages. The carpenters had, however, put their heads together and determined that they would

force wages up by threatening, one by one, to leave the plant for better-
paid jobs elsewhere. This plan was highly effective, and soon all of the
men were earning 25¢ an hour. The strike worked no particular hardship on
the Flugels, for Mr. Flugel found outside carpentry work which kept him busy
during almost the entire period.

It was in 1916 that Mr. Flugel requested time off to build a new
home. Mr. and Mrs. Flugel and the family of growing children had been living
in their own home, earlier built by Mr. Flugel, and now far too small for the
family. So Mr. Flugel took his wife to see a large plot of ground a little
farther out from town and in a neighborhood then largely unpopulated. When
Mrs. Flugel had given her approval, Mr. Flugel bought the lot and prepared
to build the home, a comfortably large story-and-a-half stuccoed bungalow.

After selling the other house for $1,600 he invested $6,000 in the
new home. When Mr. Flugel and the one other carpenter who was helping him
were well under way, Mr. Flugel, realizing that he would have to borrow money,
went to a real estate agent and asked for a loan of $3,000. The agent,
insistent that the loan should have been requested before work was begun on
the house, said "Alex, you've got your nerve with you!" To which Mr. Flugel
replied proudly, "I always did." The loan was granted, though the agent
said, "If I hadn't known you all my life, I wouldn't let you have it." Work
on the house was finished; Mr. Flugel went back to his job at the altar
manufacturing company at the end of 6 months; and before he lost his job at
Stevenson's in 1931, the loan was paid.

By the time that the altar company closed in November 1918,
Mr. Flugel was earning 40¢ an hour for an 8-hour day. This company had
always been a good one to work for: wages were reasonably high, and the
employer was "considerate." He arranged for night classes in architectural

drafting and arithmetic which employees might attend on the payment of minimum fees. In 2 years of night classes Mr. Flugel learned more than in "all the years" that he attended grade school. But in spite of its fairly liberal employment policies, the altar company "didn't know how to keep up with the times"; so it was crowded out. Until 1918 it had been one of the largest woodworking mills in Dubuque and had employed several hundred men.

From the altar company Mr. Flugel went immediately to the Stevenson plant. For about a year he worked as a bench hand, earning 50¢ an hour, which was considerably more than he had ever previously earned. At the end of a year or so he was promoted to a job as department superintendent. In addition to his salary, he was granted a bonus, calculated on the basis of the total production of the department. His monthly earnings always ex-ceeded $200. The Stevenson Company had some 1,300 workmen at the peak of employment; its best year was probably either 1922 or 1923. By 1928 re-trenchment had already begun; more and more men were laid off until finally, near the close of 1931, only a handful of men remained at work.

As a foreman, Mr. Flugel was among the very last to be laid off. He remembers the irony of a huge poster decorating a billboard which the Stevenson workers had to pass on their way to and from work day after day: "Business is Good: Keep it Good." At the end of the working day, the foremen and superintendents used to meet opposite this poster: "Bill, how many men were laid off in your department today?" "Forty; how many in yours, Alex?" "Fifty; how long do you think they can stay open?" This question was answered for them in December 1931. And the poster still proclaimed "Business is Good: Keep it Good."

Mr. Flugel says that during the twenties "the wage-earners—90 percent of the population—were urged to invest money in stocks and bonds to feed the other 10 percent," when frequently they were buying only "water." Overspeculation and overcapitalization of industry Mr. Flugel sees as two of the causes of unemployment. He thinks that Roosevelt has "tried" and "has done all he can" to help the working man, but he has "too many antagonists."

The NRA was a fine piece of legislation, except that it was perhaps "too big" an undertaking, and code regulations did not allow enough leeway for variations in methods of production. Still, the law could probably have been made to work. Mr. Flugel, "just a common working man" and "no college grad," can't be "expected to understand" all of the current legislation or to know what changes should be made, but he says that he has done some thinking on his own. The best programs recently inaugurated are, in Mr. Flugel's opinion, the Works Program, the housing legislation, and the Social Security Act.

But the Social Security Act should have been passed 30 or 40 or 50 years ago. Legislators must have been "blind" to the needs of the people not to have recognized the necessity for such legislation long ago, especially when pioneering in the field had already been done by European countries. Had a social security program been initiated years ago, Mr. Flugel believes that there might now be a reserve large enough to pension all employees over 60. Mr. Flugel thinks that there has been much unfair ness in the administration of old-age assistance programs by the separate States. Property owners have been at a disadvantage and have frequently refused to accept assistance when they have learned that homes must be "mortgaged."

Mr. Flugel believes that recently too much attention has been given to the needs of the farmers and not enough to the needs of the working men. "To hear some of the politicians talk, you'd think that 95 percent of the American people are farmers." He has noticed that when the majority of industrial workers have been employed at reasonably adequate wages, farmers have had no difficulty in selling their produce at reasonable prices. Perhaps now the problems of farmers might best be solved by the solving of the problems of industrial unemployment. In theory, Mr. Flugel favors wage and hour legislation, but fears that it may result only in raising prices for the consumers instead of shifting the responsibility for payment of adequate wages to the employers.

Mr. Flugel's experiences as a member of the carpenters' and the millworkers' unions have convinced him of their potential worth, but he thinks that now the labor unions "have to be watched, too." Certainly union strength should not be divided into two camps, for "united we stand; divided we fall," and undoubtedly some of the union men are more interested in their "profits" than in the well-being of the working men. Nevertheless, Mr. Flugel cannot hold unionists solely responsible for such "racketeering" as they may have engaged in. "After all, they are human beings, too, and they've seen politicians grafting and industrialists grafting; no wonder they do a little grafting of their own.

Mr. Flugel believes that the millworkers' union in Dubuque has not developed much strength because of the opposition of the managements of the large factories.

Mr. Flugel favors the Works Program and thinks the projects should have been more extensive. He was annoyed by the refusal of the State employment office to refer him to any project on a nonrelief basis.

From the time the employment office opened he kept an application on file in
the hope of getting private employment or project work.   When he first filled
out an application, he answered "twenty thousand and forty questions," and
was told that with his experience as carpenter and his knowledge of drafting, he "would get a job sure."

Then one night, one of the employment office men whom Mr. Flugel
has known all his life telephoned at 8 p.m. and asked him to come in the
next morning to see about a job. He answered the "twenty thousand and forty
questions" all over again, and while he sat waiting his turn to talk with
the man who was assigning one person after another to various projects, he
kept thinking, "I wonder where I'll be sent." But when his turn finally
came, he was told that he could be given no assignment because there was
"too much income in the family."

Mr. Flugel had of course told the interviewer that two of his
daughters were working, each earning $14 a week, but this didn't mean that
he had an income of $28 a week.   The girls did meet current expenses for
the entire family group, except while John was at CCC camp, but they had to
have some spending money for themselves, and they had to dress nicely.

In "all the 7 years" since the closing of the Stevenson plant,
Mr. Flugel has not been referred to any job by the State employment office,
except when he was called late one winter evening to report for work the
following morning at the Dubuque locks. Only when the weather was excessively
cold, when the forms were covered an inch thick with ice, and when the employment office was having difficulty in finding carpenters who would stick
at the work, was Mr. Flugel offered a job.   "So I said, 'John, you go to
hell' — excuse my language, but that's the way I felt." He did not report
for work the next morning.

Except for brief carpentry jobs, Mr. Flugel had no employment from December 1931 to the spring of 1936. He was too old to find factory jobs readily, and there was little private construction work. Mr. Flugel thinks that it would be impossible to estimate how much the family's expenditures were reduced during the period of his unemployment. For one thing, there was a great variation in income. At the time of the Stevenson closing only one daughter was employed; by the time he got work as cemetery caretaker, four of the daughters were working. He disliked having to depend on the earnings of his children, but there was "nothing else to do." Since so much money had been invested in the house, Mr. Flugel had no savings at the time that he lost his job. He was carrying three insurance policies which remain in force.

In the spring of 1936 Mr. Flugel got the job at the cemetery through the influence of friends. During about 8 months of the year he works 8 hours a day at 40¢ an hour. In the winter months there is occasional work, such as grave digging, but most of it goes to younger men. When Mr. Flugel is not regularly employed, he finds plenty of work to keep him busy. This winter he has put in several weeks at indoor carpentry work, for which he usually gets the regular carpentry wage of $1 an hour. Just now he is painting and varnishing the floors and woodwork of the family's home. In summer months he puts in a lot of time at his gardening.

At 65 Mr. Flugel expects to continue work for some years to come. He is well and strong and can work as effectively as ever, except that he could not hope to maintain the speed now required in factory production. Following Mr. Flugel's brief illness about 10 years ago, the doctor warned Mrs. Flugel that he had a serious heart condition, might drop dead

any time, and shouldn't be excited or overworked. Nevertheless, Mr. Flugel
has continued to do heavy work. His parents both lived to be more than 80
years old. He hopes to live as long as they, and to remain at work for the
rest of his life.

Employment Chronology for Mr. Flugel

1885 – 1888 –	Delivery boy, grocery store.
1888 – 1890	Helper, brass foundry.
1890 – 1895	Carpenter, private contractor.
1895 – November 1918	Bench hand, altar manufacturing company.
November 1918 – December 1931	Bench hand and department superintendent, Stevenson Radio and Phonograph Company.
December 1931 – Spring 1936	Unemployed.
Spring and summer, 1936 and 1937	Laborer, cemetery.

<u>KOCH</u>

At home

Mr. Koch   68
Mrs. Koch   65
Albert   19

Away from home

Adolf   21
4 married daughters

Interviewing completed
February 17, 1938

  "I've got a job when I'm 68," Mr. Koch explains proudly. He
is a vigorous man for his age, even though he is thin and haggard and sometimes crippled with rheumatism and neuritis. He talks rapidly and force-
fully, his little gray mustache twitching as the words tumble from one side
of his mouth. A native of France, of German and French parentage, and a
citizen of the United States, Mr. Koch speaks with a German accent, and the
phrasing of his sentences frequently follows the German word order. He
has worked since he was 14 years old, at a great variety of jobs, in France,
in Algeria, and in United States.

  After the Dubuque railroad shops, where he had been employed
all told for about 23 years, closed in the early summer of 1931, he had no
regular employment for more than 2 years. Still he couldn't just "lay
down; jobs you couldn't get very well, so I went contracting." His irregular earnings at the landscape gardening for which he contracted were
supplemented from the family's savings, some of which also went to help a
widowed daughter and to support a married daughter, her two children, and
her husband, who was unemployed for several months in 1931. Two sons were
still living at home when Mr. Koch lost his job in the shops.

  Since July 1933 Mr. Koch has been regularly employed at the
Julien Foundry as a boilermaker and as a watchman. The family has always

managed to get along on Mr. Koch's earnings and savings.   Even when he has earned little, he has regularly tried to save something; "if you want to get along, you have to make a budget, like the Government does, and the budget must include savings."   Mr. Koch says with great pride, "There has never been a Koch on poor relief, and I won't be the one to break the record."

Though now eligible for a railroad retirement pension, he does not know when his "turn" will come; it may not come for 2 or 3 years. He hopes, and expects, to be able to continue working at least until the pension is granted, and he isn't "wasting any time worrying" about what will happen if he loses the job at the foundry. If he can't find another job, he "can make one."   Even now, when he is working 3 nights and 2 days a week as watchman, he picks up odd jobs to keep him busy 1 or 2 days a week. To- morrow, he is to prune some fruit trees for a neighbor.

He can usually find farm work in the summer months; he makes and sells rose arbors from time to time; he is "good at buying and sell- ing," and sometimes buys huge cheeses, which he cuts into small portions and sells at a tidy profit; he has two large gardens—one taking up most of the space of the front lawn and "still a bigger one on the island"—from which he sells some produce. He lives economically: raises his fruits and vegetables, cuts his own wood in wood lots near Dubuque, and carries, in sacks slung over his shoulders, small quantities of coal from "empty cars" on railroad sidings to his home.

He delights in showing visitors his garden and his plantings. Along one side of the house are rosebushes which Mr. Koch brought from France in 1920, when he returned to visit his parents and his brothers whom he had not seen for more than 30 years. At the front gate, there are two cedar trees transplanted from Wisconsin. There are grapevines, strawberry

plants, currant and raspberry bushes, and many varieties of fruit trees.
Mr. Koch would "go without meat" to buy some special shrub.

Mr. and Mrs. Koch and the one son who remains at home occupy
the second floor of their two-story frame house, with a double-decker porch,
built tight against the hillside.   Fruit trees, rows of grapevines, and the
garden plot extend from the front porch of the house to the hedge bordering
the sidewalk. Three downstairs rooms of the house are rented to a relief
client, who theoretically pays a rental of $8.50 a month. Four different
families which have occupied those rooms owe the Kochs a total of about $100.

Mrs. Koch is a huge woman. Her thick legs are swollen and
knotted with varicose veins; she walks heavily and awkwardly.   She is exceedingly friendly and as talkative as her husband. She was born in Bavaria
and came to the United States when she was 18 years old. Until her marriage
thirty-odd years ago, she did housework, and immediately afterwards, when
Mr. Koch was earning only $1.25 a day, she "took in washings every day."

The Kochs have had nine children, six of whom are living. Only
the two youngest boys are unmarried. Adolf, almost 21 years old, who spent
2 years in CCC camp, has now been in Washington, D. C., for more than a year.
Because he could not find private employment in Dubuque after his return
from camp, he went to Washington in July 1936 to work in a garage operated
by his brother-in-law, who has since died. Adolf is now an elevator
operator in a Washington hotel. Mr. and Mrs. Koch are much pleased with his
letters which describe his work and his hopes for the future. In the past
few years he has become quite a different person from the restless boy whom
Mr. Koch arranged to have sent to CCC camp to "get him off the streets."
The camp experience was "good for him," and in Washington he has "learned

to be a chentleman."

Albert, the 19-year-old son still at home, is crippled as a
result of infantile paralysis. Mrs. Koch explains that, except for his
twisted hips and legs, he is strong and husky and "in A-1 condition." He
walks without cane or crutches, but with an awkward stumbling gait. Mr. and
Mrs. Koch have both been much concerned about him and anxious for him to
have regular work. Mr. Koch, hoping to arrange for him, too, to be sent to
CCC camp, went to the relief office and "laid the matter out to" the director
of relief, to whom he explained, "I can feed him, but eating alone don't
raise a boy"; a boy needs "an occupation as well as food and clothing."

The director of relief was most sympathetic and helpful, and
tried in every way possible to have Albert sent to camp, but three times
plans fell through at the last minute because the family was not eligible
for relief. For the past several months, Albert has been working 12 hours
a week on an NYA project for the protection of wild life; Albert considers
the project pretty much "a waste of money," but at least it gives him something to do and a monthly income of $16, most of which must be spent for
shoes and for repairs and gasoline for his little open coupe. Since he walks
on the side of one foot, he wears out a pair of shoes almost every week.
Because Albert "can't keep up with the other boys" if he walks, Mr. Koch
has bought him the car which he drives to work and to school. He finished
10th grade work 2 years ago, last year went to part-time school, and is now
attending night classes, as he works several afternoons each week.

Mr. Koch, who has many friends in Dubuque and "some influence,"
has tried to help Albert to find factory work, but most of the factory jobs
involve standing for long hours, and there are "so many straight" boys
available for work. Mr. Koch has also considered buying a small farm for

Albert. In 1933 he took all of his remaining savings—$685—out of the
bank preparatory to bidding on a 10-acre farm for sale in Dubuque County.
He had $200 due from a railroad pension, and knew that he could borrow
enough money on the home to put in a bid of $900. After Mr. Koch had
learned that the farm would not be sold, and while the money was still in
the house, the entire sum of $685 was stolen.

Mr. Koch has never been much of a "family man," for he has
always liked to be on the go. He has traveled all over the United States
and Europe. When he was 14 years old he ran away from home and found work
on the construction of fortifications for the French Government. When he
was 16 he was sent to Algeria, where he remained for another 2 years working
for the French Government. From Algeria he returned to France, and from
France he set sail for America with the expectation of going to an aunt in
Minnesota. He had saved the $60 for his passage from his earnings of $1 a
day at construction work. Since prices were so low that his food cost only
about 30¢ a day, it had been easy for him to save money. But he spent so
much in New York City that he had left only enough for his train fare, and so
arrived in Minnesota one July day in 1887 without having eaten for 3 days.
That very afternoon, he was put to work pitching hay on the farm owned by
his aunt and uncle.

For his first month of farm work, he was paid $20; for the
second, $18; for the third, $16; during the winter months he was given only
his board and room. So the following spring, he left the farm and got a
job with a stonemason, who paid him $1.25 a day in addition to his board.
Finding the work too heavy, he quit the job at the end of a year or so and
went to New Orleans. On his way back to Minnesota he stopped in St. Louis,
and for 4 months, he picked apples on a farm near there. He was paid $12 a

month and maintenance.   From St. Louis, Mr. Koch again set out for Minnesota,
but once more he paused along the way—this time to see relatives in Dubuque.
He returned to Dubuque in 1892, when he worked briefly for a wagon works,
and again in 1900, when he came back to Dubuque to stay—except for trips to
France, Colorado, and New Mexico; in New Mexico he bought some land to which
he wanted to take his family. He still regrets having given up the New Mexico
property; had he held it, he might today be a "millionaire," for oil was
struck on the land after he had sold it.

   Concerning the years from 1889 to 1900 Mr. Koch "isn't talking." He couldn't possibly recount all the many jobs he held, for he
"never stayed in one place long enough to get a letter." He worked as a
miner in the Black Hills, as a farm hand in several different States, on
construction gangs, and as a loader of Lake Superior boats. After returning
to Dubuque in 1900, he worked in a lumberyard at $12\frac{1}{2}$¢ an hour, $1.25 a day,
until the company folded up a few months after he started work. He next
went to the railroad shops, where he worked for a year or so as a handy
man, earning $27\frac{1}{3}$¢ an hour. In 1901 the railroads had little business, and
Mr. Koch was one of the many men laid off at the shops. He was then employed for 2 or 3 years at the iron works, where his earnings varied from
$80 to $90 a month; he sometimes saved as much as $50 a month from his
earnings.   From the iron works, he went to a charitable institution as a
stationary engineer.

   In 1906 he returned to the railroad shops, where he worked as
a boilermaker until 1928, except for several months in 1920, when he traveled
in Europe, and several months during the 1922 strike. His highest earnings
at the shops were 80¢ an hour. Once, while working in the shops, he was

offered a better job as stationary engineer for a Dubuque academy; he refused
the job when he learned that he would be displacing a man who had worked there
for 9 years. Besides, Mr. Koch was well satisfied with his work in the shops;
he left the job only when he was laid off early in 1928.

Just after the 1928 layoff Mr. Koch was ill for 5 months. Following
this serious illness, though scarcely able to work he insisted on looking for
a job, and in July he was employed at the Julien Foundry. Here, he earned
only 45¢ an hour. Laid off in October 1928, he immediately got a job running
an electric drill for a contractor who was building river docks. This work was
highly unsatisfactory, as Mr. Koch had to work out of doors when the temperatur
was well below zero. He wore high hip boots, as he was standing in water much
of the time, and more than once he "fell in the river."

Nevertheless, he stayed with this job until February 1929, when he
was promised work with the Electric Power Company. As it happened, the construction work on which he had expected to be employed could not be undertaken
because of a lack of materials; so Mr. Koch again applied for work at the Julie
Foundry. He was taken on almost immediately. He continued at the foundry unt
the following June, when he saw an announcement in the paper to the effect that
the railroad shops were rehiring. He was, of course, anxious to return to the
shops, both to maintain his seniority rights and to earn 80¢ an hour instead of
the 45¢ an hour he was being paid at the foundry. This time, he stayed on at
the shops until they closed in 1931; he was among the last to be laid off.

From July 1931 to July 1933 Mr. Koch had no regular employment. In
March of 1931 his married daughter had returned to the home, and the four members of her family remained with the Kochs until "warm weather." Though he ha
savings enough to enable the family to "exist" over a considerable period, he

was unwilling to remain idle. And so he began his landscape gardening. As his
work was most irregular and of a highly seasonal nature, it was necessary for
him to supplement his income from his savings.

He estimated that he would have had to earn $900 a year to support
his family adequately; but, since his annual earnings were less than $900, he
spent perhaps $600 or $700 of his savings for current living expenses over a
2-year period. During this same period of unemployment Mr. Koch did extensive
gardening for himself. He put in "40 hours a week" at gardening, and he sold
some produce. He also built an addition to his home which cost $1,800; he did
all of the work himself. He has borrowed $500 against the home, which repre-
sents a $5,000 investment, and is still paying off this debt. From his present
earnings of $14.50 a week, he manages to save about $1. For 4 or five weeks in
1932 or 1933, Mr. Koch worked for the railroad, helping to rebuild a bridge
which had been washed out. It was never necessary for the Kochs to lower their
plane of living, and Mr. Koch was not particularly concerned about his unemployment, as he has always had great confidence in his ability to get along. He was,
though, worried about the unemployment of his sons.

In July of 1933 Mr. Koch was reemployed at the Julien Foundry, partly
through the influence of friends. Mrs. Koch thinks that it is "just by accident"
that he is working now. In the fall of 1933 when work was slack in the foundry,
Mr. Koch was laid off, but soon he was given a job as watchman. When a burglar
alarm system was installed, he was transferred to a job as watchman in another
of the factory buildings. Told to report on the new job, he asked, "Do you
gonna lay another man off?" The superintendent tried to reassure him by explaining, "You got more rights as the other man," for Mr. Koch was an older
employee. When Mr. Koch insisted that he would not deprive another man of his
job, the superintendent promised that this watchman, a younger man, would be

transferred to another job. Well, "that gave" Mr. Koch "satisfaction," and he
took the job.

Mr. Koch has continued to work as watchman up to the present time.
According to Mrs. Koch, he puts in "ungodly funny hours"; he worked 3 nights
and 2 days each week. **When the foundry employees were out on
strike in the fall of 1936, Mr. Koch** worked for 4 or 5 weeks in the
railroad shops in Milwaukee, Wisconsin, so as to establish his eligibility
for a railroad retirement pension.

Mrs. Koch states that her husband tires easily, and sometimes, after
being on his feet almost all night in the factory, he is scarcely able to walk
home. But Mr. Koch prides himself on his capacity for work. He is much more
concerned about the state of the Nation than about himself. He is well-read
and well-informed, and he discusses general problems with a facility born of
long practice.

There are "no two things about it": the introduction of labor-
saving machinery is largely responsible for unemployment. Mr. Koch cites
numerous examples to prove that machines have displaced men in all of the
many industries in which he has worked. In the mines electric drills have
been substituted for sledge hammers. On the railroads a crew of five men is
now responsible for a train twice the length of the trains once handled by
the same five-man crews. Today, a farmer buys a tractor; if he has five sons,
he keeps only one at home, and "sends four to town," instead of having all the
boys work on the farm. In the sash and door factories so much labor-saving
machinery has been introduced that now "everywhere you look, there's a door
coming out. It's plain enough; now the work don't go around."

And why is the unemployment problem less serious in France than in the United States? The answer is simple: "France still has many small shops, small businesses, and small farms, while in America it's all big shops or big corporations." Mr. Koch fears that the industrial situation in the United States will "never come back normal." In order for the country to grow and to expand, the "population must increase"; yet an increasing population may mean only that there will be more unemployment. However, Mr. Koch believes that the United States will need a "big population" since war with Japan is "inevitable"—"there're no two things about it"—and perhaps America might just as well fight Japan now and "get it over with" as to postpone the inevitable for 5 or 6 years, and end by fighting a more difficult war involving "more casualties."

Mr. Koch believes that the United States is "way behind" in social legislation. He reviews the social security legislation of various European countries, giving the dates of the enactment of the earliest old-age insurance laws in Germany, France, and England, and explaining the differences in coverage of the old-age benefit provisions of the Social Security Act and of the old-age insurance program in England. He is heartily in favor of the Social Security Act, but thinks that its coverage should be broadened and that pensions should be granted to persons of 55 or 60 instead of 65. The lowering of the age limit would help to decrease unemployment. The old-age assistance programs as administered by the various States have "put property owners at a disadvantage." Mr. Koch thinks that the taking of liens on property by the State is "depriving the children," who may have helped with building and maintaining the home, "of their income,"

"Roosevelt is the greatest man we've ever had; I admit it,
and he's my man all right, but the country is so big as he can't
know everything as is going on." The Kochs do not consider the President responsible for abuses of the relief and Works Program, but they
believe that there has been "a lot of unjustice done." Mr. Koch has
"studied" the question of work relief "pretty carefully," and has gone
to the scene of various projects to watch the men at work. Though
there are "good men amongst them," there are, too, those who will
never again have jobs in private industry. The Government would have
done better, in Mr. Koch's opinion, to create new employment by open-
ing up new markets in South America, the West Indies, and China, where
American goods could readily be sold in large quantities if prices were
kept at a minimum.

Mr. Koch sees some hope in unionism. "Labor unions in America
today aren't as strong as they should be, but the country would be in
worse trouble yet if it weren't for the unions." Mr. Koch thinks that
there is little essential difference in the aims of the CIO and the AFL.
Lewis is a "better fighter" than Green, who is "too old" to head the AFL
and has lost interest in the needs of the working men. Today, "doctors,
lawyers, and business men are better organized than the working men."
And this brings Mr. Koch to another comment on what is wrong with
America. "The younger Americans don't take their Government seriously,"
are not well-informed about current problems, and in their thinking
seldom go beyond the assumption that America's a great country. If the
working men can come to an understanding of their common problems and
work together toward some solution, Mr. Koch believes, great things may
be accomplished, but not soon. Because of his genuine interest in the
labor movement, Mr. Koch has retained his membership in the boilermakers'
union, even though he is no longer working at his trade.

There is a striking contrast between the pessimism evident in
Mr. Koch's discussion of national problems and his optimistic certainty that
he will be able to work and to provide for his family for many years to come

Employment Chronology for Mr. **Koch**

1883 - 1885 -	Laborer on **Government fortifications,** France.
1885 - 1887	Laborer on Government fortifications, Algeria.
July 1887 - spring 1888	Farm hand, Minnesota.
Spring 1888 - spring 1889	Stonemason, Minnesota.
1889 - 1900	Apple picker in Missouri; miner in South Dakota; farm hand and construction worker in several different States; loader of boats, laborer in lumber yard.
1900 - 1901	Handy man, Dubuque railroad shops.
1901 - 1904	Helper, iron works.
1904 - 1906	Stationary engineer, charitable institution.
1906 - 1928	Boilermaker, railroad shops.
July - Oct. 1928	Boilermaker, Julien Foundry.
Oct. 1928 - Feb. 1929	Electric drill operator, construction company.
February - June 1929	Boilermaker, Julien Foundry.
June 1929 - July 1931	Boilermaker, railroad shops.
July 1931 - July 1933	Unemployed except for landscape gardening.
July 1933 - fall 1933	Boilermaker, Julien Foundry.
Fall 1933 - present	Watchman, Julien Foundry.

STILL WITHOUT JOBS

RAYBURT

Mr. Rayburt   53
Mrs. Rayburt   49
Margaret   20

Away from home

Milton   25

Interviewing completed
January 19, 1938

"I find it very trying not to have a penny of my own, but I am
more worried about my husband," says Mrs. Rayburt. She is "so sorry for
him," and thinks it is unfair that he can't find a job when he is so anxious
to work and be independent. He has never been a drinking man. He is always
a conscientious worker, his first interest being for his family.

Mr. Rayburt is approaching his 53rd year. He is heavy-set, but
well-built; the top of his head, bald and shiny, is fringed with gray hair
clipped short. He is intelligent; and he speaks of his situation objectively
and without bitterness, although he is discouraged and not a little frightened.
He seems to welcome the opportunity to talk frankly to an outsider though
he has difficulty at times in controlling his emotion; in the presence of his
family he puts up a brave front and acts cheerful. A clerical worker for 28
years, 16 of which were spent with the railroad, Mr. Rayburt has been unemployed since 1932, except for 7 months on emergency projects on a nonrelief
basis. Now he is beginning to despair of ever getting back to work, though
he continues his search for a job.

The Rayburts and their daughter, Margaret, a senior in college,
live with Mrs. Rayburt's three single sisters and a bachelor brother.
Milton, the Rayburts' oldest child, has not lived in Dubuque since he was
graduated from the university 5 years ago. Two of Mrs. Rayburt's sisters,

in their 50's, one a nurse and the other a teacher, are the sole support
of the family of seven. Another sister, an invalid, has never worked. The
brother, 50 years old, a machinist by trade, has been unemployed since the
railroad shops closed in 1931.   The family occupies a very neat two-story
frame house in the north-end residential section. The home was built more
than 50 years ago by Mrs. Rayburt's parents.   The mortgage was paid off,
after the parents' death, by the two sisters who now own the property.
Mrs. Rayburt, the youngest of her family, is the only one who has married.
Though the Rayburts have always lived in the home with Mrs. Rayburt's people,
Mr. Rayburt had paid his share of the household expenses until he became
unemployed. Now he and his family are dependent on Mrs. Rayburt's sisters.
The sisters are educating Margaret, who wants to be a journalist.   They have
also financed Mr. Rayburt in his search for work. At first, he did not mind,
as he looked on this assistance as a loan, but now as the prospect for reemployment has grown more remote he has become sensitive about his dependency.
While talking about his predicament he is overcome with emotion and leaves
the room to gain control of himself.

Mrs. Rayburt senses that the worry is beginning to tell on Mr.
Rayburt, though he never discusses his situation with her or with other members of the family.   She has warned her sisters and brother to be careful
in what they say to him, lest he take it too much to heart. The Rayburts
had "several hundred" dollars saved up when he became unemployed but "that
was used up 2 or 3 years ago." Now they have only their insurance, on which
the sisters pay the premiums.   Mr. Rayburt has been able to keep up his
insurance and service rights in the union of railway clerks by paying $1.50
a month.

After completing a commercial course at the age of 19, Mr. Rayburt was employed for 2 years in a county office. He was let out, however, when a new official was elected. For the next 3 years he worked in the shipping department of a local factory, then for another 2 years with a loan company. From February 1912 to May 1917 he was employed in a railway ticket office, earning $55 a month. In May 1917 he got a job as a station auditor with an oil company. After a year at this job he was hired as a cost clerk in the office of the railroad shops, where he remained until 1927, when there was a reduction in the office force. On this job he was paid $100 a month. In less than 1 month after the shop job had ended he was employed by the Mid-western Foundry Company as an office clerk at $100 a month. Early in the depression, however, this wage was cut to $80 a month. Finally, in 1932, after a number of local banks had closed, the foundry shut down temporarily and Mr. Rayburt was never called back. He was unemployed until January 1936, when he was placed as a WPA worker on the business census for 3 months. Again in November 1936 he was assigned to a WPA project as timekeeper for 4 months. He has had no employment since, except for a few months when he tried unsuccessfully to sell electrical equipment on a commission basis. He enjoyed the project work, especially the business census. His pay on these projects was $70 a month.

In 1934 Mr. Rayburt entered the race for a city office, but he was defeated. He ran again in 1936 but was defeated in the primaries, though he received nearly 3,000 votes. He says, "I guess I'm just not a good enough handshaker to make the grade"; he now feels that his running for office was probably a mistake as $200 of the family's savings were used in the 1934 campaign.

Mr. Rayburt has kept in close touch with the State employment office, though he "knows they can't make jobs." He had hopes of getting back at the Midwestern Foundry Company, but their system of rehiring workers according to seniority with the company has ruled Mr. Rayburt out so far, as he had been with the company for only 4 years. He has a very good reference from the foundry. He has taken four civil service examinations and is on two lists. He has been given little encouragement, however, as the "quota for Iowa in the apportioned service is filled." However, he has been in communication with a number of people in respect to his civil service status, and exhibits a folder of correspondence which includes letters from prominent officials.

Mr. Rayburt feels that all of the recent social legislation has been worthwhile, though some of it was "pretty well sterilized by Congress before it got to the people." He now wonders why the American people "stand for Congress wasting so much time and money." For example, the filibuster over the antilynching bill he "considers a disgrace." While he considers the Social Security Act a fine piece of legislation, he doubts if he, personally, will benefit by it. He blames labor-saving machines for much of the wide-spread unemployment. He agrees with an article he read a number of years ago advocating Government interest in all patents for labor-saving machinery. According to this plan the Government would receive royalties in proportion to the money earned by these machines. This money would then be used by the Government to finance a public works program to employ the men thrown out of work through the introduction of the machines. Mr. Rayburt also feels that States would be in a better position to care for their unemployed people if more attention were paid to the development of natural resources and new industries. Dubuque, for example, was originally settled because of the lead deposits in this vicinity. Mr. Rayburt feels certain that lead mining would again be profitable today. States that are financially able to assume responsibility for unemployment relief should be forced to do so, but the Federal Government should continue to assist the States unable to care for their unemployed.

The administration of relief is a difficult problem, in Mr. Rayburt's opinion, as some people will invariably try to "chisel in where something is being given away"; other "more timid souls" won't even make their needs known. People who had received relief before they "got a break" should reimburse the relief office. Mr. Rayburt believes that many people who come into "inheritances" or find good jobs never think of reimbursing the relief offices. He reads a great deal. In fact, he has read and thought so much about unemployment that he feels he should start writing about it himself. He has been interested in following the fight between the A. F. of L and CIO and believes that they will get together only on a basis whereby the officials in both organizations will be assured equitable jobs in the merger. Lewis, Mr. Rayburt believes, aspires to be president and "he might not be a bad choice; after all the best way to make a conservative out of a radical is to elect the radical to office." He feels that history repeats itself every so often; the fight now waged against the CIO by "the big capitalists" is comparable to the fight against the Knights of Labor when that organization became powerful politically.

While Mr. Rayburt believes economic conditions have greatly improved during the last few years, he finds conditions in Dubuque very discouraging. This situation he blames on a few manufacturers who control the Chamber of Commerce and the banks. "What the town needs is a concern not dependent on local banks or policies, and big enough to absorb two or three

thousand men." Though Mr. Rayburt has never worked outside of Dubuque, he
has traveled in all parts of the United States and Canada, as he always
took advantage of his annual pass while working for the railroad. In
some ways he would like to get away from Dubuque now, but would have no idea
where to go and has no money to pay for travel. He realizes that his chances
for employment in other towns would be even less than in Dubuque, as most
towns look out for their own residents first.

Three nights a week Mr. Rayburt teaches boxing to the youngsters
of a church society. He enjoys this activity and feels that it helps to
keep him cheered up. He spends several hours each day looking for work,
and reads extensively in an attempt to avoid idleness. Mr. Rayburt "has
done a lot of thinking" about his situation and realizes that the future
looks pretty dark for him; it has become increasingly difficult for him to
keep up his morale. Mrs. Rayburt thinks that if her husband "could only get
a job, even a part-time one, it would be like a miracle from Heaven."

Employment Chronology for Mr. Rayburt

1904 – 1906	Clerk, county office.
May 1906 – August 1909	Shipping clerk, factory.
October 1909 – November 1911	Clerk, loan company.
February 1912 – May 1917	Railroad ticket agent.
May 1917 – April 1918	Station auditor, oil company.
April 1918 – December 1927 January 1928 January 1932	Cost clerk, railroad shops Office clerk, Midwestern Foundry
February 1932 – Present	Unemployed except for 7 months on emergency work projects.

Mr. Donner	53
Mrs. Donner	48
Louise	14
Dick	12

Interviewing completed
March 15, 1938

In good years, while Mr. Donner had his own printing business in Chicago, it "was nothing" for him to take the children downtown on Saturday afternoons and spend $2 or $3 on trivalities for each of them, and Dick and Louise "never thought of going into a drug store" without having sundaes or sodas. When, in the early thirties, the business started downhill, both Mr. and Mrs. Donner were even more concerned about the children than about the business. Though they tried not to let Louise and Dick know how worried they themselves were, they did explain that now there was less money to spend because "business was bad." As it happened, the children surprised their parents by their casual acceptance of deprivations. They used to tell their father not to buy the things they especially wanted unless "business was good." They did, though, expect Christmas toys in 1933, for they still believed in Santa Claus.

Mr. Donner has had no private employment since the spring of 1934, when he finally gave up the printing business which he had owned and operated for 15 years. Then he and Mrs. Donner and the two children came to Dubuque to Mrs. Donner's parents. Since the fall of 1934 he has been employed most of the time on emergency work projects. He is now a WPA timekeeper.

He looks the part of the business man that he has been. He is broad and well-built, well-dressed, and well-groomed. Both Mr. and Mrs. Donner are cordial and gracious and talk rather freely about their depression experiences.

When Mr. Donner was 13 years old his family moved from Dubuque to Chicago. After completing a 2-year business college course in 1907, he began work in the office of a Chicago insurance firm. He was soon promoted to sales man; he continued at this job until 1918, when he took over a Chicago printing establishment. His mother had inherited the business from her uncle, and Mr. Donner purchased it from his mother. He continued to make payments to his mother until 1931; the business was paid for only "just before it was lost." Through the twenties the business had prospered. Mr. Donner employed from 12 to 30 men; "at a conservative estimate" the business was worth $15,000 in 1929, and Mr. Donner's income averaged about $300 a month.

Awareness of the depression came early to the Donners, who had savings in one of the first banks to fail after the 1929 stock market crash. The Chicago bank that went under early in November 1929 paid only 30 percent of the total deposits. Through 1930 and 1931 Mr. Donner's business was fairly good; he considered himself rather fortunate, for many of his friends had already begun to suffer heavy losses.

Mr. Donner continued to hope to meet "prosperity just around the corner" as long as he dared, but the time came when he could no longer wait for prosperity. He thinks now that he held on too long, but he had no way of knowing that the depression would last so long, and that in the end he would save nothing from his business. He hated to discharge his employees, so kept as many as possible as long as possible. He also hated to see his huge presses standing idle. All of the family's assets were converted into cash to be put into the business, and besides, Mr. Donner borrowed from relatives money which he has only recently succeeded in repaying. The Donners gave up the large home which they had been renting but had hoped to buy as soon as the business was paid for, put their furniture in storage, and moved into furnished rooms. The furniture has now been reclaimed, but it "just missed" being sold for storage.

Finally, Mr. Donner had fired all of his employees, sold some of his presses, and rented a part of the floor space. But he still couldn't give up altogether. He was gathering up what orders were to be had even when he did the printing, the delivering, and the bookkeeping all alone. He was worrying so continually and so excessively that he lost 35 pounds in a few months and couldn't sleep at night.

Mrs. Donner had lived in Dubuque until her marriage. Her parents still have their Dubuque home, a huge but somewhat ramshackle place in a good residential neighborhood. Mrs. Donner and her parents had been urging Mr. Donner to give up his business and move to Dubuque over a period of some 6 or 7 months before he finally consented to do so. He had been thinking that if he couldn't support his family in Chicago, what chance would he have in Dubuque? But there were at last only two alternatives; either the Donners would go on relief in Chicago or they would come to Dubuque to Mrs. Donner's parents. Neither possibility was a very happy one, but above all things Mr. Donner was anxious to remain off relief rolls; so he came to Dubuque in the spring of 1934.

Mrs. Donner's family had the second floor of their home made into an apartment for the Donners, who have their own entrance. The apartment is roomy and airy and attractively furnished. For about 5 months after coming to Dubuque, Mr. Donner was unemployed, though he managed to keep busy---he was so anxious to have "something to do"---by painting the doors and window

frames and sashes of the family's home. He had kept in touch with the employment office, as well as with "every factory in Dubuque." His first job
came when he was assigned as a common laborer, on a nonrelief basis, to the
Dubuque lock and dam project. His work consisted largely of gathering up
lumber and carrying it to, or away from the scene of operations.

Although Mrs. Donner was glad enough for her husband to be working
at anything, it hurt her to see him put on overalls for the first time in his
life. "He had never had a pair of overalls, not even when he was a little
boy." Mrs. Donner managed not to say anything until he was out of the house,
but as soon as he had gone she ran into the bedroom and began to cry; she
thought she "just couldn't stand it." When her brother insisted on knowing
what was the matter, and she told him, he laughed at her for worrying about
Mr. Donner; his putting on the overalls and going out on a job like that just
"showed the stuff he had in him." Mrs. Donner thinks that only the "strong-
minded" have lived through the depression without becoming either too bitter
or too resigned.

Mr. Donner continued to work on the locks until he got a brief-lived
job with a tanning company, then hiring many extra persons to handle Government orders for leather mittens and jackets to be distributed among the relief clients. Mr. Donner understands that most of the employees were assigned
on a relief basis, but the company had the privilege of hiring a certain proportion of nonrelief employees. For his work as packer and, later, as cutter
Mr. Donner was paid 40¢ an hour. This work, too, was quite different from
anything he had ever done in the past; he had scarcely even seen factory
machines in operation. The first day he operated a ripping machine, he pushed
one hide a little too near the needle, which ripped off a finger nail. After
having worked for several months for the tanning company, Mr. Donner was laid

off, along with many other workers, when the special orders were filled.

His next job was as timekeeper on a WPA project; he was assigned
on a nonrelief basis through the employment office. Mr. Donner attributes
his assignment to one of the better jobs to his "good education" and to his
experience as bookkeeper when he had his own business. For the past 2 years
he has been working as timekeeper on WPA projects.

Mr. Donner feels that the depression really hit hardest the families
like his, who had been used to a relatively "high standard of living." For
25 years Mr. Donner's earnings had averaged not less than $300 a month. Since
he now earns only about $90 a month, he thinks that his income has been re-
duced, proportionately, more than that of the average WPA worker. He is
nevertheless sympathetic with relief clients and especially with the WPA
workers who earn "a few dollars a month" less than he.

These past several years, the Donners have heard a great deal about
the unemployed men who don't want to work and won't look for jobs and about
the "shovel-leaners" on WPA jobs. "Of course," Mr. Donner says, "there are
a few loafers on WPA projects; but there are also a few loafers on jobs in
private industry." But on the whole, as Mr. Donner knows from having seen
hundreds of WPA workers come and go, they are most eager to have employment
and to do what is expected of them, or even "more than is expected." "Besides"
Mr. Donner explains, "several factors should be taken into account before any
of the WPA workers can be criticized for not doing a first-rate job: many of
the men working as common laborers haven't been accustomed to hard physical
labor; a good proportion of them have large families to support on their
earnings of $12 a week and are always undernourished. And the men really
shouldn't be expected to do $25 worth of work for $12."

Mrs. Donner, too, has noted how eager the men are to have work. It was she who now recalled that some of Mr. Donner's former employees, unable to find work elsewhere, came again and again to his shop asking to be put to work at anything and at any wages. Unfortunately, he had nothing to offer them; he supposes that some of them are still unemployed. When men were first put to work in the Dubuque County stone quarries, it made Mrs. Donner "feel good" just to see so many men with jobs once again. "Of course, it was too bad that they had to work in the stone quarries," but there it was—and it was good that they had something to do. Even when they began work at 8 a.m. Mrs. Donner could see them coming to work in the quarry just across from the family's home 20 or 25 minutes before starting time. "And talk about men not wanting to work—why, one day last month when the weather was very cold, and the streets were coated with ice, and one of the trucks which carried the WPA workers to their jobs refused to start, one man walked 2 miles to the project on the frozen-over Mississippi River." Mr. Donner believes that some men have applied for relief before it was absolutely necessary to do so; on the other hand, many have waited to apply until there was no alternative.

Mr. Donner says that he doesn't "know what the country would have done without the WPA." One thing is fairly certain: "there would have been a revolution." The WPA projects have been advantageous in many ways; not only have men been given work but also cities have had, at only a small proportion of the total cost, improvements which they might otherwise not have had for years. Dubuque, for example, now has a municipal swimming pool, built as a WPA project, a recreation pavilion, and "the largest man-made rock garden in the world, a good advertisement for Dubuque," in Eagle Point Park. Mr. Donner puts no stock in the criticism, which he has frequently heard, that expenditures for materials used on PWA and WPA projects have been excessive.

The rock used for the building of the recreation pavilion cost only 10¢
a ton, a bid of 12½¢ a ton having been turned down as "too high."

"Even though most of the WPA workers," Mr. Donner believes, "feel
deep down in their hearts that they have been given work which doesn't
absolutely have to be done, they can still feel that the work is worth-while."
Some of it would perhaps have been necessary later on, if not just now; other
projects, if not strictly essential, have added new community resources to
those previously available. The chief deficiency of the WPA program, accordin
to Mr. Donner, is that the money poured into WPA has not served to improve
business conditions or to create new jobs in private industry, perhaps partly
because WPA earnings have been too low; most WPA workers can buy only the
barest necessities. Still, higher wage-scales might have validated the
criticism that "government is competing with private industry" and encouraged
men to remain on WPA rolls.

Mr. Donner does not see any immediate prospect of his leaving the
WPA rolls. Business today is little better than when Mr. Donner returned to
Dubuque more than 3 years ago, and "numbers on WPA rolls in the county are
increasing." From his correspondence with friends in Chicago and other cities
Mr. Donner gathers that conditions elsewhere are much the same as in Dubuque.
In his opinion, the recession has been the result of "spite work" on the part
of certain industrialists; he does not anticipate that it will last very long.
"The depression of the early thirties" he thinks, "was bound to come sooner
or later when there was so much overspeculation, and overcapitalization, and
an excess labor supply" resulting from long years of unrestricted or little-
restricted immigration and the "displacement of men by machines." He thinks
that perhaps unemployment could be minimized by limitation of the amounts of

stock issued by corporations and payment of dividends only on actual investments.

For many years, Mr. Donner has been interested in social legislation
he approves of the Social Security Act in general, though he is dubious about
the need for so large a reserve for the old-age benefits fund. As one having
some knowledge of insurance, he believes that such a reserve is greater than
necessary to meet all demands that would be made on the fund over any given
period of time, and would "take too much money out of circulation."

What Mr. Donner would really like is to return to Chicago and go
into the printing business again. If business is again "as good as it was
last summer when most of the Dubuque factories were working 24 hours a day,"
there may be some possibility of his returning to Chicago; in the meantime,
there is none. He has done everything he can to find a job other than on
WPA projects: he has taken four civil service examinations, and has kept
applications on file with the State employment office and with all of the
local factories. There is nothing more to be done. He is not particularly
hopeful of finding work; neither is he particularly discouraged. There is
no bitterness or resentment evident in his expression of attitudes and opinion

Employment Chronology for Mr. Donner

1907 - 1918 -   Insurance salesman.

1918 - spring 1934- Own printing establishment.

Spring 1934 to date- Unemployed except for
                     emergency work; now on WPA.

CONSTRUCTION WORKERS

WHEATON

Mr. Wheaton	59
Mrs. Wheaton	54
Bert	25
Jack	21

Away from home

Margaret	22

Interviewing completed
December 15, 1937

Mr. Wheaton, 59 years old, is a tall, erect, proud-looking man of few words. While his wife vivaciously recounts their depression experiences, Mr. Wheaton reacts to her emotions, laughing with her at some of the more humorous episodes and even crying a little when she tells of the family's utter destitution and actual hunger.

Mrs. Wheaton, in contrast to her husband, is short, plump, white-haired, and ruddy. In her own words, "I do the talking while the mister does the thinking." She is more practical than her husband and has always managed the family's business affairs; being more of a realist, she was the one who set out to find assistance when the family no longer had food in the larder.

Mr. Wheaton, a carpenter for 30 years, has been unemployed except for emergency work during the past 7 years. Jack is the youngest of the three children. Since his graduation from high school in 1935, he has supported his parents and his older brother Bert. The daughter Margaret is taking nurse's training in a Chicago hospital.

Mr. Wheaton's father was a caretaker for a public institution on the outskirts of London. With his small earnings, Mr. Wheaton, senior, was barely able to care for his nine children, who found it necessary to drop out of school and begin making their own way at an early age. Alfred

Wheaton, the oldest child, completed the eighth grade and then worked at

various odd jobs over a period of 10 years. For much of this time, he was

employed at common labor at the institution where his father worked and at

other institutions; he finally saved enough to pay his passage to America.

          Immediately following his arrival in the United States, Mr.

Wheaton came to Dubuque, where an aunt had established a home. In 1905,

soon after his arrival here, he got a job at the railroad shops, polishing

the metal fixtures used in coaches. He is unable to recall his earnings or

hours of work on this job, but he thinks he worked at the shops for about

2 years.

          One day, he saw an "ad" in the paper for a man to learn carpentry.

He secured the job and began his apprenticeship as a carpenter at the age of

29. He stayed with the same employer for 4 years. With the exception of

one winter at the railroad shops in 1919, he has followed his trade ex-

clusively, keeping busy about 8 or 9 months of the year, and never earning

more than $1,200. He has usually worked for the same contractor for

stretches of 4 or 5 years. Mr. Wheaton especially liked the last contractor

for whom he worked because this contractor arranged the work so that there

was always inside finishing to be done during the winter months. Because

of this, Mr. Wheaton did not lose so much time. While the work was

seasonal, he kept busy, except for short layoffs, until 1930 when the

building trade collapsed in Dubuque. Since then he has had no employment

except for emergency work projects; and even this work has been very

irregular.

          Although the Wheatons managed on his earnings, they never found it

possible to save anything. They lived very economically and never went in

debt until after 1930. For 24 years they have lived in the same house,

which has few modern conveniences, but has the advantage of location in one of the better residential neighborhoods. The Wheatons pay $20 a month for their half of the house; Mrs. Wheaton's parents and sister occupy the other half. After 1930 the Wheatons got behind with rent in the amount of $150. The landlord has permitted Mr. Wheaton to pay this amount and also current rent by keeping the building in repair.

During Mr. Wheaton's unemployment in 1930 the family borrowed $100 on the household furniture from a finance company, which charged $6 a month on the loan, and "continually hounded us with threats of foreclosure." After the Wheatons went on relief 2 years ago, an investigator for the relief office looked into the matter and the Wheatons "haven't heard another word from that finance company." Mrs. Wheaton's father, who is 75 years old, is a contract painter but has had no work since 1930. Bert had dropped out of school in 1929 to help his grandfather on painting jobs, but after 1930, Bert too, was unemployed. Mrs. Wheaton's unmarried sister, who is employed as a clerical worker at $15 a week, has been the sole support of her aged parents for the past 7 years. In addition, she helped the Wheatons as much as she could after Mr. Wheaton lost his job which was the same year that her father became unemployed. Margaret and Jack were at that time still in high school and had to have clothing and books.

Insurance policies were carried on all members of the family. Mr. and Mrs. Wheaton each had a $1,000 policy; one policy had been carried for 12 years and the other for 5 years. Insurance policies amounting to $300 were carried on each of the three children. The family got behind on the payment of premiums, so in 1931 a $300 policy was cashed to pay up the back premiums, but all policies were finally allowed to lapse and the family now has no insurance.

Early in 1931, before the emergency relief office was established, Mrs. Wheaton went, in desperation, to the county supervisor of the poor, but she was told that the family would have to get help from the church. The

church to which the family belong and the Red Cross gave some clothing for
the children. The big problem, however, was food. The superintendent of
the high school knew about the Wheatons' situation and arranged to have
them helped with food by the St. Vincent de Paul Society. Mrs. Wheaton
considers that it was very fine of this society to help a Protestant family,
when there were so many Catholic families in need.

The family struggled along with a little help here and there,
often "actually going hungry" until Mr. Wheaton's placement by the State
employment office on the CWA airport project in January 1934.

Mr. Wheaton thinks that he is probably "bitten with false pride"
but it would have "killed" him to ask for "charity." If Mrs. Wheaton had
not taken the initiative, he doesn't know what would have become of them.
Mr. Wheaton had picked up a dollar or two now and then from odd jobs, but
this was hardly a "drop in the bucket for a family of five." Mrs. Wheaton
reminds him that even the occasional 50¢ given to the family by Mrs.
Wheaton's sister looked "like a lot of money." According to Mrs. Wheaton
the family seldom saw money of any denomination for nearly 3 years. It was
an "awful struggle" to keep the children in school, but the Wheatons decided that the two younger children should finish their high school education, as Bert had profited little by dropping out of school to go to work.

The family managed "just fine" from the time Mr. Wheaton was
placed on CWA in January 1934 until his layoff early in 1935. On the airport job Mr. Wheaton worked at common labor and received $12 a week. When
this job was completed in April 1934, he was placed by the State employment
service on the Guttenberg dam project. On this job, he sometimes had to
work in water "up to his shoulders"; so he requested, and was granted, a
transfer to the locks and dam project in Dubuque. For a while, he earned
$1.20 an hour as a carpenter on this project. "Everybody wanted to do
carpentry work in order to earn this rate; so pretty soon there were too

many carpenters and a lot of us got transferred to form-building at 80¢ an hour." The latter rate "was good pay, but it didn't seem so good" compared with $1.20 an hour.

In January 1935 Mr. Wheaton was laid off when the carpentry work was completed at the dam, and was not reassigned to a project. Mrs. Wheaton had saved a little out of every pay check; so the family managed to get along on these reserves and a little help from Mrs. Wheaton's sister for about 3 months. By May the sister had additional expenses because of illness and was unable to help the Wheatons. Mr. Wheaton and Bert had been trying every place to get work but couldn't find even odd jobs.

By June the family was without provisions, and Mrs. Wheaton made application for relief at the emergency relief office. She telephoned every day, requesting that an investigator be sent out immediately as the family was out of food. Four days passed before the investigator visited the Wheatons. In the meantime, they had been living on bread and molasses. The investigator was shocked to find the family entirely out of provisions and got an emergency grocery order to the Wheatons the same day. The family was also given surplus commodities, including cheese, which Mrs. Wheaton considered wonderful. "You can't imagine how good those things tasted to us after going without so long." Margaret and Jack had cheese sandwiches in their lunch boxes, and Jack could hardly wait to get home to tell his mother, "Guess what, Ma, nearly every kid at school had cheese in his lunch today." This is the first Mrs. Wheaton knew of "the numbers" of people in the neighborhood on relief. She and Mr. Wheaton had feared that their poverty would be embarrassing to the children. Jack had only two shirts, which Mrs. Wheaton kept washed and darned so that he "looked as well off as the other kids." Clothing was continually turned and made over for Margaret—"I never sewed and darned so much before in my life."

Mr. and Mrs. Wheaton feel that they were well-treated by the
relief office, but Mr. Wheaton never got over hating to go down for "slips.
Taking the slips to the grocery store was also galling to Mr. Wheaton.
"There might not be a single customer there when you arrived, but if a
dozen people came in before your order was filled, you had to wait until
they were all taken care of." As surplus commodities had to be picked up
at a different place each time, Mr. Wheaton often had to walk several miles,
"but we didn't mind that because those commodities were usually a real treat
for us." The best treat of all was bacon which was given out only once.
One day after the relief investigator had visited the Wheatons, Jack asked
his mother, "Ma, don't you think that's a lot of questions to answer for a
little food?" Mrs. Wheaton replies, "I didn't mind; I guess I am used to
giving my pedigree for a little food."

Margaret and Jack were graduated from high school in June 1935,
and Jack was immediately assigned to a CCC camp, where he had remained a
little less than 6 months when the Dubuque Woodworking Company called him to
work. Jack had made application at all the factories before he left for
camp, but Mrs. Wheaton thinks that the superintendent of the high school had
something to do with Jack's getting this job. Mr. Wheaton also brags about
Jack's keeping his job while older and more experienced men were laid off
during recent months.

Jack, the only wage earner in the Wheaton family, is a husky,
blond lad of 21, but looks 5 years younger. According to Mr. Wheaton,
Jack gets along with people and is always well-liked. Jack studied wood
work in high school and enjoys his job because he has a chance to use his
tools. He is a benchman in the assembly room, adjusting the frames that do
not fit. Jack is glad that he is not "stuck on some monotonous job." He
was able to make more money, though, when he operated a nailing machine for

a few months. Jack asked to be transferred because this machine was operated by a foot pedal and the repetitive motion was very tiring, as Jack's right knee had been injured in football play. Jack likes everything about his present job except the "pay." His rate is 30¢ an hour, and he usually works 40 hours a week. Jack feels that the millworkers union has not been very fair with the young fellows. When an increase in pay was granted, the company decided to cut out the bonus for all helpers, which included all the young fellows. Jack thinks the union should have opposed this action, but "they didn't." Because of the failure of the union to stand by the younger workers, Jack and most of the other young fellows have not "signed up." Jack considers the present 50 percent unionization in the plant very unsatisfactory anyway--"either an outright closed shop or an open shop policy would be better," he thinks.

When Jack began work at the mill, relief was discontinued, except for occasional surplus commodities. Jack gives his mother $25 a month and helps his older brother to some extent. Jack has a girl friend, but he "doesn't spend anything on her." Soon after Jack went to work, Margaret began a nurse's training course in a Chicago hospital.

Bert, 25 years old, has been unemployed most of the time since 1930. Mrs. Wheaton has worried a lot about him. She was always nervous lest he lose out on a job if he didn't go down and make the rounds every morning; when he returned "with a sour face," she "felt bad." He couldn't settle down to reading or anything, but spent his time walking back and forth to the drug store, the filling station, and the grocery store in the neighborhood. He wasn't eligible for employment on emergency work projects so long as his father was employed, and now that the family is off relief, he can't get WPA work. He had bad luck too: last January, he got work at the Dubuque Woodworking Company, but after about 3 months he was placed on short hours, and expected every day to be laid off. A man who was working

up a crew to erect telephone poles through the country "made a lot of big
promises"; so Bert quit his part-time job to join this crew. The man
was "fired" and the crew was never sent out.

Now that Jack and Margaret are able to care for themselves, and
Jack is supporting the rest of the family, Mr. and Mrs. Wheaton feel that
the sacrifices they made to keep them in school have been worth-while. All
three children have decided against marrying until they see "better times
ahead," and Mr. Wheaton thinks this is as it should be.

The Wheatons have a large garden space back of the house and last
summer Mrs. Wheaton canned 92 quarts of tomatoes and about 100 quarts of
other vegetables and gooseberries from the garden. A lot of gooseberries
went to waste because Mrs. Wheaton couldn't afford to buy sugar. Though
the family had always had a garden, they had never thought of canning such
quantities of vegetables before the depression.

Mrs. Wheaton feels that the depression has taught people "a good
lesson." Now the Wheatons know what it is like to be absolutely destitute.
Mrs. Wheaton says, "And believe me, if we ever get on our feet again, we
are going to save even the pennies." Mr. Wheaton regrets that he lost his
pension rights in the carpenters union through nonpayment of dues for 5
years. Although he was reinstated last year by paying $25, he will not
again be eligible for a pension for several years and cannot go to the home
for retired carpenters. Mrs. Wheaton reminds him that the pension amounts
to only $12 a month, but that "the home is a pretty good things because
they take care of couples." Mr. Wheaton has been a union man for nearly 30
years. He is strongly opposed to the CIO because "they want too much power--
it is best to let well enough alone."

Mr. Wheaton feels that his age is decidedly against him in finding
reemployment in the carpentry trade because the insurance companies consider
older men bad risks on jobs that require climbing and, in consequence, boost

the rate for their coverage, not because the contractors object to employing them. In fact, Mr. Wheaton thinks many of the contractors prefer the older, more experienced carpenters.

Mr. Wheaton's fondness for reading has been a great help during his enforced idleness. He never "just sits" or spends time "gossiping around the street corner." As long as he has a book or paper in his hand he is happy, according to Mrs. Wheaton. He reads all the current magazines at the public library and borrows free library books to read at home. He is not particular about the type of literature but reads fiction, history, biography, or economics indiscriminately. Mrs. Wheaton wishes Bert enjoyed reading for she thinks he might be "so much happier."

Mr. Wheaton does not contribute much to a discussion of the family's actual experiences during recent years, but he talks about more abstract philosophical subjects with enthusiasm. While he considers himself a strong supporter of the working man's cause, he believes that the Government must have the backing of the capitalists; "money power, from the beginning of time, has ruled. Every time the big fellows are taxed, it comes out of the little fellows' hides, you can depend on that." He considers the Social Security legislation "a very fine thing for the younger generation." Though not expecting to benefit personally from this legislation, he is happy to know that his children will have more security when they reach his age. He fears that some of the young people don't share his views, but "those who complain most about the deductions from the pay envelope would spend twice the amount in one evening on hootch and think nothing of it."

In Mr. Wheaton's opinion, the Federal Government, the State, and the county should share the responsibility of relief for unemployed people. He is not sure that he considers responsible for the widespread unemployment of recent years; "some books blame overproduction, while others say it is

underconsumption --so I don't know what to believe." The future looks
"very dark" for Dubuque. "What she needs is a large nonmilling industry
which would employ large numbers of men." The small industries which have
recently moved in employ too few men to help the general situation. So
long as the milling industry predominates, the town will "go flat" every
time there is a slump in building. But with the present "control of the
town by a few manufacturers," large worthwhile industries "will be kept
out. Ford wanted to establish a plant in Dubuque, and the Cream of Wheat
Company might just as well located here instead of in Cedar Rapids, had
the Chamber of Commerce offered them sufficient inducements."

Mr. Wheaton does not consider that he would be much better off
elsewhere unless he had acquaintances there. In Dubuque he at least knows
the contractors and thinks that he may be able to get work if the State
plan for participation in the Federal Housing program goes through, as
extensive building is scheduled for Dubuque. Mrs. Wheaton thinks the State
of Iowa is a "little slow" and will very likely lost out on the "housing
money."

Mr. and Mrs. Wheaton know that they can get along on very little,
if the children "look out for themselves." They would be able "to manage"
if Mr. Wheaton could only average $20 a month. "After I am really too old
to work," Mr. Wheaton thinks, "maybe the children will be able to lend us a
hand."

Employment Chronology for Mr. Wheaton

1895 - 1905	Common labor, public institutions.
1905 - 1907	Polisher of brass fixtures, railroad shops.
1907 - 1930	Carpenter.
1930 - present	Unemployed except for emergency work.

PUTNAM

Mr. Putnam	50
Mrs. Putnam	48
Wilbur	21

Interviewing completed
January 19, 1938

Twenty-one-year-old Wilbur Putnam, the only boy at home, nervously chews his finger nails. He has had no employment since leaving school 5 years ago, except for 27 months in a CCC camp. Sent home 3 months ago because he had served the limit of time allowed for CCC camp service, he does not know what to do with himself. Though he is registered at the State employment office and makes the rounds of the factories every few days, he has had little encouragement. He frequently ejaculates; "Gee, what's a guy to do when he can't find a job?"

Although Mr. Putnam is only 50 years old he sees little hope for reemployment. Mr. Putnam, a cement finisher by trade, has been unemployed except for emergency work since 1932. With the exception of brief periods on direct relief during the transition from one emergency program to another, he has worked steadily on work projects from the beginning of CWA, in the fall of 1933, to the present time.

Mr. Putnam is dapper, small, and dark. He is extremely spontaneous and dynamic, expressing opinions positively and with force. In his own words the depression has made him "just a bit radical." Mrs. Putnam, though she shares her husband's point of view, sees more humor in their situation than does her husband. She is meticulously accurate and does not hesitate to argue her husband down on questions pertaining to dates and other controversial points, even producing substantiating evidence in the nature of entries

on calendars and in notebooks, to prove her points. In appearance, Mrs. Putnam
is attractive and neat. Her dark wavy hair, only slightly gray, is bobbed. Her
blue eyes twinkle, and she smiles easily, even as she argues with Mr. Putnam.

The Putnams occupy the downstairs portion of their attractive shingled house located on the top of a hill, in a very good residential neighborhood
of small homes. The upstairs of the house is rented to a married daughter.
The rent is applied on the monthly payment to the HOLC on a loan obtained 3
years ago to save the home from foreclosure. The $25 a month from Wilbur's
work at CCC camp had paid back taxes and, until the upstairs was rented to
the daughter a few months ago, had taken care of the HOLC payments. Mr. Putnam'
earnings of $48 a month from WPA is barely enough to buy food and fuel and
keep up the family's insurance premiums of $7 a month.

Mr. Putnam is proud that he is of "straight American stock for three
or four generation." Until he was 23 years old he farmed with his father in
Wisconsin. He came to Dubuque in 1910 and worked for about 7 months for the
Midwestern Foundry Company. He was then employed at the railroad shops for
about a year before the shops closed for a brief period. During the next year
he worked as general handy man at the cemetery; then he returned to the shops
in 1912 for 2 years of employment as a drill press operator at 24½¢ an hour.
For the next 2 years he did cement work on some of the new buildings at the
woodworking mills, earning 35¢ an hour. He returned to the shops in 1917,
remaining this time for 5 years. As this work paid only 24½¢ an hour, Mr.
Putnam left to work with cement contractors for the next 3 years, earning from
30¢ to 40¢ an hour. From the beginning of 1925 until the latter part of 1929,
Mr. Putnam was employed at the Mid-western Foundry Company as a grinder. This
he considers the best paid job he has ever had, as he worked on a piecework
basis, averaging 69¢ an hour. However, the company not wanting the hourly

rate to exceed 40¢, instituted a system of group piecework. The men in the
department objected to this system, unless they were allowed "some say" as
to the men assigned to the department; one poor worker could bring down the
earnings of the group by several cents an hour. The argument became so heated
that finally Mr. Putnam "got mad and walked out." He immediately went to work
for a contractor on a cement job and had never tried to go back to the foundry
until 2 years ago when men were being hired. As Mr. Putnam was not called to
work, he thinks there is perhaps "a bad mark against him" at this plant.

Early in 1930 Mr. Putnam had started to work on a new building as
a cement finisher, but after he had worked for only a few months, his right
hand was crushed. The wound became gangrenous and one finger was amputated
to save the hand. He was laid up 18 weeks as a result of this injury. He
was paid $454 in workmen's compensation for this accident, but received only
$280 in a lump sum, as the balance had been received in weekly payments while
he was unable to work. As soon as the hand was healed Mr. Putnam worked on
another building for about 1 year for the same contractor. On the completion
of this job, in November 1931, Mr. Putnam invested the $280 in a small tailor
shop with another man. He sold new and secondhand clothing, and did cleaning,
pressing, and mending. For about 1 year the business prospered, especially
just after the veterans received their bonus payments. Mr. Putnam would buy
up a $500 shipment of clothing in Chicago and postdate the check he gave the
wholesale house. Within 10 days the shipment was usually sold out and adequate
funds in the bank to cover outstanding checks. Mr. Putnam was making about
$130 a month during this time. When banks began to close early in 1932, the
wholesale houses in Chicago became increasingly wary of checks, requiring
that shipments be delayed until checks were cleared. About this time

a "cleaning war" started in Dubuque. One tailor shop cleaned five suits for
$1 and did free mending.

By July 1932 the tailor shop was no longer profitable, so Mr.
Putnam gave it up. Mrs. Putnam had saved a few dollars each month while
business had been good, but she had only $100 when they gave up the business.
At that time there were five in the vamily, and by October all the money had
been used. Mr. Putnam's only insurance was carried in a lodge and had no
cash value. Insurance policies amounting to $2,000 had lapsed, though small
policies have since been taken out. Mrs. Putnam became increasingly alarmed
about their situation and suggested that Mr. Putnam make application for relief as many of their acquaintances were receiving county aid. Mr. Putnam,
however, was "too proud at this time to ask for relief." For more than 1
week the family lived on potatoes and "jelly bread." At each meal Mrs. Putnam
"waited" for Mr. Putnam to complain about the food so that she could emphasize
the necessity for relief; Mr. Putnam, however, made no comments about the food.
Not until the potatoes and "jelly bread" were almost gone did he finally make
application for relief. Mr. Putnam had always dressed well; and he had good
clothes left over from the tailor business. A neighbor suggested that Mr.
Putnam should wear old and worn clothes down to the relief office in order to
impress the investigators with his need, but Mr. Putnam thought, "I'll be
damned if I'll go down there like a beggar." Now he believes that his absolute
frankness made the people at the relief office respect him and believe in him.
At different times his opinions have been sought during special investigations.
After the emergency relief office had been established, Mr. Putnam was sent
out to check up on surplus commodity deliveries in the homes of relief clients.
When the director of relief asked Mr. Putnam how he found conditions in the
homes he told her about some of the particularly bad conditions, but expressed

the opinion that "poverty was no excuse for filth."

Though Mr. Putnam had felt that he "would sooner be shot than apply for relief," once the first application was made he didn't find it so bad. Relief was granted immediately. According to Mrs. Putnam, they were so hungry that the first meal after the grocery order had been received was "something of a feast." Almost every time Mr. Putnam went to the relief office he met old friends he hadn't seen for years; many of them had been prosperous when Mr. Putnam had last known them.

The Putnams received direct relief from November 1932 until Mr. Putnam was assigned to a CWA project the latter part of November 1933. While the Putnams were grateful for direct relief, Mrs. Putnam found it very difficult to manage on the budget allowance. Taxes and interest on the mortgage held by a building and loan company were 1½ years in arrears, and the home was in danger of foreclosure. After Mr. Putnam was assigned to CWA, the family managed much better, and he was delighted to be "earning cash money." From the beginning of CWA to the present time, Mr. Putnam has been employed on projects, except for very brief periods during the transition from one work relief program to another; his employment has never been on a budget deficiency basis. He has been paid the usual rate for common labor, and at present receives $12 a week on the brush clearing project. He believes he has worked on nearly every project ever in operation in Dubuque. Though he would much prefer private employment, he takes his project work seriously and believes he works just as hard as he ever worked on any job in private industry. "A few men loaf on the job and give all WPA workers a bad reputation."

Mr. Putnam is registered with the State employment office and has

made application at some of the factories. His age is against him at the
sash and door factories, where "they have adopted the policy of employing
very young boys," except in the case of former employees. Even the old employees past 50 have been laid off in some instances. Mr. Putnam feels that
his best chance for reemployment is in the construction industry, because he
considers himself a good cement finisher and a fair carpenter. Should there
be an extensive building program in Dubuque as a result of the housing legislation, Mr. Putnam feels sure that he would have work.

Mr. Putnam practically rebuilt his present home. He had bought a
home about 20 years ago and owed only $1,000 on it when it was traded, in
1926, for the present home situated in a more desirable neighborhood. In
this trade, Mr. Putnam received $800 which was invested in general repair,
shingling, and installing of plumbing and steam heat. He did most of the
labor himself. When taxes and interest on the mortgage were 2 years in
arrears, he obtained a loan of $1,800 from the HOLC. For 3 years he paid
interest at the rate of $7 a month. Now the monthly payments are $17, as $10
is applied on the principal. Had it not been for Wilbur's CCC camp allowance
for 2 years, the Putnams would have found it difficult to pay the interest
on this loan and the taxes of $65 a year. Since Wilbur's return from camp
the daughter, who was married last summer, has rented the upstairs rooms for
$15 a month. Her husband is employed as a beverage salesman earning good
commissions during the summer but not a great deal during winter months.
Mr. Putnam considers the HOLC loan a "legal debt" and can't understand the
"stupidity" of people who obtained HOLC loans with "no idea of paying them
out." He believes that all of the recent social legislation has "helped to
bring recovery a little closer," and if the American people will give the
President a chance "he will bring them through the depression."

Mr. Putnam had belonged to the union when he worked at the shops, but dropped his membership when he started to work for building contractors. He "admires Lewis" and feels that the CIO has been worthwhile, even if it accomplishes no more than it has already done in "waking up the AFL." Mr. Putnam sees little hope for industrial workers in Dubuque as long as the town is "dominated by a few selfish manufacturers." He feels that the Chamber of Commerce actually made no effort to keep the railroad shops in Dubuque. The small plants brought into the city by the Chamber of Commerce "employ too few workers, and pay wages too low, to make much difference in the industrial situation."

Mrs. Putnam is concerned about Wilbur, as he is becoming so bored and restless since his return from CCC camp. Though he preferred work to camp life, he considered camp life preferable to idleness. Now he is becoming somewhat cynical and "doubts if he will ever get a job." Mrs. Putnam hopes that Mr. Putnam will not be taken off WPA because it would be impossible to keep up their insurance should they go back on direct relief; she would "hate to think of being buried by the county." At present, Mr. Putnam has two life insurance policies amounting to $800 and Mrs. Putnam has a $300 policy.

Mr. Putnam, in spite of a fairly stable employment record, has no experience he can now capitalize on, except in the building trade; unless there is a decided upturn in that industry, he has little hope for reemployment.

Employment Chronolgy for Mr. Putnam

Until 1910	-- On father's farm.
1910 -- 7 months	-- Laborer, Midwestern Foundry Company.
1910 - 1911	-- Drill press operator, railroad shops.
1911 - 1912	-- Handy man, cemetery.
1912 - 1914	-- Drill press operator, railroad shops.
1914 - 1916	-- Cement worker, building construction.
1917 - 1922	-- Drill press operator, railroad shops.
1922 - 1925	-- Cement worker, building construction.
1925 - 1929	-- Grinder, Midwestern Foundry Company.

January 1930 - October 1931 -- Cement finisher, building construction.

November - July 1932 -- Owner and proprietor, tailor shop.

July 1932 - present -- Unemployed except for emergency work; now on WPA.

309.

                                    BOER

                        Mr. Roer   40
                        Mrs. Roer   37
                        Theresa   13
                        Francis   11
                        Anna   14 months
                        Mrs. Flannagan   60

Interviewing completed
February 17, 1938

    Frank Roer, a bricklayer for 18 years, has been employed on emer-
gency work projects most of the time since 1932. His wife, much worried over
the family's poverty, somewhat tactlessly tells of her expectations of a comfortable living when she married Mr. Roer in 1922 while he was earning $1.65
an hour, "but we've got poorer and poorer every year." Mr. Roer rejoins,
"Well, I didn't lose a hundred thousand dollars, or hang myself like some
fellows---and there are people worse off than us."

    Gaunt and weatherbeaten, Mr. Roer looks fully 10 years older than
his 40 years. He is partly bald; his neck is greatly enlarged from a goiter,
and his face is deeply wrinkled. His work clothes, patched many times, are
practically in tatters and his coarse shoes are in need of repair. He is
unreserved and spontaneous, expressing his opinions freely. Each year since
1932 he had hoped that the next year would be better, but instead, the Roers'
situation has grown steadily worse until now they are "just existing and
that's all." Mr. Roer's monthly WPA pay check of $45.60 after $2.40 is deducted for transportation provides only the barest necessities. He is beginning to doubt if he will ever get back to his trade again, unless, of
course, there is a pick-up in building.

    Patricia Roer, a domestic before her marriage, is 3 years younger
than her husband. She is thin and scrawny, and her features are sharp; her

hair is frizzy and somewhat untidy. She speaks with a decided Irish brogue in a high-pitched nervous voice. The Roers have three children: Theresa, 13, and Francis, 11, attend school; Anna is a very quiet, serious-faced baby of 14 months.

The five Roers and Mrs. Roer's mother, who earns $4 a week at a hotel laundry, occupy a very old, somewhat dilapidated, five-room brick house in the south end of town. The rooms, which rent for $10, are dingy though neat; the scant furnishings are old and worn; the large heating stove, furnished with the house, is covered with rust. The atmosphere of the house is altogether depressing. The Roers have wanted to move, but have not been able to afford a better place.

Mr. Roer, born in a small town near Dubuque, dropped out of school, when he was 14, to work in a lock factory for 3 years. When he was 16 he was "doing a man's work" and was paid $2 a day. In 1914 he started to learn bricklaying, the trade followed by his father and elder brother. This trade required a 4 year apprenticeship, which Mr. Roer had just completed when he enlisted for service in September 1918.

After 5 months in the army, Mr. Roer returned home and worked as a bricklayer for various contractors in Iowa and Illinois until 1932, when there was no more work to be had in the building trades. He had always had fairly steady work for about 8 months a year and had averaged from $1,200 to $1,800 a year up to 1930, when the work became slack; 1929 had been a good year, but from 1930 through 1932 jobs were increasingly scarce. When Mr. Roer was married in 1922 he had $1,100 saved up, but as his work often required him to live away from home and pay board and as his family increased in size, it became impossible to save anything. Within a few years after his marriage the $1,100 had been used to pay medical bills and to pay household expenses during the winter months of unemployment.

The Roers had moved to Dubuque soon after their marriage in 1922,
when Mr. Roer was hired to work on a big school building. After 2 years,
however, the Roers moved back to their home town. They remained there until
1931 when Mr. Roer was again employed on a building job in Dubuque, where the
family has lived ever since. On returning to Dubuque, the Roers moved in with
Mrs. Roer's mother, with whom they still live.

Though Mr. Roer had had very irregular work, mostly on odd jobs,
during 1931 and 1932, and the family had had a difficult time making ends meet,
he did not want to ask for relief. "In those days it was a disgrace to be on
relief, but now it's different." Mr. Roer's adjusted compensation of $212
had helped a lot, but the family had no other resources to fall back on. Two
insurance policies for which the annual premiums amounted to $10.40 had been
allowed to lapse without the family's having borrowed anything on them.

Early in 1933 Mr. Roer applied for veteran's relief and received
$2.25 a week for 2 or 3 months until he was assigned to one of the county
projects at $16 or $18 a month. "I hated like sin to be on relief, but there
just wasn't any other way out." Finally, in December 1933, Mr. Roer was assigned to CWA, first receiving $15 a week and later $12.50. He was very thankful for this work, and the family managed fine, as prices were so much lower
than they are now; "a quarter bought twice as much as it buys today." Mr.
Roer continued on CWA at common labor until March 1934, when he was employed
by a PWA contractor on a school building in a neighboring town for 6 months.
On this job he received $1.20 an hour, but he had to pay for his board and
room.

When he returned to Dubuque September 1, he had saved $165, which
kept the family going until around Thanksgiving time when Mr. Roer re-applied
for relief, "and be danged if I didn't have to wait 5 weeks before they would

give me anything." Now Mr. Roer feels that he made a mistake in waiting
until all of the money had been spent, as the family "almost starved to
death" before relief was granted. Had it not been for the mother-in-law's
meager earnings of $4 a week, he doesn't know what they would have done.
After 2 or 3 weeks on direct relief, Mr. Roer was given work relief on a
budget deficiency basis until his assignment to WPA in the fall of 1935.
Surplus commodities were greatly appreciated by the Roers; the canned beef
which Mrs. Roer prepared with potatoes and onions was especially liked by all
members of the family.

On WPA, Mr. Roer worked on the airport road and the swimming pool
and at Eagle Point Park. For about a year of the time since he has been on
WPA, he has worked at skilled labor and received from $70 to $72 a month.
Since last summer, however, he has worked at common labor, receiving only $48
At present, he works on the brush-clearing project 3 days a week. From this
project he gets most of his fuel by paying $2 a load for the hauling; during
his free days he cuts it into pieces suitable for the heater. Mr. Roer deplores the fact that so much of this wood is destroyed by burning when it
might be used for fuel. He can't understand why the city or the relief office did not arrange for a woodyard to which this wood could be hauled for
chopping and distribution to relief families.

While Mr. Roer is grateful for emergency work, he is critical of
some of the projects; he feels that it would have been better to invest more
money in roads and less in airports. Expenditures for public buildings,
however, are, in his opinion, justified. As to the accusation that WPA workers
loaf on the job, Mr. Roer feels that most of them don't have the right kind
of food for the heavy work required on some of the projects.

He has noticed that when the men at the brush-clearing project gather around the fire with their lunch pails, meat is seldom seen. Usually the men have jelly on their bread; "when men do that kind of heavy outdoor work they need meat." Workers with big families, however, can't afford to buy meat with an income of only $48 a month. Mr. Roer knows, because his family does not have meat on an average of more than 2 or 3 days a week. When Mr. Roer gets his pay check, he buys a shoulder, or about 10 or 14 pounds of some meat "on special," and it has to last until the next payday. Just after payday the family really has enough to eat, but for a few days before payday "it is mostly potatoes." Mr. Roer "knows darn well" that none of the family is getting "enough of the right kind of food." The baby drinks a quart of milk a day but, even so, they frequently find her earing the calcimine off the walls.

The Roers use each week a bushel of potatoes, boiled for lunch and fried for supper. After selling several bushels of potatoes from his garden last summer, Mr. Roer put away 25 sacks for his own use, but at the rate of present consumption, they won't last much longer. The Roers had a fine garden plot on the hill, but they didn't try to can any vegetagles this year since they have no satisfactory place to keep them; all of their canned stuff froze in the cellar last winter. Mr. Roer, however, realized quite a little from the sale of garden truck. He is wondering now if he will have enough money to buy seeds this spring. The seeds given out by the relief office are "OK for your own use" but no good if you expect to sell garden produce. While Mr. Roer much prefers work relief to direct relief, he feels that his family is really no better off financially than families on direct relief who get rent, fuel, clothing, and medical care, in addition to groceries.

Mr. Roer considers this winter the worst he has experienced since the beginning of the depression; every other winter he was either receiving higher wages or realizing something from odd jobs, and prices were not so high. This winter, Mr. Roer has not been able to pick up a "single odd job"; there is enough needed repair work in Dubuque, though, to keep all the skilled men busy, if people only had the money to spend. The discussion of odd jobs reminds Mr. Roer of "another inconsistency of the relief office; some investigators want people on relief to pick up odd jobs, but others raise a big howl and subtract the earnings from the relief slip."

The school children, Theresa and Francis, need clothing. Theresa's one uniform and Francis' one suit are cleaned and pressed at night in an effort to keep the children looking presentable, in spite of their poverty. Mr. Roer feels very bad about the children's not having the things they need. He doesn't mind going without himself, but he thinks it is very bad for children to be brought up in such poverty. Mr. Roer also needs work clothes, but he doesn't want to ask the relief office for them.

Mr. Roer feels that relief has been harmful for a lot of men who have almost forgotten how to work. Then, too, some men on WPA have reached the point where they prefer a 3 day work week to a 5 or 6 day week in some of the local mills, at little better pay. On the other hand, Mr. Roer feels that the WPA workers would take more interest in the job and turn out better work if they were employed every day instead of every other day. "At least they wouldn't have so much time to worry and get more discouraged."

Mr. Roer cannot see much hope for relieving unemployment so long as the purchasing power of workers is kept so low and new machinery and the speed-up system constantly reduce the number of workers required. "Higher wages and shorter hours would help some, but not enough. Wars won't help either, only to give some of the capitalists a chance to make more money." Mr. Roer supposes, however, that "if war is declared there will be just as many young fools in America as there was in 1918. The World War was insane and utterly useless. And you can just bet that some of the big capitalists are behind that big navy appropriation bill."

Mr. Roer holds only one thing against President Roosevelt: "the destruction of those pigs a few years ago when there were so many poor people in need of food." In Mr. Roer's opinion, all the economic theories in the world don't explain or excuse the destruction of food. In fact, he can't see much point in any of the farm legislation. "Farmers and working men should stick together, but the big fellows see to it that they don't."

The Dubuque Chamber of Commerce and a few of "the big shots who call themselves good business men are to blame," in Mr. Roer's opinion, "for the low wages in Dubuque. And wouldn't you think they would be smart enough to see that the low wages hurt the whole town?" Mr. Roer had always belonged to the bricklayers' union until he was no longer able to keep up his dues. He had to join again in order to get the building job in 1934, but his member- ship has again lapsed; "I can't squeeze $3 a month out of the present pay check." He can be reinstated by paying $50, and just one or two jobs at bricklaying would make it worth his while to join again. Mr. Roer is "ashamed to admit" that he does not keep up with current events, but he cannot afford a newspaper since the price has been raised, and the family has no radio.

An eastern company is building a big factory in a nearby town this spring; Mr. Roer plans to try to get on the job. He fears however that the contract will go to an eastern firm and that outside labor will be brought in

for the job. If Congress "ever gets around to passing" the housing bill,
the building trades in Dubuque should "get a break." Mrs. Roer muses that
she had almost forgotten about Mr. Roer's having been a bricklayer, as it has
been so long since he worked at the trade. Mr. Roer wonders "if it really
does any good to hope for better times." What he would like better than anything in the world would be a small chicken farm near town. He would follow
his trade, sell poultry and eggs, have a cow and a few pigs, and raise enough
garden produce for his own use. "That way we would always have enough to
eat." Mr. Roer doubts, however, that he will ever get enough ahead to realize
this dream.

                      Employment Chronology for Mr. Roer

                      1911 - 1914 - Laborer, lock factory.

                      1914 - 1918 - Apprentice, bricklayer.

                      September 1918 -
                      February 1919   U. S. Army

                      February 1919 -
                      November 1932   Bricklayer

                      November 1932 -
                      Present   Unemployed except for
                                        emergency work.

CRUMBAUGH

At home

Mr. Crumbaugh	58
Mrs. Crumbaugh	48
Marlene	24
Antony	22
Patience	20
Philip	14
Lynnet	11
Rose	7
Martha	4

Away from home

Lucy	28
Dora	26
Harold	18

Interviewing completed
January 18, 1938

Mr. Crumbaugh, with his shaggy snow-white hair, looks older than
his 58 years; a network of little broken veins shows through the skin of
his cheeks and nose; the pupil of one eye, its vision lost when Mr. Crumbaugh
was only 7 years old, is slightly smaller than the other, and the eyelid
droops. He is a broad and heavy-set man, who moves and talks with a heavy
slowness. Having some difficulty in remembering details of past experiences,
and likewise some difficulty in expressing himself, he pauses long before
answering any direct question; then, as often as not, he begins his response
with "Well, that's pretty hard to say."

In 1930 after he had been forced to sell the last 114 acres of his
farm--a mortgage on 100 acres had been foreclosed in 1926--Mr. Crumbaugh came
to Dubuque with his wife and the seven children then living at home. Two
daughters were married and away from home, and Antony stayed behind to work
for a while on a neighbor's farm.

When he came to town, Mr. Crumbaugh had about $1,200, the amount
realized from the sale of the farm beyond what was necessary to pay off the
mortgage; he hoped that this fund would tide him over until he could find
work in Dubuque. But he has had no private employment except a few odd
jobs, none lasting so long as a week. When this sum and amounts secured
by cashing in insurance policies had been exhausted, Mr. Crumbaugh applied
for relief. Since 1933 the family has been at least partially dependent
on direct relief grants, work relief, and Mr. Crumbaugh's CWA and WPA employment. For more than 2 years he has been steadily employed on WPA projects.

His acceptance of the present situation has in it something of
defeatism; he is not wholly satisfied with his present job or with his
present earnings, but he "wouldn't know where to look" for other work. In
fact, he has never applied for factory work in Dubuque; it has been his feeling that there were no jobs available. He is handicapped by his age and by
his lack of any sort of experience as an industrial wage earner. Perhaps he
is still more handicapped by his feeling of helplessness; he does not know
how to look for a job, or where. Though he feels that this one sightless
eye never lessened his effectiveness as a farmer and does not think of it in
terms of a physical handicap, Mrs. Crumbaugh and the oldest son, Antony, believe that it would preclude the possibility of his being employed in any local factory; the factories can find plenty of unhandicapped and experienced
men to take over what few jobs are open.

Mrs. Crumbaugh's fatalistic outlook somewhat resembles her husbands,
though she is not quite so resigned as he, for her resignation is tinged with
bitterness. She is a pleasant, friendly woman, too stout, a little nervous
and fidgety, and not very well. Since she has never been satisfied with

living in town, she would like now to take the younger children to a farm.
Mrs. Crumbaugh is somewhat irritated by her husband's failure even to express
any interest in planning to go back to farming, though she states that unless
he had some money to invest, Mr. Crumbaugh could not go to a farm except as a
hand, in which case no provision could be made for the family to be with him.

No one of the three children of employable age now at home has full-
time work. All of the older children have evidently made considerable effort
to find jobs, and, for the most part, have not been entirely unemployed. But
they have shifted from job to job with some frequency, and their earnings have
been consistently meager.

It was in 1909, the year of his marriage, that Mr. Crumbaugh purchased his first farm land—114 acres. Until the early twenties his farming
was profitable, especially during the war years, and from time to time he
made a number of new investments: in additional acreage; in livestock, farm
equipment, and buildings; in stocks, bank accounts, and insurance policies.
He purchased 100 more acres of land at $135 an acre, built a $1,000 house and
a $3,000 barn. He explains jestingly that since the first two children "un-
fortunately were girls" he regularly employed farm hands before the boys were
old enough to help with the work. His chief crops were corn and oats. He
estimated that the value of the farm, including livestock and equipment, was
at one time $50,000. Once he was offered $250 an acre for the entire farm.
Perhaps he should have sold then, but he did not even consider giving up farming; besides, in those days when land values were high, he, like other farmers,
anticipated that values would rise even higher.

By 1920 Mr. Crumbaugh was carrying a mortgage $25,000, the first
loan having been secured when he planned the building of the new house. From
1920 on, he had ever increasing difficulties. That year a tornado caused

losses involving about a thousand dollars. One or two summers later all
but three of the hogs died of cholera. Meanwhile, during the depression
of the early twenties land values were steadily declining and prices of farm
produce going lower and lower. Within this same period, the bank in which
he had a savings account failed and paid out only 15 percent of the total
deposits. This bank had loaned as much as $200 an acre on farm lands.

In 1926, Mr. Crumbaugh thinks it was, a mortgage was foreclosed
on 100 acres of his farm. At the same time, he sold a part of his personal
property in order to settle all of his debts except the mortgage on the remainder of the farm. Thus, for a while, the family was relatively secure,
but much too heavy a mortgage was now being carried on the 114 acres. In
1930, burdened with debts and threatened with foreclosure, Mr. Crumbaugh
sold his farm; he realized enough to pay off the mortgage and other debts,
and he had remaining about $1,200. The family then moved to Dubuque; there
was "nothing else to do." Looking back on his farm experience, Mr. Crumbaugh
is not certain that he had any greater feeling of security on the farm than
he has had during the past 7 years, for "farming was always a gamble." His
description of past experiences is consistently noncommittal. He occasionally
reveals a nice sense of humor but expresses no regrets.

Mr. Crumbaugh does think that he "might have held on a little longer
if he had not bought stocks which were later valueless. He had 50 shares of
stock, valued at $3,000, in a Dubuque packing company when it failed in 1921.
A dividend for the first half of 1920 netted him about $173; he believes this
was the last dividend declared. He also lost money invested in stock in a
Rockford packing company. Mrs. Crumbaugh calls sinking money in stocks
"foolish stuff"; city stock promoters sold shares to farmers who "didn't know
enough" about investments to evaluate the worth of stocks. For her husband's
"foolishness," the whole family now "has to pay."

From the spring of 1930 until the spring of 1933 the Crumbaughs
lived on the amounts secured from the sale of the farm and from the cashing
in of insurance policies, plus earnings from odd jobs. Mr. Crumbaugh worked
a few days for a construction company, a few days for the city water works,
a few days here and a few days there, but earned almost nothing. He had
carried 20-payment life insurance policies, with face values totaling $5,000,
for himself and a 20-payment life policy of $1,000 on Mrs. Crumbaugh. These
policies had a total cash surrender value of some $800 or $900. The only
other policy was Marlene's; this policy, on which $50 or $60 had been paid,
and which had no cash surrender value, was allowed to lapse. Mr. Crumbaugh
estimates that while the family was living in Dubuque and before he found it
necessary to apply for relief, expenditures totaled about $100 a month.

Since expenses on the farm covered quite different items, he can
make no precise comparison of the family's expenses on the farm and expenses
in town, but total living costs were probably about the same. In town the
Crumbaughs were now paying $30 a month for rent. They spent little more than
previously for groceries, even though the garden in the backyard did not compare with the truck garden on the farm, for prices were now much lower. The
Crumbaughs' expenses are not so high now as they were in 1930 and 1931. Since
1932 Mr. Crumbaugh has had a fairly large garden on the island--land owned by
the city and gardened rent-free -- and Mrs. Crumbaugh has done a great deal of
canning. The family has moved to a house renting for $21 a month. The Crum-
baughs' present home is in a neighborhood of small frame houses all very much
alike. It is a little shabby but in fairly good repair, furnished somewhat
sparsely but comfortably.

When the Crumbaughs applied for relief in 1933, they had exhausted
available resources, and run up grocery and doctor bills. Two of the

children were working: Antony had managed to go from one farm job to another,
keeping rather steadily employed, and sometimes contributing a little to the
family; Marlene, who had gone to country school until she was 16 but had never
attended school in Dubuque, was earning $3 a week at housework. The younger
children were still in school. Mr. and Mrs. Crumbaugh are both anxious to
make it clear that they did not apply for relief until it was absolutely necessary to do so. But, having come to this necessity, they applied for assistance without any special **reluctance** --"there was nothing else to do."

Though Mrs. Crumbaugh found it difficult to manage on the meager
food allowance with the seven children in the home, she "didn't complain"
about the relief grants. Mr. Crumbaugh inclines to the belief that there
was a good deal of "partiality" and "preference" in the distributing of relief; persons with "the most guts" got most in the way of relief; others who
were "a little bashful" did not fare so well. Being among the bashful ones,
the Crumbaughs made few requests.

Before the inauguration of the CWA program Mr. Crumbaugh had some
work relief, for which he was paid only in grocery orders. Then for several
months he worked on the CWA airport project, earning $15 a week. The Crum-
baughs consider this work the first "real help" they were given. On completion
of the CWA project the family received direct relief until Mr. Crumbaugh was
assigned to a WPA project in November or December 1935. Mr. Crumbaugh is
rather proud of his record of having missed only 1 day of work in almost 3
years of CWA and WPA employment.

During the past 2 years he has worked on various WPA projects--in
a county stone quarry, on park clearing projects, and "out in the sticks"
clearing brush. Working 3 days a week, he earns $48 a month. Out of his
wages he must pay $2.50 a month for transportation to and from work. Mr.
Crumbaugh much prefers WPA work to direct relief; as he says, "I like working

for what I get, but I would like to get more." Mrs. Crumbaugh believes
that "there's nothing like private work," and that the family could manage
much better if Mr. Crumbaugh had one of the factory jobs, some of which, she
understands, pay as much as $100 a month. The Crumbaughs would consider even
$80 a month a reasonably adequate income.

Mr. Crumbaugh thinks that he could not have managed so well during
the past few years if he had not had "good kids." But he is sorry that none
of his children have done very well, or been much interested, in school. He
feels that young people nowadays need good educations in order to find jobs.
However, the four oldest unmarried children have all helped the family to
some extent.

Marlene, 24 years old, thin and pale and tired looking, has had
only one job aside from housework since she left school some 8 years ago.
Her highest earnings at housework were $4 a week, with some meals included.
While working she has always lived at home. Marlene is quiet-mannered but
friendly and poised. She gives considerable attention to her appearance; her
clothing is inexpensive, but neat; her hair is curled in tight little ringlets.
Last August she began work as a power sewing machine operator at the Hall clothing factory. Since she has always liked to sew--at home, she makes clothing
for the younger children--and since the pay was higher, Marlene much preferred
this job to housework. On a piecework basis her earnings at Hall's averaged
about $2.50 a day, but she frequently worked only 2 or 3 days a week. When
the Hall factory closed early in December for inventory-taking, she was laid
off altogether and has not been called back. She has kept an application on
file at the State employment office, but she thinks that this office makes few
placements. Recently, having heard that the battery factory planned to hire
about 200 people, she went to the plant to make application. Thus far, she
has not heard of anyone's being taken on.

Antony, 22, has been at home for the past several days "looking around" for a job in town to last until the spring when he can again find farm work. His father feels that it will be even harder than usual to find a job in town this winter, for most of the factories have laid off some of their regular employees. If he does not find a job in a few days, Antony will return to the country, where he can probably work in return for his board and room, as he has done during several other winters. He is proud of never having been totally unemployed for more than "a week and a half" at one time. Sine he has worked on Iowa farms for about 8 years, he knows many farmers and can pick up jobs easily. He has done many kinds of farm work, for which he has been paid variously, in cash or in maintenance only, by the month or on the basis of output. This past fall, he spent several weeks picking corn at "so much" per bushel. He likes farm work better than factory employment, for he cannot get used to the "inside work." His highest earnings for farm work have been about $50 a month, in addition to room and board.

During the early part of 1937 Antony worked for 3 months as a clean-up man at the Midwestern Foundry Company. Mr. Crumbaugh thought it hard for his son to work alone in the factory at night, but Antony insists that he did not mind working at night or being alone. He did object to standing all night long, for he has had some trouble with his feet for several years. The extremes of temperature were also disagreeable. His job was a combination of the work which had once been done by two men: In addition to the clean-up work he hauled frozen sand from an unheated shed to the furnaces where it was heated for use next morning in the making of molds. Around the furnaces, he worked only in his undershirt; while shoveling and hauling the sand, he had to be warmly dressed.

Antony got his job at the foundry through a foreman whom he knew fairly well; he believes that "pull" is the primary requisite for getting any job. For the factory work, he was paid $90 a month, wages which he considered no more adequate than his highest wages for farm work. In the early spring, as soon as Antony anticipated that farm jobs would be opening up, he left the foundry.

For some time Antony has "hankered to join the navy," like his brother, Harold. A year ago he was rejected because of his fallen arches, but, hoping that "they aren't so particular now," Antony plans to make one more effort to get into the navy before he leaves Dubuque again.

Harold left school when he was 16. The following summer he was sent to a CCC camp. Both parents were glad for him to be in camp, for there was little chance of/finding private employment, and they feel that young people who have no work become discouraged even more easily than older men and may "get into mischief." At camp the boys had "good food" and learned a great deal in various training courses. Though the work was strenuous, Harold is such a husky fellow that "it didn't phase him." And Harold's earnings at camp were a great help to the family. Harold left the camp only at the end of 13 months and because he was determined to join the navy.

Mr. Crumbaugh was pleased with Harold's camp record, especially when he received a letter from the director, who stated that Harold might return to camp if he was not accepted for the navy. More than a year ago Harold enlisted for 4 years of service. He is now stationed in the Hawaiian Islands. Mrs. Crumbaugh worries because she does not hear from him very often and fears that he may be sent to China. But the Crumbaughs did not attempt to discourage him when he wanted to enlist. They have warned Antony that, if he joins the navy, he will have to stay for 4 years—he can't "run away"— and he may have to engage in actual fighting. The final decision, however, is left up to Antony.

Patience, 20, left school 4 years ago, partly because the Crumbaughs could not afford to keep her in high school. Like Marlene, she has had a variety of housework jobs, one of them paying only $1.50 a week. In July 1936 she was given an NYA assignment. She now works in the public library two afternoons a week, for which she is paid $16 a month, besides doing housework two mornings a week. She has not been able to find a full-time job. Mrs. Crumbaugh wishes now that Patience had completed her high school course, but Patience does not want to return to school, as she would be so much older than others in her class.

Three of the four youngest children are in school. Philip, 14 years old, a tall, pale lad, not "overly strong," has reached only the eighth grade, for he "doesn't learn so good." The two little girls, Lynnet and Rose, also attend grade school. The baby, who will be 5 years old in the spring, will go to kindergarten next year.

Though the Crumbaughs as a family group do not share in many activities (for they have little recreation of any kind), the children apparently get along well with each other and with the parents. Marlene and Antony are sympathetic with their father in his inability to find work. Marlene thinks that he is discouraged, as "any man would be" when he can't earn enough to support his family. She understands, too, her mother's wish to return to a farm, though Marlene herself would prefer to remain in town. But, because Mrs. Crumbaugh has not been well for the past several years, Marlene believes that she would be less happy on a farm than she anticipates. Though Mrs. Crumbaugh would like to raise chickens and have her own garden once again, she would probably not be strong enough to do more than the housework.

The Crumbaughs go regularly to church, but Mrs. Crumbaugh says despondently that "people won't even be able to go to church" now that the

pastor has asked every adult to contribute 10¢ each Sunday. Mrs. Crumbaugh
seems to be more discouraged than her husband. If Marlene had only kept her
work at Hall's, the family could probably have managed to get along during the
winter months; Mr. Crumbaugh's and Patience's earnings combined are not enough
to meet minimum expenses. Now the Crumbaughs are getting farther and farther
behind with rent and water bills. The water bill, Mr. Crumbaugh may be able
to work out, as he has done several times in the past, but no arrangement can
be made about the rent.

Mr. Crumbaugh, though not very articulate at any time, shows more
interest in a discussion of his farm experience and in the problems of farmers
than in any consideration of industrial situations or his own chances of finding private employment. He approves of the present administration because it
has "at least tried to help the farmers." He believes that the AAA accomplished its purpose of increasing farm incomes, but does not approve of having
lands "lay idle" or "taken out of production." Though he has heard many people
"hollering about over-production," Mr. Crumbaugh thinks that if all employable men had jobs paying reasonably good wages, they would be able to buy
everything that could be produced. He speaks of the "new depression" which
has already seriously affected Dubuque. As far as he can see times are no
better than they were in 1930, when he first came to town. Certainly he has
no greater hope now than then of finding a job in Dubuque.

Employment Chronology for Mr. Crumbaugh

1909 - 1930   -   Farmer.

1930 - present   Unemployed except for
                    emergency work; now
                    on WPA.

MURPHY

At home

Mr. Murphy	59
Mrs. Murphy	51
Bill	19
Jim	18
Felicia	15
Ruth	13
Pete	12
Margaret	9

Mr. Edw. Murphy	21
Mrs. Edw. Murphy	19
John	2
Barbara	2 months

Married and away from home

Mrs. Casey	26
Mrs. Dooley	24
Mrs. Smith	23

Interviewing completed
March 4, 1938

Peter Murphy, his wife, Kate, their six single children, and a married son's family of four live together in seven upstairs rooms in the downtown factory district. Though the stairs and halls leading to the flat are dirty and dilapidated, the Murphy's living room, comfortably and neatly furnished, is cheerful and attractive. The family is lively and gay; the numerous grandchildren romp about, and the grownups laughingly exchange witticisms. The two married daughters who live in Dubuque bring their five children to visit the grandparents almost every day. In order to reduce expenses the Peter Murphys and their married son, Edward, have for several months lived together and pooled resources. Edward earns from $10 to $18 a week as a garage helper, and Mr. Murphy receives $45.60 a month for his WPA work after $2.40 has been deducted for transportation. Nineteen-year-old

Bill, who is employed on NYA, turns over to his mother each month $5 of his
$16 pay check. None of the three sons-in-law earns enough to assist the
Murphys. The most prosperous son-in-law, a surveyor, receives only $110
a month and has a family of four to support; another is employed at the
Iowa Garage at $75 a month, and the third is on a ranch in Oregon. Peter
Murphy, 59 years old, is a grizzled, wiry little man. His parents came
from Ireland and settled on a farm in Iowa, where Peter was born. Peter
speaks with a decided Irish brogue. He has a keen sense of humor, and a
cheerful outlook on life despite his extreme poverty. After being "burnt
out" on the farm, where had lived all his life, Peter moved his family to
Marquette, Iowa, 14 years ago. In 1929 the family moved from Marquette,
where he had been employed in a roundhouse for 6 years to Dubuque. Aside
from two short factory jobs, Mr. Murphy has been unemployed except for emergency work since he came to Dubuque.

Kate Murphy, 51 years old, of German and Irish descent, is vivacious
and pleasant. She is still handsome, except for her teeth: several front
teeth have been extracted and no false teeth substituted. Mrs. Murphy is
devoted to her 10 living children and to her 9 grandchildren. Eighteen-year-
old Jim has not had a job since he quit school after completing the eighth
grade 1½ years ago. Four of the children attend school: Felicia, 15, never
.very strong, now in the eighth grade, is anxious to get a job; Ruth, 13, is
also in the eighth grade; and Peter, 12, and Margaret, 9, are both in the fifth
grade. The three married daughters all worked in Dubuque factories prior to
their marriage. Alice, now married to Jack Casey, the surveyor, was always
big and strong and "worked alongside the men" as a machine operator at the
Julien Foundry and at the Midwestern Foundry Company; she sometimes earned as
much as $22 a week. Mr. Casey had saved money for furniture, which he and

Alice had already selected. When they went to draw the money out on their
wedding day, the bank was closed and in consequence the furniture order was
canceled; the young people moved in with Mr. Casey's parents. When the
youngest son-in-law, Howard Smith, could no longer find work in Dubuque, he
and his wife went out west and are now comfortably settled on a ranch in
Oregon. Their glowing reports of ranch life on the west coast have raised
certain hopes for the Murphys, who now see in Oregon a sort of promised land;
they plan to go out this summer if money can be raised for transportation.

Peter Murphy never had much schooling, as he was often kept at
home to help with the farm work; when he had completed the fifth grade he
dropped out. At 19, Peter decided to "strike out for himself"; so he got
a job as general handy man in a "fine hotel" in Sioux City. During threshing
seasons he went to the Dakotas for about 6 weeks each year. In those days
steam threshers were used and the season lasted about 40 days; now, however,
the farmers all have modern machinery and the threshing lasts no more than
10 days. After "knocking about" for 5 years, Peter was married and rented
a farm of his own. For the next 20 years the Murphys made a fair living at
farming but never saved anything, as the family increased rapidly, and rents
soared higher and higher. In 1920 they were paying $800 rental; so they de-
cided to start buying the farm by paying an additional $200 a year. Just 2
years later the Murphys lost everything they had in a fire.

Discouraged with farming and anxious to be near good schools, the
Murphys moved to Marquette, where Mr. Murphy had "the promise of a job" at
the roundhouse. For more than 5 years he worked as a stoker at the roundhouse
7 days a week and 8 hours a day. During the 5 years he lost only 2 days and
that was at the time of the death of one of the children. On this job Mr.
Murphy was paid 40¢ an hour. By 1929 work at the roundhouse had become quite

slack and he was expecting to be laid off any day. A sister in Dubuque got him a job in the Julien Foundry; so the family moved to Dubuque in 1929. For 8 months Peter worked at core making and brass blowing; he was paid 40¢ an hour. He worked 6 days a week and from 8 to 10 hours a day. Peter found this work much more interesting and not so strenuous as the roundhouse job, but he was laid off at the end of 8 months. After being unemployed for 2 years, he was hired at an insulating factory where he worked for 6 months, operating a machine. He was paid 35¢ an hour and usually averaged $17 or $18 a week.

Since he was laid off from this job in 1933, he has had no other private employment. "Then it was relief for us." The Murphys felt "disgraced" over asking for relief, and Mrs. Murphy had to "hound" Mr. Murphy for 3 days before he would go to the relief office to make application. The Murphys had always considered that only "no-count" people asked for charity, but now people ask for relief "just as matter of fact as they eat their dinner." During the 2 years that Mr. Murphy had been unemployed following his layoff at the foundry two of the daughters had been working and the family had managed satisfactorily. In the meantime, these two daughters had been married, and when Mr. Murphy lost his job at the insulating factory no one else in the family was working. As there were 10 of them, Mr. Murphy's pay of $17 or $18 a week had been just enough to meet current expenses, and when that income was cut off there were no reserves to fall back on. The Murphys had small insurance policies on all members of the family, but none of the policies had any cash value.

The Murphys had no difficulties in getting relief, though Mr. Murphy "did have to answer a million questions." An investigator visited the home the day after Mr. Murphy made application and relief was granted immediately. While on direct relief for 3 or 4 months before Mr. Murphy was assigned to CWA, the family received a grocery order of $14 every 2 weeks, rent every other

month, and a ton of coal a month. Mrs. Murphy found it practically impossible
to feed 10 people on $7 a week; she says, "It was a feast, then a famine."
During the last days of the 2-week period "it was mighty skimpy." Then, too,
the relief office policy of allowing rent only every other month caused the
Murphys to fall so far in arrears that they were finally evicted. The Murphys
feel, however, that they were well treated by the relief office in spite of
the fact that "nosey people tried to make trouble." Once when one of the boys
was hired to play the guitar at a neighborhood tavern, Mr. and Mrs. Murphy
went over to listen to the music for a little while. A neighbor ran to the
relief office with a story that the Murphys were spending money in a beer
tavern.

The Murphys are still about $300 in debt. Before applying for relief
the family had run up a grocery bill of $40, and since going on relief, a
medical bill of $150 and an electrical bill of $20 have been incurred, in
addition to rent amounting to $50. One day recently the doctor came to see
Mrs. Murphy about the family's clinic bill, but when Mrs. Murphy told him
that Mr. Murphy was working on WPA and had to support a family of eight, the
doctor said, "Lady, just forget that bill."

While the Murphys feel conscience-stricken about their unpaid bills,
they have decided that they "can't eat and pay on them." Edward's earnings at
the garage are uncertain; one week recently he drew only $10 and he usually
averages no more than $15. Bill buys his own clothes, takes care of his tran
portation, and gives his mother $5 out of his monthly NYA pay check of $16.
He is on a willow-cutting project on the island. Mr. and Mrs. Murphy conside
that the NYA program is a fine thing; it not only helps financially, but also
keeps the youngsters off the streets. Eighteen-year-old Jim has also been
certified for NYA, but has never been assigned to a project. His idleness

worries Mr. and Mrs. Murphy. They feel that most of the crimes in Dubuque
are committed by jobless young fellows who become rebellious over not having
any money to spend. The Murphys also consider the CCC camps a very worthwhile
undertaking. Edward was sent to a CCC camp before his marriage, but came
home after 5 days. He had never been away from home before, and when he was
told that he would be transferred to a camp in Arkansas, he became ill from
worry, and finally hitchhiked home. Mr. Murphy was very much disgusted with
him, but Mrs. Murphy tolerantly remarks, "He was just 18 and had never spent
a night away from home before."

Since the fall of 1933, Mr. Murphy has been employed at common labor
on emergency work, and he is at present on the brush clearing project. He has
enjoyed the work but would like it better if "there was more money in it."
But at any rate, "it is much better than direct relief." Mr. Murphy believes
that the men, at least those in his crew, work as hard on WPA as they would
work on any job, and the working conditions at the brush clearing project are
none too pleasant, as the men stand in mud and slush up to their ankles. One
day last week "a man broke through the ice up to his waist."

Mr. Murphy thinks that most of the criticism of the Works Program
comes from "a one-way thinking group of people" who know nothing of deprivations themselves and object to any assistance to destitute families. "WPA
workers are paying taxes the same as other people and the work they perform
is of public benefit." While Mr. Murphy favors the Social Security legislation, he does not expect to receive any benefits personally. When the farmers
drive up to the feed stores across the street "in fine new cars," the Murphys
wonder if they did not make a mistake in giving up farming. They feel that
Government aid during the last few years had made it possible for Iowa farmers
"to get on their feet again."

Mr. Murphy blames machinery for wide-spread unemployment and doubts
if there will be any improvement in the situation, inasmuch as the introduction of labor-saving machinery is on the increase. Mr. Murphy resents the
fact that the Nation's wealth is controlled by a "mere handful of men." While
he feels that there should be a more equitable distribution of wealth, he has
no notion as to how such a change could be brought about.

In Mr. Murphy's opinion, "Dubuque is the deadest town in Iowa and
there is no hope of a resurrection as long as the big mills are in control.
Everyone will tell you those fellows run everything. All Dubuque needs now
is a monument on the hill." Mr. Murphy believes that "labor unions will not
accomplish anything in Dubuque as long as there are so many idle men ready
to scab." He does not blame men for taking any job they can get, even if it
does mean scabbing. Mr. Murphy does not approve of the violence in connection
with strikes. "That kind of stuff ain't right." Mr. Murphy feels that his
age is against him in the factories; the man "around 60" is considered a
"poor insurance risk" and in consequence, coverage rates are boosted. Mr.
Murphy has no hopes of private employment in Dubuque; he asks "Why doesn't
the Government send fellows like him out to some of the idle farms where
they could at least make their food?"

The Murphys feel that the children would be much better off in the
country than in town where work is so scarce. The Murphys are anxious to
leave Dubuque as they can see no future for any of them here. The daughter
and son-in-law in Oregon want the family to come out there this summer. The
son-in-law is sure that Mr. Murphy and the boys can find employment on the
ranch. While the Murphys have no reserve cash, and have no idea how they
will "get to Oregon," their faces brighten as they talk enthusiastically of
the prospects which are still somewhat vague. The son-in-law has offered

to help all he can; as he has recently purchased a car, the Murphys think
he will probably come after them, but "how are nine people to ride in one car
with baggage?" Edward wants to take his family, too; that would mean four
more.

Mr. Murphy has an idea that it would be best for one of the Murphys
to go out first to look the situation over before the whole family moves, but
Mrs. Murphy thinks they couldn't help but like it. "The children have beef-
steak for breakfast, deer meat, wild turkey, and sage hens and the scenery is
wonderful." The son-in-law earns $4 a day, in addition to milk and other farm
produce. All of this sounds like a dreamland to the Murphys and helps to
brighten their hopes for the future.

                    Employment Chronology for Mr. Murphy

          1897 - 1903   Hotel porter and farm hand.

          1903 - 1923   Farmer.

          1923 - 1929   Stoker, railroad roundhouse.

          1929 - 8 mos. Core maker and brass blower,
                              Julien Foundry.

          1930 - 1932   Unemployed.

          1932 - 6 mos. Shredder, insulating factory.

          1933 - Present Unemployed except for emergency work;
                              now on WPA.

DILLING

Mr. Dilling	25
Mrs. Dilling	21
Beatrice	3
Helen	6 months

Interviewing completed
February 5, 1938

John Dilling, at 25 years of age, has never had a job lasting
more than a few months. Slender, and of average height, he has strong
features and makes an excellent appearance. He has a forthright manner, and
discusses his situation without reticence, though he is a little resentful
of being on relief. Alma Dilling, his wife, is a pretty, frail little thing.
She is only 21 and looks even younger. Friendly and straightforward, she
makes no attempt to conceal their poverty or to create a favorable impression, though she does apologize for the topsy-turvey appearance of the room.

The Dillings, with their two children, Beatrice, 3 years, and
Helen, 6 months, occupy one room on the third floor of a dilapidated rooming
house, rented by Mr. Dilling's parents. The room is crowded and disorderly.
A double bed, two small children's beds, a dresser, two chairs, a small
table and a two-burner gas plate comprise the furnishings of the room. Toys
clutter the floor; one of the two chairs is filled with empty milk bottles
and coffee tins; clothing is strewn about the room, and the window sills
are laden with food, as the Dillings have no icebox.

For 3 summers prior to Mr. Dilling's graduation from high school
he had worked with his father at painting for a railroad. Mr. Dilling,
senior, had been employed in the maintenance and ways department of the railroad service for some 30 years, and he had had fairly steady work until 1929,
when his work was reduced to 3 months during the summer. John had always

wanted to take up electrical engineering; after he completed high school, he used his railroad pass to go to California to visit relatives and try to find a job at the university. He had saved, from his summer work, almost $100. After entering the university he was unable to find work to help with expenses, as practically all the students were working their way. By the end of the first quarter John's savings were gone, and as his relatives were unable to assist him, there was no alternative but to return to Dubuque.

After returning to Dubuque, John drove a truck 6 months for a construction company and 4 months for an ice company, with 2 months of idleness between jobs. For the next 3 months he had irregular work driving a truck for a produce company at 25¢ an hour during their busy season, followed by 5 months of hauling lumber.

John used his own truck while employed by the lumber company and was paid according to the amount of lumber hauled. The truck had been bought secondhand on the installment plan for $140. John was again unemployed for several months before he got work with a creamery during the summer of 1935. During the winters of '34 and '35 he worked a few days hauling for the airport project, and in April 1936, he did some trucking into Wisconsin for 3 or 4 weeks. From June to September 1936 John worked with his father at painting for the railroad. After another period of unemployment, lasting 4 months, he was hired by the Dubuque Woodworking Company February 5, 1937. Here he worked for 3 months on a saw and at assembling screen doors and was paid 33¢ an hour.

This was John's first experience at factory work. He was greatly impressed by the monotony of many of the jobs, though his own work was not particularly monotonous as he made frequent trips to the storeroom for

materials. One man who stood all day feeding small blocks into a saw lost
four fingers on his right hand when he absentmindedly placed his hand too
near the saw. In Mr. Dilling's opinion, "most of the so-called safety de-
vices just don't work, and many of the accidents occur on the monotonous
jobs." Several hundred men were working at the Dubuque Woodworking Mill
while Mr. Dilling was there. About half of these men, like Mr. Dilling, had
been taken on for only a few months during a particularly busy season. After
his layoff at the Dubuque Woodworking Mill in May 1937, Mr. Dilling began
work in June with his father on the railroad paint jobs. For the railroad
work Mr. Dilling was paid 64½¢ an hour, and usually he averaged $130 a month.
After the layoff from the railroad in September, he and his father contracted
for three or four paint jobs. Since November 1937, however, he has been unemployed except for WPA work to which he was assigned in December.

     After John's marriage in 1934 he brought his wife to his parents'
home, where they lived for more than a year. His parents received relief
early in 1935, but John and his wife were not included in the budget, as he
was able to manage on the odd jobs he picked up. After the parents moved to
a cheaper house John and his wife moved to furnished rooms where the rent
amounted to $20 a month. As John's work became more irregular, they got
behind with the rent and the landlady asked them to move. They lived for
a while with John's sister, but that didn't work out; since April 1934 they
have moved six times. The Dillings had three insurance policies totaling
$2,000; two of these policies lapsed in 1935; one $1,000 policy, however,
has been kept in force. By December 1935 the Dillings owed a medical bill
of $85 and milk and grocery bills amounting to $25, in addition to several
months' rent.

In order to reduce indebtedness he sold the truck for $25; $15
was paid on milk and grocery bills. Not until January 20, 1936, did he and
his wife ask for help, and they would not have made application then had it
not been for the child. In fact, John is inclined to think that he "would
have managed somehow if there had been no relief office to call on." He
feels that too many people heard about other people's getting help and decided to try it too. John "guesses" he made application because he had so
many people advising him to do so. "Too many people," he thinks, "have
come to feel that the world owes them a living and try to get all they can
out of the relief office."

Mrs. Dilling says that her husband resents being on relief. He
refused to make the first application and she had to go to the relief office,
as they were out of provisions. She was unable to answer all the questions
and Mr. Dilling was sent for. She thinks that his resentment may be due to
some difficulties his parents had with the relief office. The relief office
felt that the Dillings, senior, were too demanding and should have been able
to manage on Mr. Dilling's summer earnings. Alma believes that the parents
were trying to pay off back debts while on relief and in consequence pro-
voked the relief office.

During 1936 the John Dillings received relief only during the
periods when John was unemployed; when he got a job he would notify the
relief office and the grant would be discontinued. No relief was received
from February 1937 until November 1937 when John reapplied and was assigned
to the WPA brush clearing project at $48 a month. John much prefers project
work to direct relief, but he is anxious to find private employment.

The Dillings were never able to manage on direct relief; they
ran up a big milk bill and got farther and farther behind with rent, as

neither milk nor rent was included in their budget. They barely manage to
make ends meet with Mr. Dilling's WPA check of $48 a month. Two dollars
and forty cents a month is paid for transportation to and from the project
which is located some distance from town; food and milk come to $25 or $30
a month, and insurance premiums amount to $3. A little is paid each month
on the back grocery and milk bills, and whenever the budget permits, a small
remittance is made to the physician to whom $150 is owed for services at the
birth of the two children, and during the illness of the little girl last
winter.

Mrs. Dilling says, "I just never get caught up—the whole pay check
is owed before it is received." The Dillings pay no regular rent to Mr.
Dilling's parents, but give them a few dollars occasionally. Mr. Dilling's
parents have not been on relief since they rented the rooming house a year
ago. They occupy basement rooms and rent out four furnished apartments,
from which enough is realized to pay the rent and most of the other expenses.
Mrs. Dilling, senior, takes in washings to help with expenses. Mr. Dilling,
senior, is eligible for a railroad retirement pension but has received
nothing as yet. Their quarters, like those of John's family, are extremely
disorderly. Another married son was on relief until he found steady work
a few months ago. The married daughter has helped her parents and her
brother John all she could. She has taken care of John's children while
Alma worked in stores occasionally during sales and has helped a little
with clothing for the children.

Alma likes to go sometimes to dances with her sister-in-law and
other girl friends. A man who lives in the rooming house runs a dance hall;
he and his wife often take the girls along with them when there is a good

orchestra at the hall. John does not like to dance and refuses to go to
dances. He belongs to a basketball team which practices once or twice
a week.

Mr. Dilling is very affectionate with his children and seems to be
genuinely interested in their well-being.

He blames labor-saving machinery, the speed-up system, and low
purchasing power of workers for widespread unemployment. Dubuque is a "very
backward town," in John's opinion, and he would like to get away. He has
heard that a gigantic building program is planned in Florida and he would
like to make connection with a contractor down there. He would take his
family to Florida on railroad passes if he had enough to live on until he
could find work. He expects to have regular summer employment on the railroad,
but he knows that it is impossible to support a family of four on 3 months'
work a year.

Employment Chronology for Mr. Dilling

December 1933 — June 1934   Truck driver, construction
                              company.

June 1934 — July 1934   Unemployed.

July 1934 — November 1934   Truck driver, ice company

November 1934 — February 1935 Truck driver, produce company.

February 1935 — June 1935   Truck driver, lumber company

June 1935 — August 1935   Unemployed.

August 1935 — September 1935 Truck driver, creamery.

September 1935 — June 1936   Unemployed.

June 1936 — September 1936   Painter's helper, railroad

October 1936 — January 1937   Unemployed.

February 1937 — May 1937   Assembler, Dubuque Woodworking
                               Company.

June 1937 — September 1937   Painter's helper, railroad.

September 1937 — November 1937 Odd paint jobs.

November 1937 — present Unemployed; now on WPA.

DALECK

Mr. Daleck	25
Mrs. Daleck	24
Judith	6
Peggy	4
Jimmie	2

Florence Daleck 18

Interviewing completed
March 3, 1938

George Daleck and his family have been dependent on either direct relief or work relief for 7 or 8 months of each year since 1932. George has never had what might be considered a regular job, and his earnings have always been small. George was married in 1931; he now has his wife, three children, and an 18-year-old deaf sister dependent on him. The family occupies a four-room dingy, somewhat dilapidated brick house in the downtown district. The rooms are sparsely and poorly furnished. The linoleum floor covering is badly worn, and the few chairs are rickety. A new cabinet radio, a large heating stove, and three chairs are the only furnishings of the sitting room. The two little girls, Judith, 6, and Peggy, 4, chatter happily as they play with their puppy; 2-year-old Jimmie refuses to leave his mother's arms even for a moment; Mr. Daleck's deaf sister and a deaf and dumb friend carry on an animated conversation with their fingers.

George Daleck, 25 years old, is tall, slender, and rather nice looking, though somewhat unkempt. He talks easily, expressing himself with spontaneity and frankness. He discusses his own situation with some degree of of insight and intelligence; he seems, however, to have little interest in economic problems in the abstract. Mrs. Daleck, like her husband, is friendly and talkative. The family's depressed economic situation has been further complicated by illnesses during the past year. More than $300 is still owed for medical and hospital service, though George has made small

payments on these bills from time to time. The family owes other bills
amounting to $200, and Mr. Daleck doubts if they will ever get out of debt.
For about half of the time since their marriage 6 years ago the Dalecks
have lived with George's parents; after George lost his job, soon after his
marriage, he and his wife lived with his father for more than 1 year, and
again 2 years ago went to the father's home when they were evicted for nonpayment of rent.   Mr. Daleck, senior, like his son, has been irregularly
employed and on relief much of the time since 1932.

George Daleck began work when he was 14 at a glass company.   He
worked only part time, as he was required to attend part-time school until
he had completed the eighth grade.   For his work as office boy and assembler
of sets of dishes, he was paid $7.50 a week.   After working on this job for
1 year, George was employed as a farm hand for 2 years.   During 5 or 6
months in the summer he was paid $30 a month, but during the winter months
he received only his board, lodging, and laundry.

On his return to town in 1928 George worked for 6 months as a
dishwasher for the Grand Lunch Room.   Here he was paid $12.50 a week and
his meals; the hours were long, and he soon lost his appetite for this
restaurant's food.   For 4 or 5 months during the winter he was a helper on
a coal truck for the Willow Company; he was paid 40¢ an hour for a 54 hour
week.   From 1929 to 1931 George was employed as a shoe shiner and pressor
by the Quick Cleaners; here he earned from $10 to $14 a week.   It was while
he was working on this job that he was married early in 1931.   Only a few
months later the Quick Cleaners went out of business.   Since 1931 George
has worked intermittently for short periods at the Grand Lunch Room, for
various cleaning establishments during the spring cleaning rush, for the

Willow Company during 2 or 3 winter months, and since 1933 he has worked
on emergency work projects for 4 or 5 months each year.

The Dalecks first received relief while they were living with Mr.
Daleck's parents in 1932. The Dalecks, senior, had requested relief and
George's family was included in the budget. At that time there were 11 in
the father's home and no one was working. George much prefers work relief
to direct relief, but he is always delighted to get off project work when
jobs, no matter how brief, are available in private industry. Two years
ago, while George was working for the Willow Company, his ankle was fractured
when a truck ran over him. He was unable to work for 3 months, but drew
workmen's compensation of $11.80 weekly for most of the time.

George is now employed on the brush clearing project, but expects
to get 2 or 3 months work with the Service Cleaners as soon as spring housecleaning starts. He has worked for this company for 2 or 3 months each
spring for 3 years. He works only on rugs and draperies and has had no experience cleaning clothes. On emergency work projects, George has worked at
common labor. He thinks it is foolish for workers to look on project employment as regular work, because "in reality it is just one form of relief."
About a year or so ago workers on a project struck for higher wages. George
considers this action "very stupid" and adds, "but you can find some awful
foolish people on relief." "Some of them," he thinks, "would stay on
relief 100 years if they could."

On Mr. Daleck's present earnings of $48 a month, the family just
manages to get by. Two dollars and forty cents is spent for transportation
and $11 goes for rent; food and medicine takes most of the balance. The
$29 radio, purchased on a time-payment plan a month ago, is the Dalecks' only
luxury. They are paying for it at the rate of $2 a month. George "figured"

that this was economical recreation for "the whole family."   Sometimes Mr.
Daleck gets "discouraged and disgusted; everything seems so useless." His
sister Florence has not been able to find employment because of her deafness.
She took care of Mrs. Daleck at the time of Mrs. Daleck's miscarriage last
summer and has remained in the home ever since.   Though it means one more
mouth to feed, George Daleck feels that he is better able to care for her
than is his father, who "is even worse off" than George. A deaf and dumb
friend was recently employed at a candy factory, and Florence is now trying
to get on there. Mr. Daleck says that it is "touch and go" with his pay
check. He cashes it and the "money goes immediately."   He worries about
his unpaid debts; "it makes you feel better to pay up."   Nearly every payday collectors come to see him; they are satisfied, however, if he makes
a payment of 50¢ now and then. George owes a rent bill of $40, which he
"really doesn't have to pay" as the family was evicted; George considers it
a legitimate debt, however, and intends to pay it if he ever gets on his
feet again.   The Dalecks believe that they managed better on direct relief
than on the WPA pay check, but he would not want to go back on direct relief.
"It's better to work for what you get."

        George Daleck feels that wages and working conditions are unusually
poor in Dubuque, but as he has no trade, he doubts if he would be better off
elsewhere. The unions will never accomplish much in Dubuque because there
are too many "scabs." He has never belonged to a union, but he will have to
join with the truck drivers before he can be reemployed by the Willow Company. He doubts, however, that this would be worth his while, as his work
with the Willow Company has never lasted longer than 2 or 3 months a year.

        The Social Security legislation is, in George's opinion, "all right,
but old-age pensions should be paid to persons of 60 or even younger. George

does not see that he will benefit much from this legislation so long as he works in private industry for only 5 or 6 months a year, and then only as an "extra man" for two or three different employers. He has not thought much about the causes of unemployment or remedies. Neither has he thought about the administration of relief. "But it's a cinch somebody has to help the unemployed." The men with whom George works talk a lot about war, but since George has "a battle all the time to keep the wolf from the door," and he hasn't had much time to think about war. Most of the men say that they won't fight on foreign soil, but George reasons that "if there has to be a war it would be better to mess up some other country instead of the U.S.A."

Mr. and Mrs. Daleck both feel that they have never had a chance to get on their feet since their marriage 7 years ago. Mrs. Daleck observes that "it never rains but that it pours." Last year, for instance, Judith was in the hospital for 2 weeks with a leg infection. No sooner had she recovered than Peggy was near to death from drinking kerosene. Then the baby had to have a tumor removed from his eye. He had scarcely recovered when Mrs. Daleck had a miscarriage. Two years ago Mr. Daleck had been laid up for 3 months with a broken ankle; "so it goes."

Mr. Daleck has always been interested in photography and thinks he would like to have a photographic business of his own, but "knows full well that there isn't the remotest possibility of his ever realizing such a dream. In fact, he feels that he will be "lucky to get any year-round job." George likes his work with the cleaners; he hopes that business will improve sufficiently for these cleaners to hire him as a regular man instead of an extra to be called in only during the spring rush.

Employment Chronology for Mr. Daleck

1925 - 1926 Office boy and assembler,
             dish company.

1926 - 1927 Farm hand.

1928 - 6 months Dishwasher, restaurant
       4 months Helper, coal truck.

1929 - 1931 Shoe shiner and presser,
             tailor shop.

1931 - Present 2 months each winter helper on coal truck
               3 months each spring helper in cleaning
               shop; remainder of time unemployed
               except for emergency work; now on WPA.

Mr. Otterbein   28
Mrs. Otterbein   28

Interviewing completed
December 13, 1937

Edward Otterbein, 28 years old, unemployed for 4 years and now
a salesman on a commission basis, counts himself "one of a lost race and
a lost generation, for time and civilization have gone on," leaving him
"struggling" to maintain even his present precarious balance. Partly, no
doubt, as a result of financial insecurity and unemployment and perhaps partly, too, as a result of earlier experiences, he has grown embittered. Though
he feels that he has not been personally responsible for his unemployment,
sometimes he wonders, "Am I any good?"

Edward is a cocky little fellow, slender and wiry and not very
tall. He indulges in good-natured banter with his wife, for whom he shows
much affection.

Mrs. Otterbein, small, bespectacled, and competent, can hold up
her end of an argument though she is more submissive than Edward. She teases
and scolds, but is nevertheless quite protective of Edward. For the past
10 years Mrs. Otterbein has done stenographic work for a legal firm; during
the 6 years of the Otterbein's married life she has been the chief wage earner.
She works outside the home not from choice but of necessity. Since August
1937 she has contributed to the support of her parents, with whom the
Otterbeins now live.

Edward Otterbein, one of nine children, has lived all his life
in Dubuque. His father had worked at a livery stable renting teams of
work horses until trucks and tractors crowded the stable out of business, and
Mr. Otterbein, senior, took a job in a woodworking factory. Though he always
made what Edward considers "good pay"—$35 a week as a livery stable man,

some weeks much more than that as a millworker--he was never able to save money.

Even as a boy, Edward resented his parents' inability to "take care of so much as a penny." Of course Edward "loves his parents and all that," but to this day he resents their poor management, their lack of understanding of his desire for a "good education," and the necessity of his turning over virtually all his earnings to his mother when he was working and living at home.

While Edward attended school, it was frequently necessary for his text books to be provided by the school; since these books were stamped as property of the board of education it was possible for other school children to learn of his poverty and to "throw it up to him." As a youngster, Edward wanted to be a fireman or a policeman. Later he set his heart on studying to be a doctor but when, as a high school freshman, he found that he "couldn't get any place" with his schooling, he "chucked it" to go to work.

He was not yet 16 and was therefore required to attend part-time school while he worked as a general errand boy in a department store. This work he gave up to take a job in the glue room of the Mississippi Milling Company, where he was required to present a birth certificate. Edward was still under 16, but it was "easy enough" to change the birth date from 1909 to 1908 so that he was permitted to work without attending part-time school. Standing over the glue vats made him so ill that he quit this job, for which he had been paid 30¢ an hour for a 10-hour day. He then spent some months as apprentice to a baker, who died before the apprenticeship was completed. During this period Edward also worked occasionally as a ticket taker in a local theater.

All this time there was friction in the home concerning the extent of Edward's financial responsibility to his family, and his recreation was limited by lack of spending money. So he decided to go to Rockford, Ill.,

with two other fellows who likewise wanted to get work where they could be
"on their own." Soon after their arrival in Rockford, the three boys were
arrested on a charge of vagrancy. When they had spent several hours in
the "cooler," they were released with the advice that they should hop a
freight back to Dubuque—advice which they followed in short order.

Edward next got a job with the Dubuque Woodworking Company as a
buffer. After a few months of this work, he left to go to Stevenson's
where he was employed rather regularly for about 6 years before the plant
closed. Here he worked as a ripsaw and bandsaw operator, cutting veneers,
pilasters, and other bits of decorative woodwork for phonograph cabinets.
He liked the variety of his work at Stevenson's and the feeling of responsibility and of camaraderie with other workmen. Although work was usually
slack during the winter months, Edward's earnings on the average were fairly
high. He was paid 45¢ an hour and in the busy seasons was sometimes
"permitted" to work from 7 a.m. until midnight. He always received straight
pay, for "there wasn't any union then." He heartily approves the 10-hour
day since he believes that shorter working days have given people too much
leisure, which leads them into mischief: "fellows want to lay around too
much now."

Edward's work did not lend itself to piece rates, which he believes
"ruined things" because of the high differential between piece rates and
hourly rates. When Edward, two of his sisters, and a brother all worked at
Stevenson's, his sister, on piecework, frequently earned more than he. Even
though he was fairly well satisfied with the work at Stevenson's, Edward
comments on the frequent necessity of having splinters removed from his hand
and the constant fear of running his hand into the saw.

During the time that he worked at Stevenson's, he continued to contribute the greater part of his earnings to his family. He kept only $2 or
$3 a week for himself, even when his earnings amounted to $40 or $50 for a

2-week-pay period. He used "to sit at home and cry" while his brothers and sisters went out to enjoy themselves. Even now, he cannot dance. He considers this a handicap and attributes it to a lack of spending money in his youth.

In January 1932 he was married, "and that was a funny thing, too." Edward had quarreled violently with an older brother. Though the cause of the disagreement was "insignificant," the quarrel was so vigorous that Edward still feels he would "like to kill him." Disgusted with the whole home situation, Edward once again determined to leave town. When he told the girl to whom he was engaged of his decision, she suggested that they be married immediately. They were married and lived for about a year with Mrs. Otterbein's parents.

At the time of his marriage, Edward was not working, but as this was the slack season when layoffs and temporary shutdowns of the plant were not unusual, he fully expected to be called back within a few days or weeks; however, the plant never reopened, and Edward remained unemployed except for odd jobs until the summer of 1935.

Thus, Mrs. Otterbein, who has been regularly employed during the past 10 years and now earns $75 a month as secretary to a lawyer, was the chief wage earner.

Edward has never considered his marriage "foolish," but he does resent the necessity for Mrs. Otterbein's continuing to work, and her parents' "throwing it up to him" that he is somewhat dependent on her earnings. Though he supposes he "should be glad" that his wife works, he cannot be glad. From the time of their marriage, the Otterbeins have considered her work purely "temporary"; now, he begins to feel that her working is inevitable and must go on for a long time.

Neither he nor Mrs. Otterbein believes that a married woman should work if the husband is able to support her. They consider the employment of

married women one of the causes of the extensive unemployment of men, and
suggest forcing women out of jobs which might be taken over by men as one
possible solution for the depression which is "still on." Mrs. Otterbein
says that she would give up her job in a minute if Edward's earnings were
reasonably adequate.

While he thinks this "an awful thing to say," Edward wonders sometimes what would happen to him if his wife could no longer work. Though her
health is reasonably good, she is very much underweight and is under the doctor's care. Doctor bills are an added expense, but as Mrs. Otterbein is
"the wage earner" her health is very important. In spite of his resentment
of her work, Edward is proud of her ability. If he had her brains, he could
make a lot of money. Her earnings are "too low, of course." Edward believes that "people who work with their brains should be paid more than
people who work with their hands, but in Dubuque," he says, "the difference
in earnings is very little."

Because of the difficulty of getting along with Mrs. Otterbein's
parents, the Otterbeins moved to an apartment of their own after about a
year. Edward did most of the housework and the cooking, though Mrs. Otterbein sometimes cooked on Sundays "when she felt like it." Both were much
more content with this arrangement then they had been when living with the
Damroschs.

For some months after the Stevenson plant shut down, Edward kept
fairly busy at various odd jobs—painting, paperhanging, mowing, whatever he
could find to do—but for the last couple of years he could get nothing.
He worked at a number of painting jobs with his uncle, but their job seeking
was complicated by the fact that neither was a union painter. Once they
were halted in the middle of a job of redecorating a local theater, and union
painters were brought in to finish the work. Edward did not consider it

worth-while to join the union, since he usually managed to find nonunion jobs.
And payment of union dues would have limited his earnings still further; he
knows of one painter who paid back union dues of $36 in order to get a job
for which he was paid $42.

While he was unemployed Edward had still less recreation than when
he was living with his parents. He read a great deal, and "in those days
the library was a good place to be," but reading did not often help him to
"forget."

In the early days of the depression, Edward feels, little thought
was given to the "unemployed man who could get along without relief."
Edward applied for CWA work, which he understood was available to any unemployed person regardless of other wage earners in the family group. When
he asked whether Mrs. Otterbein's work had interfered with his assignment to
CWA, he was told that this was the case. He never applied for relief or for
WPA work, as he realized that he was ineligible. Though he was gratified that
the family did not need relief, he felt that Mrs. Otterbein's working should
not have made him ineligible for WPA assignment.

In July 1935, shortly before a strike was called, Edward was hired
as a ripsaw operator at the Dubuque Woodworking Company, where he had worked
for a short time as a boy. Earnings were 30¢ an hour, which "seems to be
the good wage here." Much as he wanted to continue work, he was "forced out
on strike" with the rest. Though he approves of "good organization,"
Edward was not interested in the millworkers' union, which has "little
strength" locally. The mill strike for a "closed shop" resulted only in
wage increases of about ½¢ an hour.

During the few months he worked in the mill, Edward was granted
three increases. When he was "canned" in January 1936 he was earning 38½¢
an hour. In addition to regular wages he always received a bonus for turning out the required quantity of work. Though the raises were small, they

seemed to indicate that his work was "satisfactory." So he is at a loss to
understand why he should have been fired, "unless it was because the foreman
never liked me." In the first place, he was told only that he was being
"laid off," and when Edward challenged the foreman to admit that he was being "canned" rather than "laid off," he "wouldn't even look at me." At
this time, the mill was working full force, and another man was hired in
Edward's place. Other workmen presumed that Edward was ill when he did
not return to work, for they recognized that he was the best workman in his
department.

Edward thinks that perhaps his behavior during the strike may have
influenced the foreman to discharge him. Every day he went to the plant to
learn whether the strike had been settled. When he found the men still out,
he merely "stood around" opposite the plant. But his helper "sneaked in"
and was willing to continue work. When Edward was later asked why he, too,
had not reported for work, he explained that "the union members would have
killed me--and they would have, too."

Since leaving the mill, Edward has been selling office equipment
on a commission basis. He enjoys the work, for he likes to meet people,
can give convincing sales talks, and gets great satisfaction from making
sales, and from thinking, "I earned $24 in 10 minutes." He likes the
other salesmen and has enjoyed attending meetings of salesmen in Chicago.
But there are many discouragements: earnings are irregular and commissions
are frequently delayed for many months. It is difficult to get about in the
winter without a car; sometimes he has waded through snow waist-deep to reach
houses where he has made no sales. Perhaps if he went out with fellows to
"drink beer" occasionally, he could round up more customers, but he does not
feel free to spend money for his own recreation. He and Mrs. Otterbein do
not go out with other young people, "but every Saturday night just the two
of us go to a nearby tavern, drink beer, and have a good time."

Edward does not consider his work as salesman a regular or a satisfactory job. If he could have regular work at a regular wage, he would feel "more secure," even if his total earnings were lower. He doesn't quite know what work he wants to do, for he is confused and uncertain and "mixed up"; sometimes he feels like "crawling into a hole and pulling it in after him." He believes that he could go into a factory and learn quickly and easily to run any machine, but he adds that foremen usually expect speed and efficiency immediately.

Edward has kept an application on file in the local office of the State employment service, but he has not been referred to any job. He presumes that he has been passed up when requests have been received for saw operators because the employment office people "came to someone else's card first."

The Otterbeins maintained their own household until August 1937, when the situation in the Damrosch home made it necessary for them to return to Mrs. Otterbein's parents. Mr. Damrosch, 65 years old, feels that he can do a day's work with the best of them but he has had no private employment since he was laid off 4 years ago because of his age. Previously he had worked for 24 years for the Dubuque Woodworking Company. Mr. Damrosch worked as laborer on the Dubuque lock and dam project until August 1937, when a relief investigator insisted on his being laid off since he was now eligible for an old-age pension. To him, however, it is not a pension; he calls it a mortgage, as "they" wanted to take the deed to his home and his insurance policies, and to collect 6 percent interest on any money allotted to him. He did not even inquire about the amount of any possible grant, but he knows of a woman who is receiving $18 a month—"and you can't live on that."

Thus, Mr. Damrosch was without any income at the same time that his wife was very ill with high blood pressure. Under the circumstances it seemed that the only practical plan was for the Otterbeins to move in with

the Damroschs to help in the care of Mrs. Damrosch and the support of the
family. This they did, but only with reluctance and misgivings, and the
present situation is not a happy one. Edward is conscious of the Damroschs'
feeling that he is something of a failure; Mrs. Damrosch, who does not realize
how serious her illness is, tells the neighbors that the Otterbeins are mean
to her because they do not allow her to do the housework, and that they just
want the property.

Within certain limits the Otterbeins have made the best of a bad
situation. They have brought their own furniture to the Damrosch home. Edward has painted the house outside and in, with some assistance from Mrs.
Otterbein, and has repapered all of the rooms. Edward likes to paint, especially when he can be "his own boss"; he says that he doesn't like any job
where someone is looking over his shoulder all the time.

The Otterbeins are not much in sympathy with recent social legislation. Edward supposes that he "will benefit, in a way," from the old-age
benefits provisions of the Social Security Act, but the tax reduces present
income. And he has estimated that, if he continues with his present rate of
earnings until he reaches the age of 65, he will receive a pension of "about
$7 a month. And," he adds bitterly, "I suppose I can live on that, and my
wife can live on it, too." Besides paying his Social Security contributions,
Edward carries a $1,000 life insurance policy; annual premiums of $30 have
been paid to date.

Mrs. Otterbein, who works 8 hours a day, is hoping that the 40-hour-
week bill will be passed. She reminds Edward that he favored the 10-hour day
only because he was paid by the hour instead of by week or month. Under the
NRA Mrs. Otterbein's hours were shortened to 40 a week with no pay reduction,
but hours were increased as soon as the act was invalidated. No more work
was accomplished, however, as the girls merely "stretched the work out."

Edward thinks that "maybe WPA jobs helped to uphold morale, but every other way, the money was wasted." He thinks that WPA wage rates were "too high", and that if men were to be paid $48 or $50 a month, they should at least have been required to work "long hours." On the other hand, Edward is indignant because some of his friends have had to do "dangerous work" on WPA projects.

There are too few "white men" in Dubuque, in Edward's opinion; among the nonwhites, he includes all "wops." The deportation of "unnaturalized citizens" would help to solve the unemployment situation for people who belong here. "Or maybe a war would fix things up." Although Mrs. Otterbein insists that he must be joking, and that she would break his leg before she would let him go to war, he sticks to his point. Because he has false teeth, he believes that he would not be drafted, but could remain at home and profit by war to get a good job. Finally, Edward says that he does not believe in war and would not fight unless the U.S.A. were actually invaded; certainly he will not defend any "Chinks."

Because Dubuque is a "rotten town" as far as wage rates are concerned, the Otterbeins have always wanted to get away, but now they find themselves stuck. Mrs. Otterbein toys with the idea of getting a "real job" in Chicago, though the Otterbeins would like a big city only as a place to work, not as a place to live. The low wages in Dubuque they ascribe to the influence of the Chamber of Commerce; various new factories which would have paid reasonably high wages have been "kept out" of Dubuque. Such small factories as have recently opened in Dubuque have been "kicked out" of other States because they were on the "unfair lists."

In spite of the fact that in Dubuque "everybody knows everybody else's business, or if they don't they feel free to ask," the Otterbeins would be content to remain here, where rents and other living costs are moderate, if Edward could get "a good steady job at $100 a month," which Mrs.

Otterbein would consider "riches." "Then we could get a car---oh! a house

first, of course, and then a car."

Employment Chronology for Mr. Otterbein

1923 - 1925 -   Errand boy, department store.
                       Glue room helper, Mississippi Milling
                            Company.
                       Apprentice baker.
                       Buffer, Dubuque Woodworking Company.

1925 - December
1931   Saw operator, Stevenson Phonograph
                            and Radio Company.

December 1931 -
July 1935   Unemployed.

July 1935 -
January 1936   Saw operator, Dubuque Woodworking
                            Company.

January 1936 -
present   Salesman of office equipment,
                            commission basis

INDUSTRIAL DISCARDS

DIMARCO

Mr. DiMarco	37
Mrs. DiMarco	33
Shirley	3

Interviewing completed
January 4, 1938

Mr. and Mrs. DiMarco are both stone-deaf. Bernard DiMarco, having been deaf since he was 2 years old, does not speak at all. Mrs. DiMarco, who had learned to talk before she gradually lost her hearing as the result of an injury when she was 8 years old, speaks a little now, in a harsh toneless voice, but for the most part she depends on talking with her hands.

Since neither of the DiMarcos can read lips, conversation with those who cannot talk with their hands must be written.[1] Mrs. DiMarco is very articulate, she responds quickly and readily, and writes with facility and clarity; her spelling and punctuation are somewhat erratic, but her vocabulary is varied enough, and her phrasings are sometimes picturesque. She is friendly, eager, intelligent, quick to catch the meaning of gestures and facial expressions, which she watches intently. She is slight and pale; one leg is slightly twisted; her chin is pimply, and her eyelids red and raw behind her eyeglasses.

Mr. DiMarco is exceedingly dark, with a mop of black hair and a black stubbled chin. He does not write so fluently as does Mrs. DiMarco, and, being less articulate and less aggressive, prefers to let Mrs. DiMarco, who "knows better" than he what to say, do the talking for the family. He writes answers to questions about his employment only painfully, with many

---

1 Quotations from three written interviews with Mr. and Mrs. DiMarco have here been arranged to follow as closely as possible the time-sequence of the family's experiences. Proper names appearing within quotations have been disguised, and a few punctuation marks have been inserted for the sake of clarity.

pauses for erasing, scratching his head, and asking Mrs. DiMarco what to
say or how to spell certain words. He, too, is slight and not very husky,
and he must find his glasses and put them on before he can read or write at
all.

Mr. and Mrs. DiMarco have a strong feeling of identification with
the deaf; they distinctly feel that they belong to a group set apart, and
they do not comprehend general problems except in relation to the deaf. Unemployment to them does not imply a problem faced by millions of the hearing;
it is the special problem of the deaf. Their own problems have of course
been intensified by their physical handicap, and the DiMarcos do not dis-
sociate any of their difficulties from the deafness which has been always
with them. What recreation they have is, naturally enough, shared only with
other deaf persons. When they have sought jobs, they have hunted out plants
where other deaf persons were already employed, not only because the manager
who had hired one deaf person would be most likely to hire another but also
because they wanted to associate with other deaf people. When they consider
leaving Dubuque to look for work elsewhere, they think in terms of the numbers
of deaf persons living in various other towns, once again not simply because
there may be more jobs open to the deaf where the deaf have congregated but
also because they want to join the already established clubs for the deaf.

The DiMarcos are intensely conscious of prejudice against the deaf.
Neighbors, landladies, employers, relief workers, persons to whom they have
gone in the vain search for jobs have often, the DiMarcos feel, been unfriend-
ly and unsympathetic, or at best indifferent, because the "do not care for the
deaf."

The DiMarcos are now living in a moderately well-furnished three-
room apartment, the second floor of a brick house in a semiresidential

district of the downtown area.. When the Stevenson plant closed late in 1931,
Mr. DiMarco lost the job of disc sanding which he had held for almost 10
years, except for occasional layoffs. During the past 6 years, he has
had no regular work; for such odd jobs as he has done he has usually not
been paid in cash. Steady work on WPA projects during the past 2 years
is as near as he has come to regular employment. Job-seeking is complicated by his deafness, and he sees little chance of finding any regular
full-time work, aside from WPA, in Dubuque.

The DiMarcos have a 3-year-old daughter, a blue-eyed, tow-headed
youngster, bright and well-trained. They are exceedingly fond of Shirley,
but they try not to spoil her. Already, they are planning for her future,
and hoping to be able to send her to business school. They are anxious
always to learn from those who can hear Shirley's prattle whether she "talks
good" and are delighted when her remarks are quoted to them. Mrs. DiMarco
tries to talk to Shirley so that she can learn to pronounce words plainly;
and she also asks the neighbors to talk to her.

Bernard DiMarco was born in Italy in 1900. He writes spontaneously,
near the end of an interview, "I am naturalized. I came to U.S.A. in 1902
been in U.S. for 35 years." His father, according to Mrs. DiMarco, "ran
away from the Italian frontier. He didn't like the army and guard life so
came here and took out naturalization papers--then after he earned enough
sent for Bernard and his mother and sister." On the boat, crossing from
Italy, the 2-year-old Bernard contracted spinal meningitis, which presumably
caused his deafness. On reaching New York, he and his mother and sister
had to remain in quarantine for 3 months before they could join his father,
a coal miner in southern Illinois. The family managed well for a time, and

Bernard was sent to a school for the deaf in Jacksonville, Ill. But in 1910
the father was killed in a mine accident.

Bernard remained in school, working part-time in the shoe shop,
until he was 17, when he left to help support his mother and three younger
brothers, two of whom were deaf.

After he left school, and before he came to Dubuque, Mr. DiMarco
had a succession of jobs, none of them lasting longer than 1 year, and none
very well paid or involving much skill or responsibility. He summarizes
his employment history thus: "In Spring Valley, Ill. I worked at the
Overall factory for about 1 year, 1918-1919 -- pick overalls after the
girls sewed and tie bundles then carry & sort & bale them & weigh and address
them. I quit because the girls often went on strike so I got a job at the
Roofing Co at Ottawa, Ill--do the work at the tile yard. They shut down
after about 1 year so I came back to Spring Valley where my Home is, worked
at the Overall factory for some 6 months. Then they shut down. I got a job
at Wright store & do the cleaning & Polishing stoves. After about 6 months
they laid me so I got a job at Ottawa again stayed for 3 months so I quit in
1922 & came to Dubuque. I forgot to tell you--I worked at trunk factory in
Spring Valley, Ill., for 8 months nailed the boxes & trimmed & painted them
(wardrobes). When Harding was President I was out of work for 1 year."

Mrs. DiMarco states that Bernard came to Dubuque in the hope of
getting work with the Stevenson Radio and Phonograph Company. "He heard
of a lot of deaf working there and was lonesome alone down home so came to
see if he could get on too and he did." In Mr. DiMarco's words, "When I
was working at Ottawa, Ill., I read in Chicago paper about it Stevenson's
so I wrote to my friend who worked there and asked him if I could work--He
wrote and told me to come right away so I quit & came to Dubuque & met him

& led me to a house to board. The next morning he took me to Stevensons
& told me to see Mr. Smith, who was hiring men & women so I asked him
about work. Smith is a good man & hired all deaf men to work. There were
about more than 20 deaf men before I came. There were about 85 deaf people
in Dubuque while working there. Now there are about 18 people here. Some
of them Dead. At first I asked Smith if I could paint or Varnish. He said
Filled so he put me in where I disc Sanded."

Mrs. DiMarco is proud of Mr. DiMarco's being "the best Disc Sander
they had****They could not get the men to work on it so asked him to work or
try it and he got so adept at it they couldn't go without him." Before
coming to Stevenson's, Mr. DiMarco had never done any wood work. He preferred
this job to any of the earlier ones, and found it much the best paid. When
he put in overtime, he sometimes earned as much as $85 within a 2-week-pay
period, but "Most of times over $50---2 weeks."

"They often put him on other jobs," Mrs. DiMarco writes, "when he
got ahead on his Sanding Job and he knows quite a few jobs in the Radio
Cabinet business, rubbing, hand sanding assembling and lots of other jobs."
Work at Stevenson's was still quite regular when the DiMarcos were married
in 1929.

Shortly before her marriage Mrs. DiMarco had come to Dubuque to
work with Bernard at Stevenson's. She has been crippled since she "was 8
years old, that resulted in my deafness. The lameness first started from
what we arent sure but think I stepped on a rusty nail and blood poison
set in. Then for about 5 years I was alternately in Hospital & out---I
couldn't walk for 2 years---after about the 2 years I was able to get around
& go back to school again." Mrs. DiMarco attended public schools before
going to a school for the deaf in Chicago, where she remained for 2 years.

"I only went through 8th as my parents were poor and had a large family. They could'nt afford it."

The winter after Mrs. DiMarco had left the school for the deaf, she was asked to return to take the place of the kindergarten teacher, who had resigned in midterm. "Mother was ill when school closed and I stayed at home all summer. Then about the time school reopened no doubt I would of gone back but my left limb began bothering me again****I was in the hospital at Freeport, Ill. for 5 mo. Then they brought me home but it was 2 or 3 years before it healed up. *** I had to go back to Hospital. Some friends took me to Rockford, Ill. to a (I think it was National Fraternity Society of the Deaf) picnic, it was there I met Mr. DiMarco & he kept at me until he finally got me to come to Dubuque. He got me a job at Stevensons & I worked there one summer [the summer of 1929].

"I was with a group of girls who put stain & stripes on the Radio Case legs & shellaced them. I had to stand up a lot (nearly all day) and it was awfully hard on my left leg. I used to get terribly tired. But it paid well. However when you have to pay board & keep etc., you know how it goes. Money has wings. Some days we would be real busy & earn good wages then others not so good. On the average I'd get 30 to 35 every 2 weeks.

"We were married in 1929 just before the crash." The Stevenson plant closed late in 1931. Earlier, Mr. DiMarco had been laid off twice, each time for a peiod of several months. The first layoff came just after the DiMarco's marriage. "He had always helped his mother, so didn't have much saved up. We had thought we could manage alright as his job paid well and still help his mother some but we lost out. She went on relief like we did when the factory shut down. We were particularly hard hit as we had

bought our furniture on installments and had that to bother us. It was
worse to see prices come down on furniture & know ours had cost more. We
had to pay & pay but we got it settled at last. Just last year it was
finished. The WPA was a godsend to us."

A sewing machine was the first of the DiMarcos' purchases after
their marriage. As Mrs. DiMarco "loves to sew," she had told Mr. DiMarco
that she couldn't get along without a machine. Besides buying furniture,
Mr. DiMarco soon after his marriage had taken out an insurance policy which
had no cash surrender value in 1931, and so was allowed to lapse. "Also
we had started to save in National Bank but it closed in Jan.[1932]. We
lost on that, had $5 left not bad but I wished I had that $5 to pay the
gas & rent then." "The plant closed first in 1929. We did not get any
help for 6 mo. We went to his mothers then to my mothers trying to find
another job but nothing doing. Then the plant reopened & sent for him.
It worked until December then shut again for several months." During one
of those layoff periods, Mrs. DiMarco is not sure which, "he went home and
got a better Job Cement factory but when Stevensons reopened they sent for
him. He didn't go back so the boss went down after him. I only wish he
hadn't maybe he'd have a job now as Stevensons shut down & the Cement
factory didn't but they won't take him back now."

"Then [in December, 1931, the Stevenson plant] shut paramently &
we had to go to St. Vincent Depaul Society for aid. Nothing improved &
they dropped us. We got no aid from the relief office & were put out of
that house so in desperation when the relief refused us I went to Mr. Tabor
at the Bakery & begged for a job but he phoned [the county poor relief investi-
gator] and forced her to help us. She never seemed to like us and we didn't
get only what she had to give us. Then the C.W.A. started & I went to see

[the director of the county emergency relief office] & she gave him a slip
entitling him to consideration & they put him on C.W.A. That was the first
real relief we had---after that things didn't go so bad with us. When it
stopped we seemed to get a little more consideration. Then the W.P.A. has
been in effect and it's a lot better than relief I must say. I always
hated to go and ask for things."

Mrs. DiMarco does not remember just when the first application
for relief was made. "It was after we were put out of the first place
after Stevensons shut down anyway. The St. Vicent Depaul Society helped
us for 3 or 4 mo. before that anyway. I think it began in 1930 that they
first started helping us. Mr. Edwards offered us three small rooms of his.
He says the relief did not pay him regularly & they claim they did so after
2 or 3 years they had an argument and they came over and told me to move
out of his place so I did. We got these rooms then. Mrs. Baker our landlady here has put us out several times & changed her mind. She tells us
we must go this spring but she may change her mind, she says she wants
well to do people here not ones like us who if we lost out job couldn't pay.
Seems we are kicked around like a foot ball. There was a period just before the W.P.A. started we got behind with the rent but we made it up after
W.P.A. started. Before that period they paid the Rent regularly for us,
then they made a change of every other mo. Of course with no way to earn
it we couldn't pay the other month, that's how we fell behind."

In the meantime, while the family was dependent on the weekly
grocery order of a little more than $2, supplemented by occasional grants
of surplus commodities, the DiMarcos had been sinking deeper and deeper in
debt. Mrs. DiMarco "should say we were in Debt about $350 or So. There is

probably about $50 yet unpaid. Some of them let Bernard work some off dur-
ing his unemployment, or we made exchanges and etc. We kept pegging away
& got most of it Cancelled somehow."

Exchanges were "mostly by mutual interests. We'd meet them or
Bernard (He is restless and can't stay quiet long) would go out prowling
around & meet them & they'd ask him to lend a hand they'd take so much off,
etc. I don't remember clearly just what all he did do. This seems like a
dark cave or something we'd been walking through. I dont know how we managed yet but we cut down on the electric & water bills & everything & kept
them at a minimum. He did any & everything he could think of to earn a
little."

Both Mr. and Mrs. DiMarco tried to find work, but in Mrs. DiMarco's
words "they don't seem interested in a deaf man won't listen to us. I've
been in the Candy Factory & Halls trying to get on also and they won't talk
just shake their head as if I were a freak. I wish I could make them understand we have to live like others. I don't work out much I can't seem to
find anything I can stand as I'm not overly strong but if I could I'd sure
take it. I did sewing for people for awhile to earn a little when we had
rent & things to pay every month & were on relief with nothing else on. I
sometimes help people clean house, if I can find anyone who will take me.
The last two or three years I haven't done anything as I had Shirley to
keep."

On the CWA airport project, Mr. DiMarco earned $15 a week "dig-
ging." When this work ended, he was given employment of "2 or 3 days a
week on a sewer job for the city." A former city manager, in Mrs. DiMarco's
opinion, "never like us deaf. He come upon Bernard working once & spoke to
Bernard. Bernard told him he was deaf & he wanted him sent home but the men

on the job stood up for Bernard & he remained." On WPA projects Mr.
DiMarco has been paid $12 a week. This is Mr. DiMarco's story of his em-
ployment during the depression: "At Eagle Point Park—just help the men do
the work trucking, wheeling crushed Rock & cement for almost more than 2½
years till last Dec. 17—we transfered to Riverside Park—building fires
and raking Brushes. Relief work before W.P.A.—in quarry before Relief
work." For the relief work he was paid only in grocery orders.

He prefers WPA to relief work and to direct relief, but does not
give his reasons for the preference. He has tried to find employment other
than on WPA, but "can't get—lots of men idle here. I make a little money
by selling cartons, magazines & papers to buy clothes & groceries & pay
cash on meat." The Riverside Park project keeps him busy only 3 days in
the week. According to Mrs. DiMarco, "He is always out looking for any odd
jobs that will turn up on his off days. Watches for a chance to peddle
circulars for the stores or get empty cartons for people shipping things.
It don't pay much but every little helps out."

"He likes [the WPA work] pretty well only we'd like private work
if we could find it & better wages. The Doctor bills sometimes overcome us
& we find them hard to pay. Mr. DiMarco has trouble with boils once or
twice a year and generally has to go & get medical treatments. Then this
summer after he had a spell of them I found myself in the family way and
not long after that a miscarriage & I had to go to Hospital & it seemed
such a mess. I still owe him some on that & for medicine. Then we feel
we should pay our Old Age pension [the Iowa state tax] & don't find it possible to scrape it together also a few bills (grocery) etc. that we had to
run up before we got relief & haven't found the way to pay yet, etc."

Perhaps if Mr. DiMarco had had more education, he might be in a better position to find work now, especially "if he had had a chance to learn a special trade." "But it's awfully hard on us deaf--as they don't seem to care for a deaf person when they can get one who can hear. I would like to see him take a course in barbering or something so he could go into business himself. I'd like to learn power machine operating too maybe it would help me in some clothing factory. Not here in Dubuque as Halls don't care for Deaf but maybe in Davenport or some other town."

Mrs. DiMarco is confident of her husband's ability to do a job well, especially in view of his experience at the Stevenson plant. "I'm sure if someone would only be interested enough to try him out they would find him a good steady worker also. We can't seem to find a person who will give him a trial. Some deaf here haven't such good records. I think that injures the reputation of the rest of us. There are all kinds of deaf just like hearing people."

Both Mr. and Mrs. DiMarco belong to a Catholic Deaf Society. "We have meetings 2d Sunday of the month and then we have Confessions & he gives us instructions etc. as most of us are Catholics here. Just a few aren't. We pay 10¢ a mo. dues Sometimes we give a little party all chipping in together."

Mr. DiMarco formerly belonged to a club for deaf men, but "they decided to discontinue it as there isn't enough deaf here any more. There are about 15 deaf people here. We get together as much as we can. They are all unemployed also except for 2 or 3. Two are well off and the other has pull with relatives & they give her a job. I don't have any relatives here to help us so it was harder on us than most."

Though there is no longer any formal organization, Mr. DiMarco
still meets on occasion with a group of deaf men. Some days Mrs. DiMarco
goes "for walks etc, I like to go & see the other deaf too evenings. It's
nice to visit with friends, but oh if only some of those who are gone were
here we'd have lots more fun. I understand a great many of them are out of
work & just mooning around wishing they were back here too." She wishes she
could go to some of the conventions of national organizations for the deaf,
but as she says, "we never get to attend havn't the money but we read papers
etc.--seems they have fun." Of the 80 or more deaf persons who lived in
Dubuque before the depression and worked, most of them, at Stevenson's, "a
great many died the last 4 or 5 years--others are out of work & had to go
home. Dubuque didn't seem to care for us when the Depression started so they
went to their parents or wherever they came from. It's sad--Dubuque is the
looser. Once they had a big convention here. Around 300 or 500 came from all
over."

From time to time, the DiMarcos have thought of leaving Dubuque in
the hope of finding work in some more friendly town. "There don't seem much
else for us to do but leave sometime no future for us here than I can see.
Mr. speaks some of going to Dixon Illinois where some of my people live &
try the Cement Co or Milk Co or some of those large places. We would become
affiliated with Rockford deaf if we did--Around 80 there now. Davenport
might be a place also--I have a sister who moved there--we thought of going
down sometime & trying. There are 35 or 40 deaf there. Seems odd when we
used to have more than them to have them above us now."

The DiMarcos' preoccupation with the problems of the deaf is evident in their responses to questions relating to general problems, just as

in any discussion of Mr. DiMarco's employment, chances of getting work now, experiences during the depression, or recreation. In answer to a question as to whether Mr. DiMarco has thought about what may have caused so much unemployment, or what should be done to reduce unemployment, he writes, "I am thinking about moving out & look for better job Illinois. I get jobs easily but hardly in Iowa. In Iowa they begin not to hire any deaf men to work because of Insurance. In Cedar Rapids, Iowa there were about more than 15 deaf men but now about 5 men left. They wont hire any more." As an elaboration of his comment, Mrs. DiMarco writes, "The Deaf find it difficult to get jobs because factories have insurance & refuse to insure the deaf in their employ."

Mrs. DiMarco's own answer to a question as to whether the DiMarcos have thought about what should be done for the unemployed or to minimize unemployment was as follows: "We read what the deaf think. The National Association for the deaf think the deaf are as good risk in Insurance as the hearing and I know they should not be prejudiced against us if only we could make them understand that our other senses are sharper because we can't hear and we are mostly all able to hold our own with the hearing in nearly every job we care to tackle. We don't waste time in talking like the hearing or get interested in something else like they do because we have to use our hands if we do & that would injure the work so we keep doggedly on. Any of Bernard's bosses will tell you he can hold his own." She adds, "I am glad to help you in any way we can & the deaf in General if it will interest anyone in them God knows we need it. Do you suppose we ought to stay on here in Dubuque or try to get away. I don't know whether we'd be any better off somewhere else or not. If only I knew where there was a steady job."

The DiMarcos' hopes for the future are centered in Shirley. Mrs.
DiMarco is planning to teach her by the same methods used in kindergarten
classes in the Chicago school for the deaf. "I want her to go through High
School and if possible some kind of Business school. I'm afraid we won't
be able to but we are already trying to fix it. We make her put all the
pennies anyone gives her in a little bank & bank it. I also insured her--
25¢ a week. Hard to pay but if anything should happen--" The DiMarcos
now carry no insurance except the small policy for Shirley. "They ask too
high premiums on a deaf person & he would pay out double the mortuary sum
so we decided against it. There are some Societies for the deaf we'd rather
join if we felt we could pay them but I'd hate to join up now unless I was
certain I could keep them paid up & we would be taking an awful risk with
no permanent job and not being sure of ourselves now."

Mrs. DiMarco takes pride in keeping her home looking neat and attractive. On one occasion she wrote, "I don't think I told you the other
times you was here that we have an account for clothing and other necessities. I just got my new curtains, my old ones were in shreds. When this is
paid I hope we can get some new rugs." The WPA pay checks have been "a
godsend."

Employment Chronology for Mr. DiMarco

1918 - 1919 - Packer, overall factory.

1919 - 1920 - Laborer, roofing company.

1920 - 1922 - Packer, overall factory;
            handy man, grocery store;
            laborer, roofing company;
            trimmer, trunk factory.

1922 - December
1931   Disc sander, Stevenson
               Phonograph and Radio Company.

December 1931 -
present   Unemployed except for emer-
               gency work; now on WPA.

<u>SIBERT</u>

Mr. Sibert	34
Mrs. Sibert	33
Frances	9
Marie	8
Phyllis	5

Interviewing completed
December 16, 1937

Mr. Sibert talks intelligently and matter-of-factly about
the problems associated with his unemployment, which he sees clearly
and with some objectivity, but avoids mention of his physical handicap. An attack of spinal meningitis when he was 6 years old left him
rather badly crippled. He walks now with a decided limp; his legs are
spindly; one hip is twisted; and his chest is barrel-shaped. Except
for the deformity of legs and chest, his general appearance is attractive; his eyes are blue, his hair blond and curly, and his teeth unusually strong and white. He smiles easily and gives no indication of
undue worry about his unemployment, the family's financial limitations, or
the illnesses of his wife and the three children, although Mrs.
Sibert says that he worries a great deal when he is alone and that he
is quite discouraged and disheartened.

For 11 years, and until the plant closed in December 1931,
Mr. Sibert had worked as a cabinet inspector and stock clerk for the
Stevenson Radio and Phonograph Company. Since 1932 he has had but
two regular full-time jobs in private industry, each one lasting about
1 year. The remainder of the time, except during the first year when
they lived on savings, loans, and earnings from scattered and infrequent
odd jobs, the family has been dependent on relief grants and Mr. Sibert's

WPA employment. During the past 14 months, he has been steadily employed
as a clerical worker on various WPA projects. Though he does not consider WPA jobs the equivalent of private employment, his work is now more
regular and his earnings higher than when he last worked in a local
factory. Mr. Sibert is only 34 years old, but he has little hope of
getting work, other than on WPA, in Dubuque. Not only is he physically
handicapped; he fears that he has been "blacklisted" by the woodworking
mills, the largest factories in Dubuque, and the only ones providing jobs
for which he has had any experience. He has thought of going elsewhere
to look for work, but "going is harder than thinking about it," especially when he must consider his family responsibilities.

Mrs. Sibert is a pale, weary little person, somewhat untidy
in her makeshift clothing. She has had several serious illnesses during recent years, and has never been really well since her marriage
some 10 years ago. It is only with a tremendous effort that she cares
for the three little girls, two of them in grade school, and keeps spot-
lessly clean the five rooms of the family's second-floor flat in a
shabby business block. For Mrs. Sibert "plays out" easily, and the
children's rowdy play intensifies her "nervousness" which is immediately
evident in the continuous jerky movements of her hands and feet. She
has accepted the family's many difficulties with resignation, though
she is wistful as she recalls the good times she and her husband shared
and the fat pay envelopes he brought home when he worked at Stevenson's.
She discusses details of budgeting and of illnesses with more freedom
than does Mr. Sibert, but her thinking is less clear-cut, her vocabulary
less varied, and her grammar less accurate.

Mr. Sibert, one of seven children of a factory foreman, completed an eighth grade education and a 6 months' business college course
before starting work on a clerical job at the Iowa Foundry in 1919, when

he was 16 years old. He stayed at the foundry for only a few months.
From 1919 until November 1920 he worked for the city, first as timekeeper, later as truck driver. His earnings were $110 a month, and he
found the work satisfactory enough, until he had some difficulty with
the department head. In attempting to brace one of the truck wheels
with a stone, when the brakes were not functioning, he had crushed his
hand. The superintendent accused him of "carelessness" and threatened
to fire him. Although his explanation was finally accepted and he was
kept on, he felt that after this argument he would not get along well
with the superintendent.

So he gave up the job to look for work in Rockford, Ill.
Having found none, he returned to Dubuque after a stay of about 2 months,
and was almost immediately employed at the Stevenson plant, where he had
made application on the advice of a neighbor. He began work as a trimmer;
it was his job to put the hardware and the lids on the otherwise finished
cabinets. During the first week, while he was learning the job, he was
paid at an hourly rate; for the next 3 weeks, on a piecework basis. The
trimmers were fairly well paid; even "a poor workman" seldom earned less
than 90¢ an hour at the piecework rate.

When Mr. Sibert had been at Stevenson's for about 1 month,
he was made an inspector. Each finished cabinet had to be inspected
and approved before any worker was permitted "to take it off his bench."
Any inspector was likely to be accused of slowing up the other workers,
and of "picking" on certain men, even though he tried, as Mr. Sibert
did, to be absolutely fair; hence no one was very anxious to have the
job, which usually fell to the lot of a new employee.

In addition to making inspections, Mr. Sibert kept track of
the stock and made out the production reports for the trimming department. His earnings varied with changes in rates of pay and hours of

work. The men worked as many as 68 or 70 hours a week in the busiest
seasons, the work being staggered so that they put in 10 and 13 hours
on alternate days. Occasionally, they were called to work on Sundays.
When they worked both day and evening shifts, they were given their
suppers and 50¢ apiece in addition to their regular pays. In the
unusually good year of 1926, Mr. Sibert earned 85¢ an hour. In 1931
his hourly rate was only 65¢. In December 1931 the Stevenson plant
shut down and some 1,200 men, Mr. Sibert among them, were let out.

He had been married while he worked at Stevenson's. When
the plant closed, the Siberts had two children: Frances, then almost
4 years old, and Marie, past 2. Mrs. Sibert had had difficult pregnan-
cies, and had undergone an operation 5 months before Frances was born.
Yet despite numerous doctor bills the family had managed fairly well.
They had lived first in a three-room apartment, later in a four-room
house, and still later moved to the five-room-and-bath apartment where
they now live. Mr. and Mrs. Sibert had done their planning and budgeting together, going "50-50 on everything," but there was always some
money for Mrs. Sibert to spend on herself and as she chose. Every payday a little money was "laid away." By 1932 savings amounted to about
$400. On Saturday nights the family usually entertained some of the men
from the shop or went to parties at the homes of other Stevenson employees.
On occasional week-ends Mr. Sibert went on hunting or fishing trips, and
Mrs. Sibert liked sometimes to go along.

But "them days are gone," Mrs. Sibert explains plaintively.
The family no longer entertains or visits with friends. They go only
to church or downtown to do a little shopping. Mrs. Sibert never rides
the buses, as "that 10¢ can always be spent for something else." She
buys clothing for herself or the children on rare occasions, and then

only the least expensive things available. Sometimes Mr. Sibert wonders
if the family's purchases are "worth anything." Within the past 5 years
Mrs. Sibert has bought only one coat, "and I took care of that myself."
She had done a week's housecleaning for $5, which she invested in a
spring coat that she hopes to wear for the rest of her life.

During the year following Mr. Sibert's loss of employment,
he got a number of odd jobs, chiefly painting and paper hanging, but
these did not amount to much. His father was by this time quite elder-
ly and not regularly employed, but he picked up what jobs he could,
and arranged for Mr. Sibert to do some of them in his stead. He also
lent the family $150 from his savings. In addition to securing the
loan from his father, Mr. Sibert borrowed $100 on his insurance policy.
When savings and amounts borrowed had been exhausted, the family began
to run into debt—on rent, groceries, and gas and light bills.

In November 1932 the family moved in with Mrs. Sibert's aged
and unemployed father and her sister and brother, in the hope that both
families could reduce expenses. The Siberts made use of their bedroom
suite but stored other furniture in the attic. From the beginning the
arrangement was unsatisfactory; Mrs. Sibert did not get along well with
her sister, who is the chief support of the father, and the sister was
annoyed by the Sibert children. So in January 1933 Mr. Sibert went to
his old landlord and asked if he would prefer having someone in the rooms
to letting them remain empty. The landlord, though not anxious to rent
to a family who could no longer pay the $25 rental, agreed to the family's
return. Mrs. Sibert was now 8 months pregnant. Gas and electricity had
been turned off; so the family managed with kerosene lamps and a coal
range, the only means of heating the house. Since the storeroom directly
underneath the apartment was vacant, there was no other heat in the
building.

It was at the suggestion of the landlord that Mr. Sibert
applied for a relief grant; the landlord was anxious to have at least
a part of the rent paid, and was willing to accept the $5 a month allow-
ed by the relief worker. After the family had waited 4 weeks, a grocery
order of $2.50, from which the Siberts had also to buy kerosene, was
granted. In addition to rent and groceries they received ½ ton of coal
each month. Though it was difficult to manage on such small amounts,
the family had no complaint to make. Relief was "all right," except that
there was "too much red tape."

The third daughter was born in February 1933 while the family
was still without gas or electricity. The doctor arrived only after the
baby had been born. Mrs. Sibert was partially paralyzed for several weeks
She has refused to have a recommended operation, partly because she is
"afraid" and partly because she does not know how the children could be
cared for in her absence.

The new baby was puny and not very well, partly as a result,
the doctor thought, of Mrs. Sibert's having been undernourished during
her pregnancy. While Mrs. Sibert remained in bed, her husband did most
of the housework and cooking, and got up regularly at 4 a.m. to build the
fire in the kitchen stove.

From August or September 1933 until about 1 year later Mr.
Sibert worked as bookkeeper, earning $65 a month, for a newly-established
gasoline station. The job was eliminated, and a final pay check of
$32.50 was tied up, when the station was closed on the landlord's order.
Having no savings, and still being in debt, the family had no choice but
to return to relief rolls about 1 month after Mr. Sibert lost his job.

They remained on relief, supplementing grocery orders with occasional
odd jobs, until April 1935, when the Dubuque Woodworking Company telephoned a call for Mr. Sibert to report for work; he had filed application with the company just 2 years earlier. He now worked 40 hours a
week fitting doors.

The work was rougher than his work at Stevenson's; the men
were "pushed harder" to turn out a set quantity of work; and the pay
was less. But Mr. Sibert believes that "in these days," when workers
are more plentiful than jobs, no employer is as lenient as the Stevenson
foremen once were. At Stevenson's men could frequently turn out the required day's work in the forenoon. It was customary for the men to work
furiously during the mornings, then slow up and spend some time talking
and kidding each other during the afternoons, while at the woodworking
mill, men usually could not turn out the set quantity of work if they
"drove themselves" all day.

The work at the mill was more irregular than work had ever
been at Stevenson's. From November 1935 to April 1936, when he was
laid off, Mr. Sibert worked on an average of no more than 3 days a week.
He was also out on strike for 2 weeks in the summer of 1935. At this
time, he was a member of the millworkers' union, and served on picket
duty. Elected by the union members to membership on the shop committee,
Mr. Sibert on one occasion met with the officials to request an equal-
ization of hours of work, as some of the men were putting in 9 hours a
day, others only 6. No adjustment was made.

When Mr. Sibert was fired in April 1936, he was told that his
work had been found "unsatisfactory." He considered this a "poor excuse,"
especially as he had been granted three raises—from 32¢ to 38¢ an hour.
Earnings for the entire year had totaled a little more than $540. Mr.

Sibert himself attributes his being laid off to his union activity and
to his defending the union in the plant during lunch hours, when older
workers were exceedingly critical. "I was a pretty hot-headed fellow.
*** I couldn't keep quiet, no matter where I was or who was around. ***
I said too much; I know I did. *** I imagine they got the idea I was a
kind of agitator." Mr. Sibert was not an organizer and did not think
of himself as an "agitator," but he thinks that he shouldn't have talked
so much, especially to "those fellows," who were decidedly antagonistic
toward the union and "undoubtedly" reported his comments to the management.

        Mr. Sibert is no longer a union member and has not kept in
touch with activities of local unions since he was laid off by the
woodworking company. He believes that industrial unionism is the only
logical type for "the mass production industries," but that there is a
place for craft unions—chiefly for painters and carpenters. As long as
Green and Lewis fight against each other for control of unions and "the
money that's in it," there can be no real agreement between industrial
and craft unionists. Mr. Sibert thinks that some adjustment might be
made if a third person headed up a Nation-wide organization for craft and
industrial unions alike.

        After leaving the woodworking company, he filed application
with the Mississippi Milling Company. But he "made a mistake" in men-
tioning his employment with the Dubuque Woodworking Company, for he has
evidently been "blacklisted." At any rate, he has had no word about the
application filed with the milling company.

        There are only three or four local factories where Mr. Sibert
might hope to get a job as a woodworker. He believes that no one of
these plants would hire him. Furthermore, none is now working at full

capacity. At best, the work is seasonal, the rates of pay are low, and the earnings are irregular. Mr. Sibert cannot see much of an industrial future for Dubuque. He has toyed with the idea of going to another town to look for work, but knows that he could not risk doing so unless he had enough money to take care of himself for at least 2 or 3 weeks and to leave his family provided for.

Eleven days after he was laid off by the Dubuque Woodworking Company, the family reapplied for relief, which was granted in short order. In October 1936 he was assigned to a WPA road project. Only on the insistence of his doctor, who explained his inability to do heavy work, was he transferred to a clerical job. Mr. Sibert much prefers WPA employment to direct relief, for "it makes a man feel he's earning something, even if it isn't a whole lot." He adds, "besides, I like working better than sitting around the house; I don't have anything to do except read and then take a nap and then read some more, and I got bored to death."

Since October 1936 Mr. Sibert has been regularly employed on WPA projects, on the homestead tax exemption study, as an editor for the Consumers' Purchase Study, as senior clerk on a farm community survey, and as assistant foreman and timekeeper for the coding of schedules for a recreational survey. His WPA earnings have varied from $55 to $70 a month. All during last summer he was paid $55 monthly. Now he is earning $70, working 64 hours during each half-month pay period. The Siberts feel that they could have managed very well if Mr. Sibert had earned $70 monthly during the summer, when there was no fuel to be purchased; then they might have bought winter clothing for the children and paid something on the back bills, still totaling $700, including loans on the insurance policy and from Mr. Sibert's father.

As it is, the Siberts "live 2 weeks behind," paying bills for the preceding 2 weeks from each pay check. Mrs. Sibert is "almost sorry to see paydays come, because the check is gone as soon as you get it in your hands." From one check, the family pays grocery, coal, and gas bills; from the next, grocery, rent, and electric bills. The apartment rental has been reduced from $25 to $16, and the landlord accepts $12 or $14 as full payment when Mr. Sibert cannot pay more. The family has had gas and electricity since Mr. Sibert began work for the gasoline station in 1933, but during the winter months they do not use the gas. The coal range is used for cooking and helps to heat the house. Fuel bills are high and most difficult to meet.

It is difficult, too, to keep Frances and Marie in school. They must purchase their own textbooks and wear regulation middies and serge skirts, but are "lucky" in not having to pay tuition. Each girl has two middies and one skirt. Every night, Mrs. Sibert washes and irons a middy blouse, and on Saturdays she cleans and presses the two skirts. She is glad that all of the school children wear uniforms, for "some of them could afford to buy better clothes, but this way, you can't tell which is which." Mrs. Sibert isn't "lucky enough" to be able to sew for the girls, but the baby can "fall into" the clothes which the older girls outgrow.

All of the girls have had rather serious illnesses, and Frances and Marie have missed a good deal of school. The children worry Mrs. Sibert a great deal, and, with Mr. Sibert's discouragement and unemployment and inadequate income, she feels that she "will be lucky if she doesn't get a nervous breakdown out of it yet." Though she is fond of the children and knows that she will be sorry next year when the baby goes to school, she doesn't "want no more kids."

Mrs. Sibert, especially, misses the recreation which the family once enjoyed. For 9 years before she was married, she had worked as a packer for a tea company, earning $14 a week—"good wages"—during the war, and later $11 a week. She got acquainted with a great many girls, most of them still in Dubuque. But she no longer sees them, for she cannot spend bus fare to visit them. "Since they have cars," she thinks, "They can just come and see me, but they don't. In the evenings," Mrs. Sibert continues, "Instead of visiting with friends we just sit and look at each other—or else read." Mr. Sibert likes mystery stories, and he borrows books from the public library twice each week. He is fixing up a discarded rocking chair which he plans to place by the big heating stove in the middle room; "that will be his place for the winter."

Mrs. Sibert is as discouraged as her husband about the prospect of his finding private employment. She puts the emphasis on his "bad limb," which has kept him from getting several jobs for which he has applied, including a job as mail clerk. Mr. Sibert "would take a job tomorrow" if he could get one, but he can't. In Mrs. Sibert's words, "Every time the first of the year comes round, we hope things will be better, but they still ain't. But we're not as bad off as some people; most of the factory workers make less than we do."

Mr. Sibert can't consider WPA employment "steady," as he knows "the whole thing may blow up tomorrow." Still, he "doesn't blame anyone" for not trying to get off WPA rolls "in this town." During the year that Mr. Sibert worked for the Dubuque Woodworking Company, he earned only about "five-sixths as much" as he would have earned at WPA work paying $55 a month. "Besides, the factory workers aren't any more secure than the WPA workers," in Mr. Sibert's opinion.

Mr. Sibert has read that "1 percent of the people control 99 percent of the wealth" in the United States. In his opinion, it is this situation which is responsible for the depression. He is interested in wage and hour legislation, provided standards can be set high enough really to improve the lot of the working man, and is mildly enthusiastic about a modified version of the Townsend plan, which he believes would serve to create new jobs and expand business. A "2 percent revolving tax" would assure the Federal Government of recovering "at least 50 percent" of the money paid out in pensions. But Mr. Sibert would have pensions of $100 a month instead of $200, as people "wouldn't know how to spend" so much as $200. In his mind, this plan assumes the proportions of a panacea. It is one of the few things that he can discuss hopefully.

Employment Chronology for Mr. Sibert

Several months, 1919 —	Clerical worker, Iowa Foundry.
1919 — November 1920 —	Bookkeeper and truck driver, city.
Nov. 1920 — January 1921	Unemployed.
Jan. 1921 — December 1931	Trimmer and cabinet inspector, Stevenson Phonograph and Radio Company.
December 1931 — August 1933	Unemployed.
August 1933 — October 1934	Bookkeeper, gasoline station.
October 1934 — April 1935	Unemployed.
April 1935 — April 1936	Sash fitter, Dubuque Woodworking Company.
April 1936 — present	Unemployed except for emergency work; now on WPA.

<u>GLAISTER</u>

Mr. Glaister 69
Mrs. Glaister 66

Interviewing completed
February 3, 1938

Mr. Glaister, a round little man with a round face and shiny bald
head, is 69 years old. He has been unemployed since April 1937, when he
was laid off by the Mississippi Milling Company, for which he had worked
for 8 years. Now he says that he hasn't a "ghostly chance" of getting
back to work unless he can "begin again where he left off" at the mill;
he cannot be hired as a new worker at any plant, for he is "too old."

He feels that he is still able to do "a good day's work" and
that it is unfair for older men who have given their best years to their
jobs to be "thrown out" and replaced with younger men. He and Mrs. Glaister
"have to live, too." They would be content with only a very small income;
$40 a month would be enough to buy food for the two of them--they have never
had any children--and to pay the taxes and insurance on their well-kept
little frame bungalow, built in 1913, when theirs was one of the few scattered houses in the north end of town. But even a meager income is not to
be had. Mr. Glaister doubts his eligibility for the railroad retirement
pension for which he has applied. His savings are now almost exhausted, and
he fears that it may soon be necessary to apply for a State old-age pension
or for direct relief.

Mr. Glaister talks freely about his past employment and his present
joblessness and his fears for the future, but he is a little deaf and follows
the conversation with some difficulty. He becomes confused easily when he
tries to recall any sequence of events, and he tangles his recollections of
the far-distant past with his descriptions of recent experiences. Mrs,

Glaister stands by to recall his attention to whatever subject is under discussion at the moment.

Mr. Glaister, born in Switzerland, was brought to Dubuque when he was 4 years old. In Switzerland his father had been a cobbler, making shoes and boots by hand. In this country he had "hard sledgin'" and often talked of going back to Switzerland. But he was only a common laborer, with 12 children to support; so he had to stay in Dubuque. Because the family was so large and so poor, the children began work early. Mr. Glaister had "very little schooling." His first job was driving a kindling wagon for the Dubuque Woodworking Company in the days when shavings and scraps of lumber were sold from house to house.

Just after his marriage in 1892 Mr. Glaister began work as a car repairman in the railroad shops, where he was employed, though with some irregularity, until 1927. His earliest earnings in the shops were $13\frac{1}{2}$¢ an hour, and it was 5 years before his rate was raised to 15¢. But in those days, $1.50 for a 10-hour day "wasn't bad pay." Mr. Glaister at one time or another did virtually all types of car repair work in the shops. He worked underneath and "on top" the cars, on coaches and on sashes and doors and steps for engines, as a carpenter and as a bench hand. His earnings were highest during the war, when he made 85¢ an hour for an 8-hour day.

His work was steady until the general railroad strike in 1922. After the strike had been settled and the men had gone back to work, almost half of them were laid off. Mr. Glaister was laid off several times between 1922 and 1927; each time he was taken back but always as a new man. There was a "regulation" that the "six-month men" had to be laid off before the hours of the rest of the shop workers could be cut. Again and again Mr. Glaister was counted one of these "six-month men," even though he had

actually worked in the shops for almost 30 years. Probably he should have
"made a holler," but that wasn't his way; he had always believed in doing
what he was told and going where he was told. Once he worked for 2 months
on coach repair in the State of Washington, and at another time he was sent
to North Dakota, where he worked all alone in a gravel pit with the temperature 40° below zero.

Despite layoffs and transfers Mr. Glaister always liked working for
the railroad.   Wages were high — higher than at any factory in Dubuque except the Stevenson plant — and the foremen were considerate. Dubuque has
never been "really the same" since the Stevenson plant and the railroad
shops closed.

In May 1927 Mr. Glaister was once again laid off at the shops.
This time after he had been unemployed for about 1 month, he got a job
as a molder in the Iowa Foundry. He liked the work well enough, but not
the piecework system which made for too great a variation in rates of pay
for the same general types of work. It was all very well as long as the
piece rates differed for molds of various sizes, but soon the management
found that the men were making "too much money," and a flat rate was set
for molds of all sizes. The larger the mold, the more time was required to
make it; yet the pay for the large and the small molds was the same, and it
might happen that one man would work all day on only the largest molds.
When Mr. Glaister protested, the foreman promised that work on molds of each
size would be equally distributed among the men all working at the same job
in the same room. And still he found himself working always on the largest
molds.

When Mr. Glaister had earned only $3.50 for 2 days' work while
two other employees had each made about $15, he quit the job and went to
work in the cabinet room of the Mississippi Milling Company. This was in

1929. Though he had disliked the piecework system, he thought afterwards
that it was better than the bonus system in effect at the milling
company; at the foundry he could at least figure out for himself what
his earnings would be, but at the mill he never knew how the bonus was
calculated. Day after day, he turned out approximately the same amount
of work; yet the bonus "kept going down and down." Even when he asked
the "bonus man" how the bonus was figured, he was given no understandable
explanation.

When Mr. Glaister started work at the mill, he was paid $22\frac{1}{2}$¢ an
hour for 10 hours a day, 6 days a week. Later the hours were cut to 8 a
day, and even to 3 or 4 when there were not enough orders to justify
keeping the plant running full-time. He was transferred from the cabinet
room to bench work--veneering and smoothing the finished doors by hand.
His rate of pay rose from $22\frac{1}{2}$¢ to 45¢ an hour, wage increases having
been effected by the NRA and by the change in type of work.

In April 1937 he was finally "frozen out" at the mill. It is
his feeling that the management wanted to "get rid of" older employees
without firing them outright. Though it seemed to him that his work was
just as good as ever, the foreman began to keep him "in hot water all the
time" by criticizing his work and urging greater speed. So Mr. Glaister
went to the superintendent and asked to be transferred to another job if
he couldn't give satisfaction as a bench hand.

Just so long as he could go on working at something, and
earning enough to keep him and his wife, he didn't care if he was given
a job at "common labor"; he would have been willing even to "sweep
floors." The superintendent promised to see if he could "create a
vacancy," and with only this much assurance that he would be given other
work Mr. Glaister quit the job as bench hand. He has not been given

another job at the Mississippi Milling Company or anywhere else.

Mr. Glaister feels sure that there is work that he could do well, if only he were given a chance, and he thinks that he should be given a chance. Manufacturers profit from the production of "the working class men" and should certainly try to place their older workmen on suitable jobs instead of "throwing them out." Now Mr. Glaister doesn't even ask for a full time job; 2 or 3 days of work each week would be "enough." But he can't find anything at all to do.

This morning he received a card from the State employment office asking him to call at the office to renew his registration; this afternoon, he will go down to the office, but the card states that there is no guarantee of employment, and he isn't "expecting anything." He has kept in touch with the Mississippi Milling Company, but to no purpose, and he has gone to the Woodworking Company "half a dozen times." Always his request for a job meets with the same response: he is "too old" to work. Since last April he has had just 5 days of work—2 days for an ice company and 3 days as a cemetery laborer.

He resents having no way to spend his time almost as much as having no income. Just now, he has "got a little job" sawing logs for fire wood, the logs having been purchased from a neighbor. Last summer he spent a lot of time making a garden on the island, but his plot of ground was so dry and sandy that nothing did very well. He might have been better off if he had spent his money for "groceries instead of garden seeds."

During brief periods of unemployment, Mr. and Mrs. Glaister have always lived on the amounts saved from Mr. Glaister's earnings during the good years. For 3 years while he worked only half-time or less at the Mississippi Milling Company it was necessary to supplement his earnings, sometimes as low as $9 for a half month period, from savings.

The Glaisters have never asked for credit or for assistance of any kind. Though they have not had a bank account for several years, they had something like $200 on hand when Mr. Glaister gave up his job last April. On these savings they had managed up to the present time but without paying the 1937 taxes on the home, and savings are now almost exhausted. What they will do when they can no longer manage at all, they do not know. Mr. Glaister is still hoping that he will be given some sort of work at the Mississippi Milling Company.

Mr. Glaister has applied for a railroad retirement pension, for which he is eligible in terms of length of service, but he has heard nothing from his application. He understands that a regulation establishing eligibility only for the men working for the road in August 1935 will automatically bar him. At various times, he has tried to establish his pension rights, but the railroad shops in Dubuque now employ only 30 or 40 men, and he had no way of paying his transportation to Milwaukee, Wisconsin, when men were being taken on in the shops there. He did talk with a foreman in the Dubuque shops who offered to arrange for his transportation, but the plans fell through when the "head of the union" said that there was no use for Mr. Glaister to go to Milwaukee; he was "too old" to be rehired.

The Glaisters have not yet considered applying for direct relief. Mr. Glaister believes that relief is necessary—"you can't just let people starve"—but thinks it much better for men to "work for what they get." He has applied for WPA work through the employment office, but has learned that he cannot be assigned on a nonrelief basis. Though he is not sure that he would be strong enough to fell trees on the clearing project day after day, he thinks he should be able to work 1 or 2 days a week. He is

enthusiastic about the WPA program, which not only has created jobs for
the unemployed but also has saved merchants from being "frozen out"; he
knows of many shopkeepers who depend almost entirely on purchases made
by WPA workers.

Mr. Galister is reluctant to apply for direct relief and not at
all certain that he would be "eligible," for he owns his home and both
he and Mrs. Glaister are old enough for State old-age pensions. They have
carefully considered applying for pensions but do not want to "sign everything over to the State." They have worked all their lives to keep their
home in good repair, and to keep up payments of taxes and insurance on the
home. "Why should we give it up now?"

Though they know that they would still be permitted to live in
the house even if it were "signed over," they could no longer call it their
own. Nor do they want to "sign over" Mr. Glaister's insurance policy,
which is only large enough "to bury him." A more valuable insurance policy
was cashed in several years ago when Mr. Glaister was unable to meet the
premiums.

Instead of applying for pensions, the Glaisters have advertised
their home for sale. They are not hopeful of making a sale, as there is
little market for real estate. Mr. Glaister feels that it is unfair for
men who "never worked a day in their lives" to get pensions more readily
than property-owners.

Repeatedly, Mr. Glaister has gone down to the City Hall to ask
if he can work out his taxes; even there, he can get no "satisfaction,"
though he has been a "property owner for 45 years"—before the Glaisters
built their present home, they had owned another house in Dubuque. Mr.
Glaister wishes that the Social Security Act had been passed early enough
for him to be eligible now for an "earned" pension. Nevertheless, he is

glad that "our followers" will have the protection of old-age benefits
and unemployment compensation. He believes that Roosevelt has had "more
work to do" than any other President, "even Wilson," and that Roosevelt
had done more for "the working men" than any other President.

Mr. Glaister has more faith in legislation than in unionization
as a means of raising wage scales and minimizing unemployment, though he
believes that unions can accomplish a great deal "if the men will stick
together." The newly-organized factory employees have not had much practice in "sticking together," but Mr. Glaister believes that workers will
learn that their only strength lies in unity. He has a great deal of confidence in the future for younger men; for himself, almost none.

Employment Chronology for Mr. Glaister

Before 1892 –	Driver of kindling wagon, Dubuque Woodworking Company.
1892 – May 1927	Car repairman, railroad shops.
May 1927 – 1929	Molder, Iowa Foundry.
1929 – April 1937	Cabinetmaker and bench worker, Mississippi Milling Company.
April 1937 – present	Unemployed.

Mr. Hesper   74
Mrs. Hesper   70

Away from home

Rita   30

Interviewing completed
March 15, 1938

          Even at 74, John Hesper has a dynamic and forceful personality.
He is a cabinetmaker by trade, and he had worked in two Dubuque woodworking mills for 35 years prior to his layoff in 1932. Highly critical of
the work turned out under modern production methods, Mr. Hesper considers
his workmanship superior to that of most millworkers and resents having
been laid off on account of his age. Though Mr. Hesper has had no work
for the past 5 years, he and his wife have lived on their savings,
supplemented by some help from a daughter, Rita, who is employed in
another city as a stenographer.

          Mr. Hesper, though somewhat frail looking, is wiry and ener-
getic. He talks spontaneously, expressing himself with clarity. Though
he speaks with a pronounced accent in a somewhat loud, rancous voice, his
choice of words and his grammar are exceptionally good. He is meticulously neat, and his manner is refined.

          The Hesper home, owned clear for many years, is located in a
north-end neighborhood of small homes. The two-story brick house, by far
the best building in the block, is in excellent repair. The furniture
and rugs, of a superior quality, are also in good condition. Mrs. Hesper
regrets that Rita cannot live at home, as her monthly board bill would
take care of the three of them. A married son died last year, leaving
his wife with two children to support. This daughter-in-law now clerks

in a dry goods store. The Hespers have converted two upstairs rooms into
an apartment which is rented for $14 a month; this rental at least takes
care of the taxes. Mr. Hesper is scornful of the old-age pension system
in Iowa; he would not think of making application, as he would be required "to sign the home over." In his opinion this benefits only "no-
good people who have no property."

Mr. Hesper came to the U.S.A. from Switzerland, the country of
his birth, in 1884, primarily to avoid the "annoyance" of compulsory
military service. Though the requirements in Switzerland were less severe
than in Germany, Mr. Hesper had become vexed over having to spend several
weeks each summer in a military camp. After he had completed the ninth
form, the highest common school education available at that time in
Switzerland, Mr. Hesper had spent 4 years learning the cabinetmaker's
trade.

For 6 years after his arrival in America, Mr. Hesper worked in
a Chicago cabinet factory. Then he came to Dubuque, where he worked on
his own at cabinetmaking and carpentry for 7 years.

Soon after Mr. Hesper came to Dubuque he was married. Mrs.
Hesper had come to the U.S.A. from Switzerland and was living with
relatives in Dubuque.

In 1897 Mr. Hesper got a job at the Mississippi Milling Company,
where he remained for the next 17 years. During a slack season in 1914 he
was employed at the Dubuque Woodworking Company. Though he had intended
to return to his old employer, Mr. Hesper was paid a slightly higher rate
at the Dubuque Woodworking Company; so he continued working there for the
next 17 years until the general reduction in force in 1931. After Mr.
Hesper had been laid off by this company he made application at the
Mississippi Milling Company and was called to work there about 2 weeks

later. Mr. Hesper thinks that he was hired because he was well known
from his former work with the company as a good workman; this mill was
no busier than the Dubuque Woodworking Company. Mr. Hesper had worked 1.
year at the Mississippi Milling Company before he was laid off "for good."

Mr. Hesper feels that the speeding-up system in both mills has
lowered the efficiency of the workers. In the old days the emphasis was
on perfect workmanship; now these mills are more interested in the
numbers of doors and sashes produced. He also feels that this "greed for
numbers" has caused the management to "drive" the men and lose sight of
their welfare. One day Mr. Hesper completed six doors in the time he was
supposed to have turned out eight. When his doors were compared with
those turned out by other workers in the time specified, it was found
that Mr. Hesper's doors had four nails where the others had only three;
he had also done a much more complete finishing job. "When men are
hurried, of course they turn out shoddy work." It is difficult for Mr.
Hesper to remember his various wage rates, but he believes his lowest
day rate was $1.50 and his highest $2.50. Most of the time, however, he
worked on a piecework basis, but his piecework earnings averaged little
more than the day rate, except during busy seasons when the men put in
overtime. Though his earnings had never been high, the family always
lived frugally and managed to save something out of each pay check.

When Mr. Hesper was laid off in 1932, he fully expected to be
called back when business picked up again. The mills, however, had begun "to get rid" of the older men; so Mr. Hesper was never called back.
He feels that older workers had not been discriminated against until recent years; "15 years ago it made no difference whether a man was 30 or
60, so long as he could turn out good work." Mr. Hesper is inclined to
blame the present administration for the "squeezing out" of the older men.
Mrs. Hesper, however, thinks it is a product of the depression.

Soon after Mr. Hesper became unemployed, the Hespers lost
$2,000 which they had invested in public utility stock. They had con-
sidered this stock safe and were depending on the investment to take
care of them in their old age. They now have only $200 of their
"several hundred dollars" cash savings. Mr. Hesper is glad that the
home is owned clear; if worst comes to worst he can borrow on it. Soon
after the Hespers were married, Mr. Hesper had built a home with his own
hands and without borrowing money. In those days materials not only
were cheap but also could be bought on 90 day's credit. Eleven years
ago this home was traded in for the present home, which is valued at
$2,900.

Mr. Hesper has little sympathy with the emergency recovery program. "All this WCA, CAX, and the likes of what we never heard of before
won't stop unemployment unless they do something about new machinery."
Mr. Hesper feels that something should be done to prevent the introduction of labor-saving machines; unless there is a ban on machinery,
unemployment will become an even greater problem than it is today.
Never having been a union member, Mr. Hesper has no interest in unionization, though he is not opposed to it. He can see no advantage to the
poor man in the recent housing legislation. "It will help only the banks
and loan associations and people who could build without Government assistance." In general Mr. Hesper considers the farm legislation "a lot
of foolishness." He believes the emergency Works Program and relief for
the unemployed to be necessary and worth-while, though there have been
some abuses in their administration. Wages are low in Dubuque because of
"the greed of a few manufacturers who control the town."

Mr. Hesper can see no hope for improvement in his situation;
he expects to grow no younger, and most of his life's savings are gone.

He laughingly suggests that he might get a job by giving his age as 47
instead of 74, but soon he will be 77; then there would no longer be an
advantage in reversing the numberls. Mr. Hesper feels that he has done
the best he could, and all he now asks is that he and his wife be
permitted to finish their days in reasonable comfort.

Employment Chronology for Mr. Hesper

1884 - 1897   Cabinetmaker.

1897 - 1914   Mill worker, Mississippi
                       Milling Company.

1914 - 1931   Mill worker, Dubuque Wood-
                       working Company.

1931 - 1932   Mill worker, Mississippi
                       Milling Company.

1932 -
present   Unemployed.

At home

Mr. Feigus	71
Mrs. Feigus	55
John	19
Russ	16

Away from home

Henry	34
Thelma	32
Guinevere	29
Bert	27
Elmer	25
Rose	22

Interviewing completed
January 27, 1938

During the days Mr. Feigus has little to do except read or listen to the radio, or go, when the weather is fine, to visit his married daughter in Dubuque. On the days that Mrs. Feigus is working on the WPA Housekeeping Aid Project, he cooks his own lunch. Before 3 P.M. — though she will probably not come home until 4 or 4:30 — he begins to watch for her return. He peers at the clock, and paces again and again to the living room windows to see if she is coming up the hill.

The Feiguses' dingy frame house is perched at the very top of a steep hill where the unpaved street peters out into a narrow path. The yard is muddy and untidy, and the porches are littered with odd assortments of rubbish.

The house is no more attractive inside — though clean and fairly tidy, it is very sparsely furnished. All of the floors are bare. Mr. and Mrs. Feigus and John and Russ, the only ones of the eight children still living at home, sit around the small cookstove in the kitchen, for there is seldom a fire in the furnace. One of the few spindly chairs has a gaping hole in its cane seat. A dirty, tangle-haired little dog — "part wooly dog and part something else mixed" — and two cats play around the stove and crawl

in and out among the newspapers spread over the kitchen floor.   The house,
which Mr. Feigus built in the early twenties is to be sold next fall, because payments have not been kept up on the Home Owners loan secured in 1934.

Mr. Feigus, now 71 years old, was employed at the Dubuque railroad
shops from 1905 until 1931, when the shops closed.   Since 1931 he has had
no work except on WPA projects.   His name was removed from WPA rolls late
in 1935 because he was more than 65 years old.   For the past 16 months
Mrs. Feigus has been working on WPA.   Mr. Feigus has applied for a railroad
retirement pension which has not yet been granted.

John, 19 years old, left high school 3 years ago because the family
could not afford to keep him in school and, too, he hoped to get a job.   But
he has never had a job lasting longer than 2 weeks.   Mrs. Feigus is anxious
for Russ, a ninth-grader, to finish a high school course since the older
children have not profited by leaving school.

All of the Feiguses are discouraged and resigned; they discuss their
present situation with a rather casual hopelessness.   Mr. Feigus doesn't
"know what to do" except wait for his pension and periodically write "to
Washington" or go to the railroad shops to find out "what the matter is."
He hopes that the pension will come soon so that Mrs. Feigus "can stay at
home."

Mr. Feigus is frail-looking.   While he talks, he walks slowly,
with bent knees, back and forth from one end of the kitchen to the other,
pausing to spit tobacco juice into the trash can or the stove.   His gray
hair, streaked with the original reddish brown, is uncombed and grows long
on the back of his neck.   His ragged mustache and his stubbled chin are
stained with tobacco juice.   He talks slowly, with a noticeable German accent.
His conversation shows a certain preoccupation with old age and illness and
death.

Mr. Feigus, one of 11 children, was brought by his parents to the United States from Belgium when he was 4 or 5 years old. His father had been born in Luxembourg and had worked as a cabinetmaker in Luxembourg and in Paris. In America he continued to do woodwork. He also had his own farm, which he worked with the help of his sons. Mr. Feigus began doing heavy farm work when he was only 12 years old; he used to plow when he could scarcely reach as high as the plow handles. Later he worked on other farms. When he was in his 20's he went to "Dakoty," where he bought half an interest in a farm of "22 three-quarter sections." Except for the "uncertain weather in Dakoty, I wouldn't be here today yet." When he had trouble with his back, doctors recommended that he work where the climate was milder.

Mr. Feigus returned to Iowa, where he bought his own small farm on a time-payment plan. The acreage was mostly bottom land. During Mr. Feigus's second summer on his own farm the land was flooded, and even in the best of weather the place was damp. Again he had trouble with his back and was advised to leave the farm which he traded for a small house in Dubuque. He worked for some time, but only irregularly, as a railroad section hand. In 1905 he secured a job in the Dubuque railroad shops, where his first work was in the supply room, distributing and accounting for the supplies used.

He began work at only 16½¢ an hour for a 10-hour day. His wages had risen to $2.05 a day before he was transferred to carpentry work in 1913. On this job he was at first paid $2.45 a day, and he continued to put in 10 hours daily "till that law passed 'em going on 8 hours a day." During the war his hourly rate rose to 72¢, but "after the strike we got put down some," and when the shops closed in 1931, Mr. Feigus was earning only 70¢ an hour. He had eight children, and it took all that he earned "to run the

house, even if he did earn 72¢ an hour."   Grocery bills were $50 or $60
a month, "then the taxes, then the coal, then the clothes and shoes."

The house to which Mr. and Mrs. Feigus had come when they first
moved to Dubuque soon "got too small" for the family of growing children.
So, soon after the World War, Mr. Feigus built his own home. He did all the
work on the first story, which was finished off with a flat roof. About a
year later, with the help of another carpenter, he added a second story.
He traded two Liberty bonds for a part of the lumber. About $6,000 was
invested in the home, and when the second story was added it was necessary
for him to borrow against the property. Besides investing in the house,
Mr. Feigus had taken out insurance amounting to $2,000 for himself and his
wife. These policies were allowed to lapse after Mr. Feigus lost his job.

In the spring of 1931 Mr. Feigus was still at work in the shops.
He had always liked the carpentry work better than farming, and it was not
so hard on his back, for in the shops he was "mostly all the time bent."
Of course, he had had to "do what the boss told him," whether he liked it
or not, and he had found the riveting job, on which he worked last, not
much to his liking. It was hard to hold the drills in place from beneath,
and the sparks showered down on his hands.

After the shops closed Mr. Feigus felt that "it wasn't no use"
to look for another job; even young men could scarcely find work. He has
difficulty in remembering just how the family did manage when he no longer
had a pay check coming in. He guesses, "We lived off the boys a while
yet," for the two older sons were working regularly. Then in 1932, when
one of the children contracted smallpox and the family was "quarantined in";
they "had to live off the county."

Both Mr. and Mrs. Feigus refer very casually to this first application for relief. Mr. Feigus seems to be more interested in a discussion of
whether or not small pox is "catching" than in any discussion of relief experiences. Mrs. Feigus goes on to say that the family has been dependent
on direct relief, work relief, or WPA most of the time since 1932. Perhaps
one of the boys would have work for a while, and the family could manage without assistance. Then he would lose his job and a reapplication for relief
would be necessary.

Mrs. Feigus is proud of the children's having helped the family
when they were able to do so. She thinks, however, that she shouldn't
"expect too much" of them, and that they should have a chance to become independent. Because of the "low wages" in Dubuque and the difficulty of finding jobs, young people "have to leave town" if they want to get ahead.

John, a lanky, pimply-faced lad, says disconsolately that although
he has worked "almost every place in town," and looked for work every place,
he can't get a "steady job." When he asks for a job, the bosses "just
laugh." Over a 3-year period, he has had only a few weeks of work—for a
creamery, for a filling station, and for the Dubuque Woodworking Company.
His meager earnings have been spent for his own clothing.

Russ, the ninth-grader, has likewise had a few odd jobs. Last
summer he mowed lawns, saved his quarters, and bought two pair of school
trousers. From time to time he threatens to leave school and look for work,
but Mrs. Feigus tells him that the place for him is in school; he "couldn't
find a job anyhow."

Of the seven children of employable age, only Henry, the oldest,
has never been unemployed. He is married and has two children. He began

work at one of the woodworking mills when he was only 16. Later he was employed in a grocery store, and for the past several years he has been working
for the Dubuque Woodworking Company. The two oldest girls have also married
and now have families of their own. One is widowed and receives a mothers'
pension. Bert, 27, now employed at the Mississippi Milling Company, has
been married for the past 2 years. He had gone back and forth from Dubuque
to Chicago several times and had found it easier to get jobs in Chicago than
in Dubuque.

Elmer, 25, worked at the Mississippi Milling Company for several
months in 1930 and 1931. In 1933 he spent 6 months in a CCC camp. He liked
the woods work well enough, and the Feiguses were glad to have the income
of $25 a month, on which they managed without supplementary aid. Elmer later
was assigned to WPA work in the place of his father, who had been laid off
because of his age. Mr. Feigus himself feels that his age is not a handicap. He prides himself on having worked more effectively than many younger
men on the CWA airport and the WPA park-clearing projects, though he mentions
having sent the boys to work in his stead when he was too ill to go out in
the cold. He expresses no resentment at having been laid off.

In July 1936, after a few months of work on the Dubuque lock and
dam project, Elmer was discharged for "loafing on the job." Neither
Mrs. Feigus nor Elmer could understand this criticism of his work. When the
"inspector" — the relief worker — offered to certify all members of the
family except Elmer for direct relief, Elmer felt that he would have to leave
home. Without bitterness, Mrs. Feigus states that he would probably be at
home now if he had been included in the food budget. But it is perhaps just
as well that he has gone, for he is now working in Washington, D. C., for

Mrs. Feigus's sister, who runs a small doughnut-making establishment. He earns $16 or $17 a week. He does not contribute anything to the family.

Alice, 22, has done housework and farm work since her graduation from junior high school. Mrs. Feigus is proud of Alice's ability to do all kinds of work. Her earnings at housework in Dubuque or on nearby farms never amounted to more than $4 a week, even when she worked in the home of a doctor and had the responsibility of answering the phone and caring for the children in the evenings. Several months ago she, too, went to Washington, where she hoped to earn more money. She is now doing housework in a small town in Maryland.

Mrs. Feigus believes that John and Russ should spend for themselves whatever little money they can make. Her own earnings of $55 a month as a housekeeper on the WPA project have gone for household expenses. Recently the monthly rate of pay has been cut from $55 to $48. Especially as she has her own bus fares to pay, she does not know how she can manage on $48 a month, for even while she earned $55 it was impossible to meet all current expenses.

Mrs. Feigus enjoys her work as housekeeper. She takes a personal interest in the families she visits, and likes to discuss their difficulties. It is a part of her job to teach women to manage on as little as possible, but "it's hard to help people who don't have nothing to do with. Besides, I can't absolutely tell people what to do; other women know the needs of their own families best anyhow."

Both Mr. and Mrs. Feigus believe that WPA work is far superior to direct relief. Mr. Feigus would "sooner work as to get relief. I like to earn my living." Mrs. Feigus sees the advantages of a larger income and a cash income. They do wish that John could have private employment and that

Mr. Feigus would get his pension. He expects to have a pension of about $50 a month, which he thinks will be ample for the family's needs. If he gets his "back pension" from the date of application he will have some $900 in a lump sum. With this money Mr. Feigus would like to buy a small house in town; the city has advertised several such small homes for sale.

Mrs. Feigus has been wondering why wages are so low in Dubuque and why Dubuque boys can find jobs elsewhere more quickly and more easily than at home. She has recently "heard that the Chamber of Commerce keeps out" industries that would pay higher wages than those paid by the local factories. Such new industries as have come in have employed only "very few men," and those at "low wages." Mrs. Feigus "wondered" why the Chamber of Commerce should be concerned with keeping industries out of Dubuque until she finally "figured out" that if one new factory established higher wage-scales the older local factories "would have to raise wages" of their employees. She considers this situation largely responsible for unemployment in Dubuque, for her sons' inability to find work, and for the family's complete dependency on her WPA earnings.

Employment Chronology for Mr. Feigus

Until 1905	-- Farmer.
1905 - May 1931	-- Supply room helper and carpenter, railroad shops.
May 1931 - present	-- Unemployed, except for emergency work.

Mr. Schellen   66
Mrs. Schellen   62

Interviewing completed
January 13, 1938

Mr. Schellen looks and acts fully 10 years younger than his actual
age of 66; intelligent and alert, he recalls dates and jobs with no difficulty
and expresses himself with clarity and precision. He is meticulously neat in
appearance. His dark brown hair is only slightly gray; his dark eyes are
bright and expressive. Though he has worn spectacles for some years, his
eyesight, he feels, has not been impaired by age. His posture is erect, and
he walks with a firm, quick stride.

He considers himself as good a workman as most younger men and resents being told that he is too old to work. He was employed at the Stevenson Company from 1918 until the latter part of 1931, when the plant closed.
He has been unemployed up to the present time except for emergency work, from
which he was laid off because he was 65 and, therefore, eligible for an old-
age pension.

Mrs. Schellen, a striking looking woman with snow-white, curly
bobbed hair looks older than her husband though she is 4 years younger. She
is not very well, and has frequent gall stone attacks. The Schellens have
no children. Three married daughters of Mrs. Schellen by a former husband
live away from Dubuque. Mr. and Mrs. Schellen live alone in their own home,
a very attractive two-story frame house in a working class neighborhood. The
home had been paid out in 1919, but after Mr. Schellen became unemployed, it
was necessary to borrow money on this property for living expenses. At present

the Schellens' only source of livelihood is Mr. Schellen's old-age pension
of $21 a month.

In 1885, at the age of 14, Mr. Schellen started work in a buggy
top factory at 5¢ an hour. For 5 years he worked at this job; during winter
months he put in 10 hours a day and walked 2½ miles to and from work, for
the "munificent sum of 50¢ a day." During spring and summer months he and
his mother cultivated a truck garden and sold their produce at the City
Market.

Mr. Schellen worked at the Lasky Lumber Company in the lathe and
shingle department for the next 4 years and until the fire of January 9, 1894,
when the mill was partially destroyed. This company then sent Mr. Schellen
to their mill in Minnesota for a year until the Dubuque mill had been rebuilt.
After returning to Dubuque he worked for this company 5 years, earning from
$1.10 a day to $13 a week for a 60-hour week.

Mr. Schellen was hired as shipping clerk in 1900 by the American
Foundry, then a small concern. His rate, in the beginning, was $8 a week for
a 54-hour week, but when he left to go into the saloon business for himself
in 1910, he was earning $17 a week. After 3 years in the saloon business the
Mulct law was passed in Iowa, limiting the number of saloons to 1 per 1,000
population; so Mr. Schellen's business was discontinued. The saloon business
had not proved as profitable as Mr. Schellen had expected—he had averaged
only $18 a week for the 3 years. He then returned to the American Foundry,
where he was paid at the rate of $15 a week. "After 3 years on this job"
Mr. Schellen says, "I still had the saloon business on my mind"; so he got
a job tending bar in East Dubuque, Ill. During the 2 years on this job he
was paid from $16 to $20 a week. Tending bar in East Dubuque wasn't so pleasant

in those days, though; many of the customers became disagreeable and difficult
to wait on after a few rounds of drinks. Iowa had gone completely dry in 1916,
so the drinkers were attracted to East Dubuque, Ill., just across the river.

In 1918 Mr. Schellen went to work at the Stevenson Company in the
phonograph cabinet assembly department. He was paid 30¢ an hour for the 2
months before he had learned the job well enough to go on a piecework basis.
Sometimes when the new men complained about the rate they were told they could
go on piecework immediately. Until a man had been on the job about 2 months
it really was not to his advantage to go on piecework as he usually made less
than he would at the hourly rate. During the war when labor was scarce
Stevenson's paid from 65¢ to 75¢ an hour on piecework, but no sooner had the
boys returned from war than the rate was decreased. During the war period
Mr. Schellen earned as much as $80 for a 2-week pay period. In the early
twenties there were a number of strikes, usually in only one department. These
strikes never accomplished anything as the men in the different departments
did not "stick together"; the company also sometimes "imported labor from
outside Dubuque" to break the strikes. Mr. Schellen belonged to the millworkers union but finally gave it up after going to the union hall time after
time only to find a handful of men present. He saw no use in continuing to
pay dues of 75¢ a month, "knowing full well that the union had no strength."

Mr. Schellen was ill in 1928 and worked only 3 months during that
entire year. During the next year the plant was closed several months; so
by the time Stevenson's closed permanently in 1931, Mr. Schellen had no savings
left. In fact he had borrowed $200 against the home during his illness in 1928
and had also fallen behind with his taxes. At the time of the layoff in 1931,
Mr. Schellen had no idea that he would not find work within a few months, "what

with all the talk of prosperity just around the corner." So Mr. Schellen
kept borrowing a few hundred dollars against the home until he finally owed
$1,000 on which he could not even pay the interest, charged at the rate of
6¼ percent. The home had been purchased in 1912 for $2,100. Mr. Schellen
had $850 saved up, and by borrowing $150 from a friend he had been able to
make the down payment of $1,000. By paying the building and loan company
$15 a month for the next 7 years, Mr. Schellen had purchased the home. When
he was forced to make application for an old-age pension a few months ago the
home was "signed over to the State."[1]/

By the end of 1934 Mr. Schellen owed about $140 interest on the
mortgage and $160 on taxes 2 years in arrears. The Schellens sold their car
for $275 and cleaned up this indebtedness. In January 1936 Mr. Schellen was
required to pay $30 in addition to the regular annual interest for the privi-
lege of renewing the mortgage for another 3 years. Fortunately, he had been
assigned to WPA by this time and was able to squeeze this amount out of his
pay check. After the money borrowed on the home had been used up, he borrowed
$400 on a $2,000 life insurance policy which had been in force for many years.
This loan was adjusted by reducing the amount of the policy to $1,000. At
another time a small policy carried by Mrs. Schellen was cashed in for $40.
Mr. Schellen had also worked out a coal bill of $60 for a company he had
traded with for 20 years. He had no income from work from November 30, 1931,
until his assignment to a CWA highway project on a nonrelief basis the latter
part of November 1933. His pay on CWA was $15 a week. When the reduction
in CWA pay rolls was begun 3 months later, he was one of the first men to be
laid off, because he had no children dependent on him.

1/ The State of Iowa takes a lien on property of old-age pension applicants.

In March 1934 the Schellens were again without funds. Mr. Schellen
had never thought of asking for relief though many of his neighbors and friends
were receiving public aid. Finally he realized that there was no other way
out, but still he couldn't bring himself to the point of making application.
For a whole week he walked down past the relief office every day but "got
sick" every time he started in. When there were no more provisions in the
house the application was finally made and relief was granted a few days
later. Mr. Schellen did not object to answering all the questions, even
those about his ancestors, but he did resent the investigator's doubting his
veracity. One day the investigator called when Mrs. Schellen was not at home.
After Mr. Schellen had told her all about the disposition of his and Mrs.
Schellen's insurance policies, the investigator wanted to see the policies.
Mr. Schellen didn't know where Mrs. Schellen had put them; when he said so,
the investigator thought he was trying to cover up something.

Mr. Schellen never got over feeling that he was waiting for a trial
when he sat awaiting his turn at the relief office. "I was never tried in
court for anything but I imagine that's the way I would feel." Surplus
commodities were distributed from different points in the city. One day
Mr. Schellen walked 4 miles for a pound of rice. Another time, he was supposed
to call for a can of beef "away up on the hill." When he spoke to the commodit;
clerk about it, Mr. Schellen was allowed to substitute a pound of butter at a
distributing center downtown. The Schellens were allowed $2.50 a week for food
and managed only by skimping. "And then there were so many dasn't about those
orders; you dasn't have this and you dasn't have that."

After about 9 months on direct relief Mr. Schellen was assigned
to work relief, in December 1934, on a budget deficiency basis, earning only
$13.75 a month. He was assigned to the 16th Street sewer project, where he
was required to work in mud and water. "But I didn't mind that; I was so glad
to be paid in cash." After a year on work relief, Mr. Schellen was certified
for WPA in December 1935. At first he was paid $15 a week, but the rate was
later cut to $12. For some time after going on WPA, he continued on the sewer
project, but was later transferred to the city water project and to other
projects where the work was somewhat more pleasant. Mr. Schellen continued
on WPA until March 29, 1937, when he was laid off because he was 65 years old.
He had liked the WPA work and was distressed over being laid off. He is under
the impression that the relief office made this decision because the investigator told him "You've been investigated and found to be over 65." Mr. Schelle
feels that "an arbitrary decision" with no check on a person's ability to work
is "unfair" since there is so much difference between persons of the same age.

The family had again been on direct relief from 2 weeks after Mr.
Schellen's layoff from WPA until a month ago when he received his first old-
age pension check of $21. Mr. Schellen does not know whether or not the re-
lief office will allow them any further assistance, but he does know that they
will have a hard time managing on the $21 a month, with coal $11 a ton, and
food prices so high. They have bought no clothing or household furnishings
during the past 6 years and now clothing, linens, and rugs need to be replaced.
Though the Schellens had received some of the food stuffs distributed as surplus commodities, they had never received any of the clothing, sheets, comforters, etc., granted through the relief office. In fact, they had had only 1
ton of coal. About 3 months ago when Mr. Schellen requested this coal, the

investigator wanted to know what they had been burning up to that time. When he explained that he had cut up a tree which had blown down in the back yard, the investigator wanted to know just how much of the wood was left. He told her "just enough for 2 days"; though there was enough for a week, he knew it would probably be at least 2 weeks before the coal order came through. Sure enough, he had to wait 3 weeks and managed only by borrowing fuel from a neighbor.

Mrs. Schellen says that unemployment is very trying for Mr. Schellen, as he has always been so active. During his unemployment following the layoff from Stevenson's, he lost weight and became very nervous; since the layoff from WPA, he has again become very restless and a little "crabby." He tries to keep busy at something around the house; Mrs. Schellen even found him mending the worn places in the living room rug one day. He also spends quite a bit of time in his workshop in the woodshed, though it is unheated and not very well protected from the weather. Mr. Schellen does not have much hope of getting work in a factory again, though the American Foundry has given him some encouragement. Mr. Schellen considers this factory his best chance since he knows the foreman, and there is not so much prejudice against employing older men.

Mr. Schellen blames labor saving machinery and the speeding up system for the present widespread unemployment. This unemployment he fears will become not only a permanent problem but also a problem of increasing significance. While Mr. Schellen approves of the Social Security program he believes that unemployment insurance will be of little help in cases of prolonged unemployment, as the period during which benefits are paid is too short in most States. "And its the man who has steady work who profits by the old-age pension system" under the Social Security Act. The President, Mr. Schellen believes, has done everything in his power to give employment to unemployed people. Most of the recovery legislation has been beneficial, in Mr. Schellen's opinion, in spite of all the criticism to the contrary.

The Federal Government should continue to take the major responsibility for unemployment relief, though the States should be required to do their share too. Mr. Schellen fears that if unemployment relief were left entirely up to the States, there would be no uniformity. Some States would take care of their people, while other States might permit their needy people to suffer.

Mr. Schellen enjoys reading the stories in a 5¢ weekly, though the "biased" editorials and special articles make him "mad." He has recently read about the salaries paid some of the country's big executives; no man, in Mr. Schellen's opinion, is worth a salary of $300,000 a year. "Who but the workers make such salaries possible?" Mr. Schellen considers it ironical that some of these companies have put up such a strong fight against wage increases while the executives continue to draw fabulous salaries.

Though Mr. Schellen realizes that his age makes reemployment extremely doubtful, he is not resigned to his situation; he continues to search for work and hopes that he may yet be given another chance to show his ability to produce, and to earn his living.

Employment Chronology for Mr. Schellen

1885 - 1890 - Laborer, buggy factory.

1890 - 1899 - Laborer, Lasky Lumber Company

1900 - 1910 - Shipping clerk, American Foundry

1910 - 1913 - Owner and proprietor, saloon.

1913 - 1916 - Shipping clerk, American Foundry.

1916 - 1918 - Bartender.

1918 - November
1931   - Assembler, Stevenson Phonograph
                and Radio Company.

November 1931 -
present   - Unemployed except for emergency work.

POVERTY, U. S. A.

THE HISTORICAL RECORD

An Arno Press/New York Times Collection

Adams, Grace. **Workers on Relief.** 1939.

The Almshouse Experience: Collected Reports. 1821-1827.

Armstrong, Louise V. **We Too Are The People.** 1938.

Bloodworth, Jessie A. and Elizabeth J. Greenwood.
The Personal Side. 1939.

Brunner, Edmund de S. and Irving Lorge.
**Rural Trends in Depression Years: A Survey of
Village-Centered Agricultural Communities, 1930-1936.**
1937.

Calkins, Raymond.
**Substitutes for the Saloon: An Investigation Originally
made for The Committee of Fifty.** 1919.

Cavan, Ruth Shonle and Katherine Howland Ranck.
**The Family and the Depression: A Study of
One Hundred Chicago Families.** 1938.

Chapin, Robert Coit.
**The Standard of Living Among Workingmen's Families
in New York City.** 1909.

**The Charitable Impulse in Eighteenth Century America:
Collected Papers.** 1711-1797.

Children's Aid Society.
Children's Aid Society Annual Reports, 1-10.
February 1854-February 1863.

Conference on the Care of Dependent Children.
**Proceedings of the Conference on the Care
of Dependent Children.** 1909.

Conyngton, Mary.
How to Help: A Manual of Practical Charity. 1909.

Devine, Edward T. **Misery and its Causes.** 1909.

Devine, Edward T. **Principles of Relief.** 1904.

Dix, Dorothea L.
On Behalf of the Insane Poor: Selected Reports. 1843-1852.

Douglas, Paul H.
**Social Security in the United States: An Analysis and
Appraisal of the Federal Social Security Act.** 1936.

Farm Tenancy: Black and White. Two Reports. 1935, 1937.

Feder, Leah Hannah.
**Unemployment Relief in Periods of Depression:
A Study of Measures Adopted in Certain American
Cities, 1857 through 1922.** 1936.

Folks, Homer.
**The Care of Destitute, Neglected, and
Delinquent Children.** 1900.

Guardians of the Poor.
**A Compilation of the Poor Laws of the State of
Pennsylvania from the Year 1700 to 1788, Inclusive.** 1788.

Hart, Hastings, H.
Preventive Treatment of Neglected Children.
(Correction and Prevention, Vol. 4) 1910.

Herring, Harriet L.
**Welfare Work in Mill Villages: The Story of Extra-Mill
Activities in North Carolina.** 1929.

The Jacksonians on the Poor: Collected Pamphlets.
1822-1844.

Karpf, Maurice J.
Jewish Community Organization in the United States.
1938.

Kellor, Frances A.
Out of Work: A Study of Unemployment. 1915.

Kirkpatrick, Ellis Lore.
The Farmer's Standard of Living. 1929.

Komarovsky, Mirra.
The Unemployed Man and His Family: The Effect of Unemployment Upon the Status of the Man in Fifty-Nine Families. 1940.

Leupp, Francis E. **The Indian and His Problem.** 1910.

Lowell, Josephine Shaw.
Public Relief and Private Charity. 1884.

More, Louise Bolard.
Wage Earners' Budgets: A Study of Standards and Cost of Living in New York City. 1907.

New York Association for Improving the Condition of the Poor.
AICP First Annual Reports Investigating Poverty. 1845-1853.

O'Grady, John.
Catholic Charities in the United States: History and Problems. 1930.

Raper, Arthur F.
Preface to Peasantry: A Tale of Two Black Belt Counties. 1936.

Raper, Arthur F. **Tenants of The Almighty.** 1943.

Richmond, Mary E.
What is Social Case Work? An Introductory Description. 1922.

Riis, Jacob A. **The Children of the Poor.** 1892.

Rural Poor in the Great Depression: Three Studies. 1938.

Sedgwick, Theodore.
Public and Private Economy: Part I. 1836.

Smith, Reginald Heber. **Justice and the Poor.** 1919.

Sutherland, Edwin H. and Harvey J. Locke.
Twenty Thousand Homeless Men: A Study of Unemployed Men in the Chicago Shelters. 1936.

Tuckerman, Joseph.
**On the Elevation of the Poor: A Selection From His
Reports as Minister at Large in Boston.** 1874.

Warner, Amos G. **American Charities.** 1894.

Watson, Frank Dekker.
**The Charity Organization Movement in the United States:
A Study in American Philanthropy.** 1922.

Woods, Robert A., et al. **The Poor in Great Cities.** 1895.

MUHLENBERG LIBRARY

WITHDRAWN

DATE DUE
